AN INTRODUCTION TO CLASSICAL ISLAMIC PHILOSOPHY

Islamic philosophy is a unique and fascinating form of thought, and particular interest lies in its classical (Greek-influenced) period, when many of the ideas of Greek philosophy were used to explore the issues and theoretical problems which arise in trying to understand the Qur'ān and Islamic practice. In this revised and expanded edition of his classic introductory work, Oliver Leaman examines the distinctive features of classical Islamic philosophy and offers detailed accounts of major individual thinkers. In contrast to many previous studies that have treated this subject as only of historical interest, he offers analysis of the key arguments within Islamic philosophy so that the reader can engage with them and assess their strengths and weaknesses. His book will interest a wide range of readers in philosophy, religious studies and Islamic studies.

OLIVER LEAMAN is Professor of Philosophy at the University of Kentucky. He has written extensively on Islamic philosophy and is the author of *A brief introduction to Islamic philosophy* (1999). He is the editor of *Friendship east and west: philosophical perspectives* (1996) and *The future of philosophy* (1998) and co-editor of the *History of Islamic philosophy* (1996) and the *History of Jewish philosophy* (1997).

AN INTRODUCTION TO CLASSICAL ISLAMIC PHILOSOPHY

OLIVER LEAMAN

CAMBRIDGE
UNIVERSITY PRESS

PUBLISHED BY THE PRESS SYNDICATE OF THE UNIVERSITY OF CAMBRIDGE
The Pitt Building, Trumpington Street, Cambridge, United Kingdom

CAMBRIDGE UNIVERSITY PRESS
The Edinburgh Building, Cambridge CB2 2RU, UK
40 West 20th Street, New York, NY 10011-4211, USA
477 Williamstown Road, Port Melbourne, VIC 3207, Australia
Ruiz de Alarcón 13, 28014 Madrid, Spain
Dock House, The Waterfront, Cape Town 8001, South Africa

http://www.cambridge.org

First published as An Introduction to Medieval Islamic Philosophy 1985
Second edition 2002, Reprinted 2002

Printed in the United Kingdom at the University Press, Cambridge

Typeface Baskerville monotype 11/12.5 pt.   *System* LATEX 2ε [TB]

A catalogue record for this book is available from the British Library.

Library of Congress Cataloguing in Publication Data
Leaman, Oliver, 1950–
An introduction to classical Islamic philosophy – 2nd edn.
p.   cm.
Rev. edn. of: An Introduction to medieval Islamic Philosophy. New York : Cambridge
University Press, 1985.
Includes bibliographical references and index.
ISBN 0 521 79343 2 – ISBN 0 521 79757 8 (paperback)
1. Philosophy, Islamic.   2. Philosophy, Medieval.   I. Leaman, Oliver, 1950–
Introduction to medieval Islamic philosophy.   II. Title.
B741 .L43   2001
181'.07 – dc21   2001037349

ISBN 0 521 793432 hardback
ISBN 0 521 797578 paperback

In fond memory of my father and mother

وَعَنِ ابْنِ عَبَّاسٍ، قَالَ: قَالَ رَسُولُ اللهِ صَلَّى اللهُ عَلَيْهِ وَسَلَّمَ: "فَقِيهٌ وَّاحِدٌ أَشَدُّ عَلَى الشَّيْطَانِ مِنْ أَلْفِ عَابِدٍ"

Ibn 'Abbās (may God be pleased with him) reported that the Messenger of God (peace and blessings of God be on him) said: A single scholar of religion is more powerful against the Devil than a thousand devout individuals.

Contents

Preface to the first edition

My aim in this book is not just to describe aspects of Islamic philosophy but also to arouse interest in the philosophical problems, arguments and ideas current in the medieval Islamic world. I very much hope that readers of the book will want to go on to read the philosophers themselves. I have tried to bring out something of the range and flavour of Islamic philosophy by following a number of central arguments and issues from their origins in theology to their discussion in philosophy without attempting in any way to provide a comprehensive historical account of the period and its main thinkers. There are a number of books already which describe in some detail the cultural milieu in which philosophy developed in the Islamic world, and there are also books which painstakingly analyse the intellectual predecessors and influences upon the Islamic philosophers. By way of contrast, the emphasis in this book is on the arguments of the philosophers themselves, and the theme of the book is that this is the appropriate emphasis. It is a shame that Islamic philosophy as a topic of interest is at present largely confined to orientalists rather than philosophers. The former often have concerns and interpretative methods which are not shared by the latter, and vice versa. This sometimes has the result that the philosophical point of the argument is lost or confused. I hope that this book will serve to a degree to bring philosophers and orientalists together in a better appreciation of the nature and interest of Islamic philosophy.

It is always a difficulty when dealing with a set of arguments so firmly set within their own period as is much medieval Islamic philosophy to know how far to bring into their analysis the works of more modern philosophers. Indeed, a superficial glance at such arguments might well suggest that they bear close resemblances to later philosophical discussions. For example, it has often been argued that al-Ghazālī's critique of the Aristotelian notion of causality is rather similar to Hume's analysis of the causal relation. In addition, the conflict between al-Ghazālī and the philosophers over the character of the origin of the world is not unlike the sorts of conflict which are represented in Kant's discussion of the antinomies. It has to be said, though, that when one closely compares the medieval and the modern formulations of apparently similar arguments, the resemblance often appears slight. It is possible to understand Islamic philosophy on its own terms, as a philosophy which deals with topics which do not always appear relevant to contemporary philosophical issues. It is not necessary to relate Islamic philosophy to modern philosophical thought, nor to the continuation of the themes of Islamic philosophy among the Scholastics such as Aquinas. It would be very interesting to carry out a detailed investigation of the relation between the arguments of Islamic philosophy and more recent arguments which proceed on roughly similar lines. It would also be interesting to see precisely how Scholastic thought was influenced by Islamic philosophy. It is not the purpose of this book to explore these fascinating issues, but rather to carry out a far more modest task. This is to discuss some of the leading themes of Islamic philosophy by analysing the arguments of some of the most important philosophers concerned, and by relating those arguments to Greek philosophy on the one hand and to the principles of religion on the other. In this way I hope that the book will be accessible and useful both to philosophers who know nothing about Islam and the Arabic language, and to orientalists who are unpractised in philosophy.

I am very grateful to the British Academy for their financial help in carrying out the research for this book. Dr Erwin Rosenthal has provided sustained encouragement even (especially!) when he has disagreed with me. Both he and Dr Ian Netton have made some very helpful comments on the manuscript. The skilful bibliographical assistance of Jill Stothard from the college Library has eased its path considerably, as has the advice and assistance of Peter Edwards and of the staff of the Cambridge University Press. My thanks go to them all.

Liverpool, January 1984   O. L.

Preface to the second edition

When it was suggested to me that there should be a second edition of my *Introduction to medieval Islamic philosophy* I was initially rather hesistant to agree. It seemed to me that the book I had written some time ago might well deserve to go to its final rest without the prospect of any form of resurrection. After all, since this book I have written many other things on Islamic philosophy, and certainly changed my mind on a number of the issues which I discussed in the earlier *Introduction*. In addition, that book was written with a certain degree of passion and conviction which I find rather harder to summon up nowadays, and not only because I am older and possibly wiser. At the time of the earlier book I felt with some justification that the methodological paradigm for doing Islamic philosophy was firmly in the wrong hands, and that it was important to challenge that paradigm. I felt that Islamic philosophy tended not to be studied as philosophy, but more as part of the history of ideas or as an aspect of some orientalist project, neither of which accurately represented the nature of what I took the discipline to be. Within the last two decades it is encouraging (to me at least) that a much broader set of approaches has been adopted in Islamic philosophy, and many of those who work in the area now are philosophers and treat the material as serious philosophy. So the battle has to a degree been won, and perhaps the situation in the past was not as grim as I represented it at the time.

When I came to read my earlier book again I felt that it still serves as a useful introduction to the Peripatetic tradition in Islamic philosophy. Since I wrote it I have come to have much greater respect for the other ways of doing philosophy in the Islamic world, in particular the mystical tradition, and illuminationist philosophy. In the past I took these to be not real philosophy at all, but much more closely linked with theology and subjective religious experience. I regarded these forms of thought

as indications of a form of *Schwärmerei* or wildness which I regarded
with a Kantian disdain. I now think I was too limited in my approach
to these ways of doing philosophy, which have much closer links with
the Peripatetic tradition than I had previously realized. I have added
to the book a brief account of these schools of thought, since they are
so important to understanding the cultural context of the discipline as
a whole. Nonetheless, I think there is merit in dealing with Peripatetic
thought as a distinct entity, and this remains the aim of the book. Readers
who are interested in exploring the wider aspects of Islamic philosophy
will find many indications of where to go in the bibliography, and it is
not the claim of this book that the full extent of Islamic philosophy is
discussed here. But some of the central issues in the Peripatetic tradition
are dealt with, in particular those which use classical Greek ideas in trying
to understand theoretical issues. Although it has been argued often that
this sort of philosophy came to an end in the Islamic world with the death
of ibn Rushd (Averroes) in the sixth/twelfth century, even were this to be
true, and it is not, that would not mean that this sort of philosophy was
not of continuing interest. Nor would it mean that this sort of philosophy
did not strongly affect the kinds of philosophy and theology which then
became the leading theoretical approaches in the Islamic world.

Apart from including some introductory material about the mystical
and Illuminationist schools of philosophy, I have also revised many of
the translations and included a discussion of Averroes, who I regard as
the paradigmatic exponent of classical Islamic philosophy, in his specific
role as a commentator on Aristotle in order to try to throw some light on
the links between this kind of Islamic philosophy and the classical Greek
tradition on which it reflected. I have included some discussion of the
influence of Averroes on the wider Christian and Jewish worlds.

I have continued to discuss the Jewish thinker Maimonides as an
example of someone who although not a Muslim was firmly within the
tradition of classical Islamic philosophy, but I have reduced the amount of
space devoted to him. I hope that readers will find the account provided
here of interest and useful to them in navigating through what often seem
to be the rather choppy waters of Islamic philosophy.

Of greatest help to me in revising the first edition have been the many
students in both Europe, the Middle East and North America who have
used the book and been kind enough to send me comments and queries.
My own students in Liverpool and now in the United States have been
the most forthcoming here, and it would be invidious to name any of

them personally, since although some have helped more than others, I really have benefited from everyone's help. I have been privileged to have been able to discuss the ideas in this book with many colleagues all over the world, and I thank them all. All errors are of course my fault only.

Lexington, Kentucky, February 2001 O. L.

Texts and abbreviations

Where there are Oxford Classical Texts of the works of Plato and Aristotle these have been used, and the Oxford translation has generally been used, although sometimes modified. Translations from *De Anima* have been taken from W. Guthrie, *A history of Greek philosophy*, vol. VI, *Aristotle: an encounter* (Cambridge, Cambridge University Press, 1981), since he adopts a similar interpretation of the active intellect to the Islamic philosophers.

An. Post.	*Posterior Analytics*
Cat.	*Categories*
De An.	*De Anima*
De Int.	*De Interpretatione*
Met.	*Metaphysics*
NE	*Nicomachean Ethics*
Phys.	*Physics*

The sources of translations from Arabic and Hebrew are found in either the notes or the section on further reading, and these have often been modified, too. In the text these abbreviations are followed by a page or section number.

Comm.Pl.Rep.	*Averroes' Commentary on Plato's 'Republic'*, ed. and trans. E. Rosenthal, University of Cambridge Oriental Publications, 1 (Cambridge, Cambridge University Press, 1956)
FM	Averroes, *Faṣl al-maqāl*, in G. Hourani, *On the harmony of religion and philosophy* (London, Luzac, 1976)
GP	Maimonides, *Guide of the perplexed*, trans. S. Pines, 2 vols. (Chicago, University of Chicago Press, 1963)
TT	*Averroes' Tahāfut al-tahāfut*, trans. S. Van Den Bergh (London, Luzac, 1978)

Passages from the Qur'ān are generally taken from the Arberry version, with the sura in Roman and the lines in Arabic numbers.

In the notes, terms are fully transliterated, as are foreign terms, but not always proper names, in the text. Where more familiar Latin versions of names exist, these have been used in the text but not in the notes. The notes are designed to give readers an idea of the sorts of references they will find if they go on to read articles and books on Islamic philosophy. Given the introductory nature of this book, I have tended not to refer to the original Arabic or Hebrew text where an accurate and accessible translation exists. The original reference may readily be found by consulting the translations used.

There follows a list of texts used, with details of the Arabic editions, where these are not available in the notes.

Al-Fārābī, *Agreement of the opinions of the philosophers Plato and Aristotle – Jam'*
  bayna ra'yay al-ḥakīmain Aflāṭūn al-ilāhī wa Arisṭūṭālīs
  Attainment of happiness – Taḥṣīl al-Sa'āda (Hyderabad, Dā'irat al-Ma'ārif
    al-'Uthmānīyya, 1926)
  Book of letters – Kitāb al-Ḥurūf
  Catalogue of sciences – Iḥṣā' al-'Ulūm, ed. O. Amine (Cairo, Dār al-Fikr
    al-'Arabī, 1949)
  Philosophy of Aristotle – Falsafat Arisṭūṭālīs, ed. M. Mahdi (Beirut, Dār
    Majallat Shi'r, 1961)
  Philosophy of Plato – Falsafat Aflāṭūn, ed. F. Rosenthal and R. Walzer
    (London, Warburg Institute, 1943)
Al-Ghazāli, *The incoherence of the philosophers – Tahāfut al-falāsifa,* ed.
    M. Bouges (Beirut, Imprimerie Catholique, 1962)
  The intentions of the philosophers – Maqāṣid al-falāsifa, ed. S. Dunya (Cairo,
    Sa'adah Press, 1961)
  The Renaissance of the sciences of religion – Iḥyā' 'ulūm al-dīn, ed. 'Irāqī
    (Cairo, 'Uthmānīyya Press, 1933)
Averroes, *Decisive treatise on the harmony of religion and philosophy – Kitāb*
    faṣl al-maqāl
  Incoherence of the incoherence – Tahāfut al-tahāfut, ed. M. Bouges (Beirut,
    Bibliotheca Arabica Scholasticorum, 1930)
  Short commentaries on Aristotle's 'Topic', 'Rhetoric' and 'Poetics' – Talkhīṣ kitāb
    al-jadal, al-khaṭābah, al-shi'r
Avicenna, *Book of deliverance – Kitāb al-najāt*
  Metaphysics – Shifā': al-Ilāhiyyāt
Maimonides, *Guide of the perplexed – Dalālat al-ḥa'irīn* (Sefer Moreh
    Nebhukhim), ed. S. Munk (Jerusalem, Junovitch, 1931)
  Treatise on logic – Maqālah fi ṣinā'ah al-manṭiq

Introduction

Although this book is in no way a guide to the religion and history of Islam itself, it is as well to consider some of the main aspects of that religion before discussing the contribution which philosophy sought to make to it. We might naturally start by considering Muḥammad, the son of ʿAbd Allah and Amīna, a member of the tribe of Quraish, who was born in Mecca in the late sixth century CE. Although his parents were of distinguished lineage, they were far from wealthy, and Muḥammad's father died before his son's birth while his mother died when he was about six years old. He was brought up first by his grandfather and later by his uncle, and spent a great deal of time as a youth and young man in the hills which are near to Mecca guarding his family's flocks of sheep. His fortunes improved when in his mid-twenties he married an older and wealthy widow, whose business affairs he came to manage. Yet it is said that he often spent time alone in the hills of his youth to consider the tribal warfare which caused such great loss of life in Arabia and the idolatry and loose behaviour which prevailed in the local towns. When he was about forty years old he started to hear a voice, interpreted as coming from the angel Gabriel, which commanded him to recite the revelations which were thus made to him.

The sum of those revelations were eventually written down in the Qur'ān (or 'recitation'). This consists of a highly variegated set of elements, with pictures of heaven and hell and warnings about the consequences of immorality, legal regulations and accounts of the tasks of former prophets. The Qur'ān is a confirmation of the teachings and messages of such prophets, including Abraham who is said to have built the shrine (Kaʿba) at Mecca, Moses the legislator of the Jews and Jesus son of Mary, who was not as the Christians insist killed upon the Cross at all, since God substituted a likeness of him at the last moment. The messages which Muḥammad transmitted were critical of the arrogance and egoism of the rich and powerful, and also of the gods whose shrines

I

in Mecca made the town a place of pilgrimage and so were a source of economic power. It is hardly surprising that the messenger and his followers were eventually obliged to leave the city and take up residence in the oasis of Yathrib, afterwards named Medina (or 'the city') about 200 miles to the north. This migration (*hijra*) is the event which initiated the Muslim calendar, and it is worth noting that the start of the Muslim era is not reckoned from the birth of Muḥammad nor from the commencement of the revelation, but rather from the creation of an Islamic community. At first, this community represented just another community in the large mosaic of tribes at that time, yet by the time of Muḥammad's death his community controlled not just Mecca and Medina but was the most powerful force in Arabia. Only twenty years after his death it had overthrown the Persian empire and captured all the Asian territories of the Roman empire except the area that is now modern Turkey. Only 100 years after his death there existed a considerable empire which extended from the Pyrenees to the Punjab, and from the Sahara to Samarkand.

While Muḥammad lived there was no doubt as to the rightful leadership of the community, but when he died it became necessary to select a *khalīfah*, or successor to the messenger of God. This person could not himself be a messenger, since Muḥammad was the last one, and the criteria for selection became a controversial issue in the community. One section of the Islamic community, which later turned out to be a minority, argued that the Prophet had appointed his successor – his son-in-law and cousin, ʿAlī. This group came to be known as the Shīʿa, or followers of ʿAlī. The majority, on the contrary, took the view that Muḥammad had knowingly left the question of his succession open, passing the responsibility of deciding who would be best suited to assume the leadership to the community itself. These Muslims came to be known as the Sunnīs, or the adherents of tradition (Sunna), a description which is supposed to emphasize their following of principles rather than personalities. Yet the Shīʿī case is a good deal broader than a simple reliance upon Muḥammad's putative choice of ʿAlī and the latter's personal qualities. There is also the theoretical principle that, given God's justice and grace towards human beings, it is inconceivable that he should have left the question of leadership open. The first civil war in the Islamic community occurred when ʿAlī became fourth caliph in suspicious circumstances, the third caliph ʿUthmān from the Umayya tribe having been murdered in Medina in 35 AH / 655 CE. When ʿAlī died his supporters looked for a more appropriate representative of spiritual leadership than that available among the rich and worldly Umayyads. They naturally looked towards 'Alī's sons (and Muḥammad's grandsons) Ḥasan and Ḥusain, who were not powerful enough, however, to prevent the formation of an Umayyad dynasty. The Shī'ites argued that the legitimate authority in the Islamic community lay with the Prophet's family, and only the rule of Muḥammad's legitimate heir could bring to an end the injustice and exploitation of the existing régime and replace it with a political system based upon the Qur'ān and the example of Muḥammad. At various times Shī'ite régimes have come to dominate some territories in the Islamic empire, and the basic principles of Shī'ism have become fragmented into many different sects. The first few centuries of Islam have seen a large variety of movements who have all attempted to restore what they have interpreted as the authentic doctrine of Islam in place of the unsatisfactory status quo.

It is often argued that the Shī'a has a much more committed attitude to philosophy than do Sunnī Muslims. It is certainly true that Islamic philosophy has continued to flourish in the Shī'i world as compared with many centuries of neglect in the Sunnī world, and the Persian-speaking world has played a highly significant role in continuing the tradition initiated in the classical period. One reason might be because the sources of authority in Shī'ism do not tend to pay a great deal of attention to the *sunna* (practice) of the Prophet or the Traditions or the *madhhāb* (schools of law) of the Sunnī tradition. So reason comes to be an important principle, albeit in its role as a gift of God, and was regarded as both legitimate and necessary.

Of particular significance is *ta'wīl* or interpretation, which involves understanding the nature of revelation by returning to the original meaning and going behind the apparent meaning. This approach suggests that the divine language of the Qur'ān uses symbolic and allegorical language and needs to be interpreted if it is to be really understood. For example, the Ismā'īli thinker Ḥamīd al-Dīn al-Kirmānī (d. *c.* 412 AH/1021 CE) has a theory of language which accounts for the different forms of expression in the Qur'ān. He contrasts the contingency of language with the necessity of God, and suggests that this means that language cannot define God. But we have to use language to describe God, there is nothing else available, and we should understand that language is just a starting point, not where we should stop. We can use our intelligence to work out some features of what it means to live in a world created by God, but we must be aware of the limits of that language. It is our reason which gets us to this conclusion. This should be placed within the context of a wider debate in the fourth/tenth century among Muslim theologians and philosophers dealing with the relation between God's attributes and his essence. Many thinkers came to argue that the problems of defining God should be resolved by concluding that he is beyond existence and non-existence, that only negative properties should be applied to him (i.e. he is not finite, he is not mutable, and so on).

The notion of creation as a process is taken very seriously by many Shīʿī thinkers, and the command by God to the world to be (*kūn*) is not seen as just issued once, but part of a continual set of instructions and orders. This came to be part and parcel of the normal way in which the *falāsifa* saw creation, as is hardly surprising given their general commitment to a Neoplatonic way of interpreting the nature of reality. Of course, with Shīʿism comes the idea of divine intervention being ever-present as a direct possibility through the influence of particular imams or representatives of God. But it is important to distinguish between this and the main position of the *falāsifa*. For the latter the constant creation is not a result of a deity who intends to bring about certain results and who is as a result keeping the tap flowing, as it were. Nor is the eternal dependence of the world on the creator a sign that our fates and that of our world is at the command of a personal deity. On the contrary, the descriptions of the connection we have with God rule out such direct kinds of relationship, and the world flows from God automatically without his direct intervention at all. So there is no scope for arguing that Shīʿism is more attuned to *falsafa* at all. On the contrary, the emphasis in Sunnīsm on general institutions such as the caliphate and the consensus (*ijmāʿ*) of the community might be seen as more in line with the adherence of the *falāsifa* to general principles such as the necessary status of causality and the ability of logic to analyze the deep structure of language.

But what this shows is how misguided the question of which type of Islam is more friendly to Islam is. It is just as foolish as associating particular theological schools of thought with philosophy (Muʿtazilite) and others as antagonistic (Ashʿarite). We shall see from the case of Abū Saʿīd al-Sīrāfī that it is perfectly possible for a Muʿtazili to be opposed to *falsafa*, and we shall also see that there is no difficulty in seeing al-Ghazālī as a *failasūf* malgré lui.

The principal task of Islamic government is to establish obedience to God and his law as laid down in the Qurʾān, although in practice the Qurʾān has had to be interpreted in particular ways to cope with new situations, situations which were dealt with in terms of the Traditions (*ḥadīth*) concerning the doings and sayings of Muḥammad. The political and social upheavals so prevalent in early Islam were not regarded as merely struggles for power by different groups but as religious disputes made concrete by political and military action. Apart from the caliphs, then, another source of power and influence was to be found in those learned individuals (*'ulamā'*) who had considerable knowledge of Islamic law and who were capable of interpreting novel and difficult cases. The judgments of the *'ulamā'* were gradually built up into a system of law or *sharī'a*, which specified the way of life ordained for human beings by God. Of course, different schools of jurisprudence arose, yet within the Sunnī community no one of them was regarded as exclusively true, and where they agreed their judgments were held to be obligatory. Although the *'ulamā'* were certainly not regarded as priests, they did come to wield authority as legitimizers of régimes and witnesses to their doctrinal orthodoxy. Only the first four caliphs after Muḥammad came to be regarded as really orthodox, and many of the succeeding administrations clearly owed their position more to secular power than to religious authority. Nevertheless, the *'ulamā'* were frequently significant politically in providing particular rulers with their Islamic credentials, and as such their suspicion of philosophy became something of a thorn in the side of philosophers in the medieval Islamic world.

From the early years of Islam, then, the community was involved in a number of controversies which occasionally struck at the very essence of the religion. Disputes took place on all fronts, not just between different military powers, but also between different interpretations of the Qur'ān and its law, different views on the legitimacy of government and religious behaviour, so that the notion of the Muslim way of life became something of an essentially contested concept. But none of these controversies were *philosophical* in the sense that they embodied the sort of philosophical thinking which came later to be transmitted from the Greeks to the Islamic world. This kind of philosophy first appeared in the third/ninth century under the ʿAbbāsid dynasty, the successors of the Umayyads. The ʿAbbāsids transferred the capital of the empire from Damascus to Baghdad, a significant move since the ʿAbbāsids had gained control largely due to the support of the Shīʿite Persians, a non-Arab people with a highly developed culture of their own. Since the Umayyad dynasty, the empire had contained the whole of the area in which Greek thought had spread, with the exception of Europe still under the control of Byzantium. Under the ʿAbbāsids not only Syria and Egypt but also Persia came into the empire, all areas with a long history of Greek cultural and scientific influence. To a large extent the interest in Greek sciences such as medicine, astrology and mathematics was practical and regarded as useful among the administrative élite in these territories. It was within this context that the 'Abbāsid caliph al-Ma'mūn founded in 217/832 the House of Wisdom (*bayt al-ḥikma*), which was designed both to encourage and bring some order into the development of Greek influence on Islamic philosophy and science in his realms. This institution comprised not just an observatory but also a library, with a team of translators directed to transmitting originally Greek texts into Arabic.

We might wonder, though, how a basically Greek set of ideas, domesticated in Greek religion and culture, and expressed in the Greek language, came to fascinate intellectuals in a radically dissimilar society in which knowledge of Greek was lacking in Jews and Muslims and where the religions of Judaism and Islam were very different from the religious beliefs of the Greeks. The means of transmission were through the mediating force of Christianity and its eventual assimilation of Greek thought. Although for quite a lengthy period philosophy and Christianity were mutually antagonistic, Christian thinkers came to use philosophy, or at least philosophical techniques, in order to provide a rational justification for religion while still insisting on its divine origin. For example, the development of patristic theology in the fourth century CE by St Basil in the East and St Augustine in the West employed elements of Stoicism and Platonism in many of its arguments. The continuation of the traditional Greek philosophical curriculum in the schools of Athens, Constantinople, Antioch and Alexandria made it available to the Muslim conquerors of these areas. Especially important was the way in which the competing Syriac churches, the Nestorians and the Jacobites, adapted various philosophical texts to further their doctrinal controversies and so made these available to the Muslims who lived in the same areas.

What motives did the Christians have for incorporating Greek ideas into their thinking? Since the Bible was regarded as the criterion of truth, those Greek ideas (and there are many of them) which are, at least superficially, incompatible with biblical truth were by and large discarded. Yet many Christians were eager to represent their faith in such a way that it was possible to maintain a notion of continuity between Christianity and Greek accounts of the correct way of living. This might seem a little surprising. After all, the Christian revelation is a covenant of God's relation in history with a specific group of people, the Jews, and their spiritual successors, the Christians, with whom God has established a new covenant in place of the old. The specificity of the historical basis of this relationship is apparently opposed to the entirely general characteristics of philosophy, consisting as it does of universal rules of reasoning. The fact that Christians were interested in converting the world to their religion and thus broadening the particular relationship between God and his people to include everyone else meant that they became involved in presenting their religious doctrines in as universal a form as possible.

There were aspects of Platonism which Christians did reject out of hand as idolatrous. For example, the belief in the existence of a hierarchy of subordinate deities through whom God works in the world and communicates with his creatures was beyond the bounds of acceptability for orthodox Christians and Muslims. The orthodox position of both religions is that God is entirely apart from the world which he has made and is only available to us through such revelation of himself which he may provide. But many of the Islamic philosophers accepted the Greek view that God communicates his divinity as far as possible to the world and all its parts through the variety of immortal 'souls' lower than him, and so is accessible to a degree to all his creatures via their existing religious traditions. Despite a well-developed hostility to philosophical views which could be seen as offering competing religious hypotheses, Greek philosophy was studied by Christians seeking arguments and argument forms which would be useful in doctrinal disputes in Christianity itself and in disputes with followers of other faiths. What made the study of Greek philosophy by Muslims possible at all was the existence of more-or-less reliable translations of an eclectic range of philosophical texts into Arabic, chiefly by Christian scholars. From 150/750 to 400/1000 a large number of translations were made, some directly from the Greek and some from Syriac versions of the original. The standard is very variable, as is hardly surprising given the basic differences between Greek and Semitic languages, and the difficulty of the subject matter, yet some translations are impressive in their accuracy. The interest in Greek philosophy led to the commissioning of translations of a good deal of Plato and Aristotle, and a substantial body of Neoplatonic works. Plotinus, Porphyry, Proclus and John Philoponus were well known, as were the commentaries of Alexander of Aphrodisias. Some books were described as by Aristotle which definitely were not, such as the *Theology of Aristotle* (in reality Books IV–VI of Plotinus' *Enneads*) and the *Liber de Causis* (by Proclus). Since many philosophers were also doctors and interested in science there were many translations too of Galen, Hippocrates, Euclid and Archimedes.

Yet it would be a mistake to regard philosophy in Islam as starting with the translation of Greek texts. Interestingly, philosophical distinctions arose in Islamic theology without any apparent direct connection with philosophy, but rather through the development of appropriate rules of legal reasoning. When Islam was established in the seventh century the legal norms seemed rather elementary, with the right and wrong paths being determined by reference to the Qur'ān and the Traditions (*ḥadīth*), which embody supposedly reliable accounts of the practices and beliefs of the Prophet Muḥammad and his Companions. Interpretative difficulties were to be dealt with by a consensus of the learned and independent reasoning was frowned on. The text of the Qur'ān was taken to be decisive, as opposed to independent sources and principles. But the rapid expansion of Islam and its rule over highly sophisticated civilizations made necessary the assimilation of a great number of foreign legal elements, which initially were often subjected to a process of Islamization and identification as Qur'ānic. Foreign practices and customs were absorbed into Islam by means of legal devices. Yet Islamic law is based on religious texts and supposedly requires no further justification. In the absence of a notion of natural law in most Islamic theology, and the corresponding idea of ethical and rational values which impose themselves on God, or which he imposes on himself or which are inherent in him, there is no a priori standard by which to assess human laws and norms other than reference to some religious criterion. Islamic law is flexible enough to accept that it is difficult to claim certainty in all cases, and many jurists are satisfied with solutions which are more just than other solutions.

There are some interesting legal devices which obviously have philosophical relevance. One of these is that a figurative meaning (*ta'wīl*) may be preferred to the apparent meaning (*ẓāhir*) of a religious text if the former is normally admissible for the expression in question, is required for the understanding of the text and is supported by a convincing piece of evidence. In fact, the application of this interpretative device was strictly controlled and very limited. Another philosophically relevant distinction is between terms which are equivocal and those which are unequivocal and so have only one sense. Thirdly, a text which is rather imprecise and loose can be taken, if there is appropriate evidence, in a more precise and determined sense. The movement from the particular to the general via analogy (*qiyās*) is also very important. The sorts of issues which arise here are legion. Do the texts which refer to 'Muslims' and 'believers' cover women and slaves? The Qur'ān threatens with a 'painful punishment' those who store up gold and silver without spending them in the way of God (IX,34): is this text supposed to establish a norm that implies the deduction of the tithe from all objects of gold and silver? Does this include jewellery and precious stones? There was a great deal of controversy in Sunnite Islam over the appropriate use of analogy, with some strongly opposed to its use at all, and much argument over particular cases even when its use was agreed. The introduction of Greek logic as a rival to the established Islamic reasoning process of analogy led to a good deal of argument, too. But, clearly, even before Greek logic was available, there were philosophical arguments going on in the field of jurisprudence, disputes concerning the nature of law, analogy and meaning, and it is not unnatural to suppose that some Muslim jurists might have welcomed the contribution which Aristotelian logic could make to conceptual clarification in this area.

The development of theology became an issue when Muslims felt the need to systematize the metaphysical worldview of Islam, which meant that there was now a need to reconcile apparent contradictions and difficulties. A particular difficulty was the reconciliation of God's omnipotence and omniscience with his beneficence given the problem of the human capacity to do evil and to be punished accordingly. Another popular theological topic was the appropriate interpretation of anthropomorphic language in the Qur'ān in spite of the fact that the Qur'ān is clear in stating that God does not have a body. One might have expected that the development of interest in Greek philosophy would have led theologians to seek new logical instruments in their theoretical discussions which would be transformed by the import of powerful philosophical concepts. But this did not happen. The philosophers in the Islamic world (who were frequently known as *falāsifa*, a term significantly derived from the Greek language rather than native to Arabic) were rather contemptuous in their philosophical (although not necessarily in their theological) works of the dialectical and so inferior modes of reasoning which the theologians employed. However, the difference between demonstrative and dialectical reasoning is not between a valid and an invalid procedure, but merely between working with premises which have already been established as certain and unchallengeable, in the case of demonstration, and working with premises which are generally accepted but not logically established, in the case of dialectic. In theology the premises are taken from a religious doctrine, which the philosophers assumed could not be logically proved to be true, and so the consequent reasoning is limited and reduced to a defence of those premises without being in a position to prove them. From the middle of the ninth to the middle of the eleventh centuries CE, philosophers and theologians who were not both tended either to ignore each other or to swap insults.

The description of theology by the *falāsifa* as *kalām* or merely a dialectical and defensive line of reasoning is hardly fair. To a large extent, the difference between philosophy (*falsafa*) and *kalām* is merely a difference in subject matter: philosophers work with philosophical premises while theologians (*mutakallimūn*) apply themselves to religious texts. *Kalām* sets out to represent the speculative framework and the rational content and coherence of the principles of Islamic belief. It was necessary to resolve conflicts between revelation and practice, between for instance God's great power and the existence of innocent suffering in this world, and the issues raised are often philosophical, although not explicitly identified as such. Why not? Presumably the reason is that it was thought by many that the theoretical instruments of unbelievers could not explicitly be used to unravel problems in the doctrine of Islam. After all, *kalām* became important within a certain context. The term *kalām* means 'speech' or 'conversation' – it is based upon the idea that truth is found via a question and answer process. Someone proposes a thesis, and somebody else questions it, this form of disputation being apparent in the grammatical structure of the works of *kalām* themselves. This technique for solving dogmatic problems accurately represents the fact that from the beginning Muslim theology had to think very much in terms of defence and attack. The *mutakallimūn* had to struggle from the beginning against comparatively sophisticated Jewish, Christian and Manichean intellectual skills. Theology, says ibn Khaldūn (732/1332–808/1406), 'merely wants to refute heretics'. It is 'a science which involves arguing with logical proofs in defence of the articles of faith and refuting innovators who deviate in their dogmas from the early Muslims and Muslim orthodoxy'.[1] It acts, according to al-Ghāzalī, like a protection troop at the pilgrim road.[2] Al-Ghāzalī brings out in more detail what is unsatisfactory about *kalām*:

A group of the *mutakallimūn* did indeed perform the task assigned to them by God. They ably protected orthodoxy and defended the creed which had been readily accepted from the prophetic preaching and boldly counteracted the heretical innovations. But in so doing they relied on premises which they took over from their adversaries, being compelled to admit them either by uncritical acceptance, or because of the community's consensus, or by simple acceptance deriving from the Qur'ān and the Traditions. Most of their polemic was devoted to bringing out the inconsistencies of their adversaries and criticizing them for the logically absurd consequences of what they conceded. This, however, is of

[1] Ibn Khaldūn, *Al Muqaddimā* (Prolegomena), trans. F. Rosenthal, *The Muqaddimah: an introduction to history* (New York, Columbia University Press, 1958), III, pp. 155 and 34.
[2] Al-Ghāzalī's critical view of *kalām* may be appreciated by the fact that his very last work, finished only a few days before his death, was titled *Curbing the masses from engaging in the science of kalām*.

little use in the case of one who admits nothing at all except the primary and self-evident truths.[3]

A dramatic example of the confrontation between *kalām* and philosophy took place in Baghdad in 331/932 before the vizier. A discussion took place between the Christian translator Abū Bishr Mattā (*c.* 870–940) and the theologian Abū Saʿīd al-Sīrāfī (d. 368/979) over the respective merits of the 'new learning' which came from the Greek philosophical tradition. Mattā puts the philosophical position in this way: 'I understand by logic an "instrument" of "speech" by which correct "speech" (*kalām*) is known from incorrect and unsound meaning from sound. It is like a balance, for by it I know overweight from underweight and what rises from what sinks.'[4] His opponent argues at length that each language is a conventional rather than natural system and that they each have different interpretative principles or 'instruments' which are relevant to that specific language. So Greek logic would only be appropriate to the Greek language, and wholly useless in analyzing aspects of Arabic. Obviously, the Aristotelian move required to avoid this sort of objection is to deny that by 'speech' is meant the ordinary lexical meanings, but rather the logical principles inherent in linguistic structure and common to all languages. Al-Sīrāfī refuses to accept this point, reiterating his view that Aristotelian logic cannot do justice to the Arabic language. Al-Sīrāfī pushes the point that the philosophers do not even know the Greek language and the texts they adopt they only have at third-hand, from Greek to Arabic via Syriac. Mattā replies by expressing his confidence in the quality of the translations, and adds that it is not important that every linguistic nuance survives in translation, as long as the basic semantic values are accurately reproduced from Greek into Arabic. Yet al-Sīrāfī is so impressed with the importance of particular languages that he is not prepared to accept this suggestion, and insists again upon the uselessness of a logic being applied to anything but the language out of which it was derived.

Significantly, a strong theme throughout al-Sīrāfī's attack on the introduction of Greek philosophy into Muslim intellectual life is opposition to glorification of Greece and Greeks by comparison with the community of Islam. He suggests that admiration for Greek culture is overdone, and

[3] Al-Ghāzālī, *al-Munqidh min al-Ḍalāl* (The deliverer from error), trans. R. McCarthy, *Freedom and fulfillment* (Boston, MA, Twayne, 1980), pp. 61–114; pp. 68–9.
[4] D. Margoliouth (trans.), 'The discussion between Abū Bishr Mattā and Abū Saʿīd al-Sīrāfī on the merits of logic and grammar', *Journal of the Royal Asiatic Society* NS, XXXVII (1905), pp. 79–129: p. 112.

that no nation is superior to others in its complement of accomplishments. He also pokes a lot of fun at Mattā's failure to master Arabic itself, and thinks he would be better employed studying Arabic grammar and semantics rather than having anything to do with Greece. He does suggest, however, that a distinction can be made between speech and meaning, claiming that the former is 'natural' and mutable, while the latter is apprehensible by reason and is permanent. But he transforms the Aristotelian conception of the relation between logic and language, regarding logic as not a way of reasoning but rather a way of speaking properly. Once the method of correct expression is mastered it can be transformed into a science, that of grammar, and translated into formal rules. It may well be that these formal rules and the intelligible meanings are the same for all languages, but they can only be grasped language by language and then compared, and Mattā has admitted that he does not know Greek (and his Arabic is not perfect, either). Given al-Sīrāfī's definition of logic (a highly question-begging definition, it must be admitted) he is able to claim that the true logician must be able to express himself correctly, and distinguish correct from incorrect expressions on all levels. He pours scorn on Mattā, firing off questions at him which express the implications of his disagreement with Mattā on the basic logic–grammar distinction. Mattā's silence is supposed to represent cowed defeat, no doubt, but perhaps it rather appropriately comes over as a dignified silence when confronted with a disputant who refuses to take seriously a reasonable philosophical argument. Al-Sīrāfī appropriately ends the discussion with a flood of praise about dialectic in both its legal and theological form. These sciences incorporate a complete knowledge of a language, its logic and grammar, and employ sound reasoning to go beyond the confines of language to determine the truth between two opposing positions.

The dispute between al-Sīrāfī and Mattā over the respective merits of *kalām* and *falsafa* brings to the surface an important explanation for the problematic nature of Greek philosophy in the Islamic community. Many of the questions which philosophy applied itself to already had answers provided within the context of Islam. For example, the question of how people ought to live and act had been answered in the Qur'ān, which contains everything in the way of information required to ensure salvation and concerning religious and social behaviour. Islamic law provided details of personal and property relations, and the sorts of political structures which are acceptable. The Muslim had only to observe the Qur'ān, the Traditions of the Prophet and his Companions, and the judgments of the early caliphs. More abstract issues were dealt with by *kalām*, which argued towards certain theoretical analyses of concepts such as power, fate, God and freedom. In addition there existed a well-developed science of language of long standing. The arrival of philosophy on the intellectual scene seemed to challenge many of these traditional Islamic sciences, and threatened those who were expert in such forms of knowledge. After all, philosophy covered a lot of the same ground as *kalām* but claimed greater surety for its methods and conclusions. Furthermore, on a number of important issues philosophy presents a contrary conclusion which might seem to challenge Islam itself. Aristotle, often referred to as the 'first master', appeared to argue that the world is eternal, that there can be no individual survival of the soul after death and that God is radically removed from connection with his creation and creatures. The scene was clearly set for a major demarcation dispute between the philosophers and the rest of the Islamic intellectual community, a dispute which alternately raged and simmered in the Islamic world from the fourth to the sixth centuries AH/tenth to the twelfth centuries CE.

It is important to distinguish the controversy between *falsafa* and *kalām* from an important theological controversy which took place at around the same time as philosophy entered the Islamic world. The Mu'tazilites, who called themselves the 'people of unity and justice', presented a large number of theological doctrines which sought to define a more satisfactory *rational* basis for Islam. They argued for the unity and justice of God, for the responsibility of human beings for their actions and the necessity to try to justify the actions of God. Perhaps their most significant doctrine for our purposes was the importance of reason in guiding Muslims to a knowledge of God, and the belief in the agreement of reason with revelation. It is hardly surprising that the very same caliph al-Ma'mūn who encouraged the introduction of Greek philosophy and science was enthusiastic about the Mu'tazilite approach. Indeed, this theological school was made the official doctrine in Islam between 833 and 848, with a corresponding persecution of Muslims who could not accept the Mu'tazilite interpretation of Islam. However, the dominance of Mu'tazilite doctrine was relatively short-lived and al-Ash'arī (260/873–324/935) spearheaded the reaction by affirming the more traditional interpretation of Islam, which emphasizes the gap between the power and knowledge of God, and of his creatures. Al-Ash'arī argued that appropriate religious authority is enough to justify the basic theses of Islam, and that reason is not required to justify revelation. The Mu'tazilites insisted that reason is an important interpretative device in gaining profound insight into the Qur'ān, and that it is a condition of true faith that one should by the use of reason alone know all the following: God's existence, essence and characteristics; the possibility of prophecy and revelation; what it is to act morally and immorally; and the structure of the physical world and its relation to its maker. These facts must be reached by the use of independent reason since otherwise they must rest on authority and tradition, which are imperfect grounds for holding such important beliefs. The Ash'arites challenged this set of theses and argued that reason alone is incapable of establishing satisfactorily the basic themes of Islam. (It is worth noting that both the Ash'arites and the Mu'tazilites hold reason in considerable regard as a means of discovering important facts – a point we shall establish later.) To give an example which helps bring out briefly the flavour of the controversy, we might look at the Qur'ānic injunction against wine. The drinking of grape wine is forbidden in the Qur'ān because it is intoxicating, and so by analogy date wine is forbidden too. The connection between the reason and the rule is different for Mu'tazilites and Ash'arites. For the former, the cause or reason for the rule might help us discover the reason God had in mind when introducing the law. This would be based upon the idea of an objective system of ethics with which God would have to concur. Ash'arites, though, would argue that the cause is just used by God for a particular purpose, and it does not follow that he must use that cause or have that reason for promulgating the law.

Although the Mu'tazilites possibly derived some of their central concepts from philosophy, it would be a serious mistake to think that they came nearer to philosophy than their Ash'arite opponents. To take an example, al-Sīrāfī was a Mu'tazilite, and this did not prevent him from launching his attack upon the new philosophy. The dispute between the two theological schools frequently employed philosophical arguments, yet in its subject matter and methods it was clearly a theological dispute, characterized by dialectical rather than demonstrative forms of reasoning. Despite the strong insults and accusations of heresy which were thrown about in the dispute, it is difficult to argue that either party was involved in the defence of views which were incompatible with Islam itself.

As we shall come to see, the views of philosophers were condemned on occasion as heretical and beyond the limits of Muslim belief. It is important here to distinguish between two sorts of principle. One principle shared by both Ash'arites and Mu'tazilites is that reason is usefully employed in understanding religion. A principle that both would reject

is that religion may be usefully analyzed by the use of concepts derived
from Greek, especially Aristotelian, philosophy. The use of such philosophical concepts were not regarded as helpful in an understanding of
religion. But in rejecting philosophy the theologians were not rejecting
reason; on the contrary, they were enthusiastic concerning the value of
reason when employed in a suitably domesticated context. It is not difficult to find Qur'ānic backing for this position. The Qur'ān does not
require that people believe in its teaching blindly. Both believers and
unbelievers are invited to ponder, reflect and understand through the
use of their reason. It warns against blind obedience to one's predecessors (II,170; V,104) and repeatedly addresses itself to the understanding
of its audience (III,65; XII,2). Although the teachings of the Qur'ān are
based upon divine authority, they often seek by rational persuasion to
bring about faith. There are a number of verses which seek to prove that
God must be a unity, in particular the verse which argues that the whole
universe would have perished if there existed several gods beside God
(XXI,22). Similarly, the Qur'ān seeks to establish by argument the veracity of the Prophet, referring to the pious life which he led prior to
revelation (X,17).

The rituals mentioned in the Qur'ān are often grounded in reason
and Muslims are commanded to understand their spirit and purpose.
Many of the rituals are designed to contribute to the welfare of Muslims
themselves. For example, Muslims who pray are thereby less likely to fall
into disfavour and dishonour, since Muslims who pray remember God
(XX,14). The practice of *zakāt* or charity, although not a ritual, is designed
to prevent the accumulation of wealth in the hands of only a few people
and to spread some of it around the community (IX,60; LIX,7). We shall
see later the different explanations which the philosophers give of such
religious commandments and customs. The point here is to establish that
rational understanding is a much-valued aspect of traditional Islam even
where Muslims are suspicious of philosophy. Indeed, it might be argued
that the Prophet implies the significance of reason when he abolished
prophecy. The Prophet himself announced that he was the last of the
prophets, and so there would be no more revelations or voices claiming
divine authority. God has thus invited human beings to assume responsibility for their judgments and to employ their reason in establishing the
way they ought to behave. Of course, they will be helped by the Qur'ān
and the rest of Islamic law and tradition, but there will frequently be occasions when these sources do not comment upon particular problems
and situations. We can no longer expect a prophet to reveal the right

way to us in these circumstances, and it might well be argued that we should then have to use reason to work out a solution.

If reason and rational explanation were held in such high esteem by some Muslim intellectuals, why then did they not enthusiastically embrace Greek philosophy as the acme of rationality and employ it to make sense of problems which arose in the interpretation of Islam? A variety of tentative answers may be offered. Firstly, as we have seen, the space which philosophy sought to occupy was *already* filled by theology, the theory of language and a well-developed jurisprudence. Philosophy appeared to be an interloper into a field of problems which were being taken care of quite adequately by other theoretical devices and from different speculative perspectives. Although some Muslim intellectuals had confidence in the value of reason, this confidence was not boundless, and they acknowledged that in the last analysis faith and religious practice are justified by non-rational criteria, i.e. the commands of God. Secondly, the conclusions which philosophy seemed to offer as the only demonstratively respectable conclusions often ran against the most important principles of Islamic theology, not to mention the Qur'ān itself. When one looks at the character of the argument between al-Sīrāfī and Mattā, and arguments between theologians and philosophers in medieval Islam as a whole, one often finds yet another strain of contention emerging. This is a suspicion that philosophy is an essentially *alien* way of thinking. Muslim intellectuals were, and indeed still are, sometimes wary about dealing with pre-Islamic and non-Islamic themes which have become incorporated in Islam. For example, some of the customs and rituals of Islam are assumed to have a non-Islamic origin, being reflections of older and pagan traditions, yet accepting that such practices have pagan precedents has seemed to some Muslims impious and unworthy of the considerable religious respect in which those practices are held by the community. Philosophy clearly bore the marks of its Greek creators, and it was transmitted to the Islamic world through the good offices of the Christian community, and so in some ways it was doubly alien in character due to its *origins* even before its content was considered. It is probably in reaction to this charge that philosophy is a radically alien activity that al-Fārābī tried rather unconvincingly to provide philosophy with an Eastern pedigree, an Islamic pedigree being unfortunately unavailable: 'It is said that this science [Greek philosophy] existed anciently among the Chaldeans, who are the people of Iraq, later reaching the people of Egypt, from there passing to the Greeks, where it remained until it was transmitted to the Syrians and then to the Arabs. Everything composed by this science was expounded in the Greek language, later in Syriac and lastly in Arabic.'[5]

One of the characteristic aspects of al-Fārābī's approach to philosophy is that he regarded himself as a member of a distinct school in a particular philosophical tradition. This school is a continuation of the Alexandrian tradition in the fifth and sixth centuries CE. He refers to an unbroken line of teachers and interpreters of Greek, and especially Aristotelian, philosophical texts with their ever-developing accretion of criticisms, agreements and arguments. Indeed, al-Fārābī insists that the only genuine sort of philosophy is that which is transmitted from generation to generation.[6]

Abū Naṣr al-Fārābī was born about 259/872 in Turkestan, dying in Damascus in 339/950. He was not only a writer on philosophy and logic but also on the theory of music, and had something of a reputation as a Ṣūfī, although it is difficult to see why. He established the curriculum of the *mashshā'ī* or Peripatetic tradition of Islamic philosophy, and in particular did a great deal to put logic at the head of the philosophical process. His high standard of analyticity and clarity led to his frequent appellation as the 'second master', second, that is, to the *shaykh al-ra'īs*, Aristotle (Arisṭūṭālīs). It is difficult to overemphasize his contribution, since he not only worked in areas of philosophy but really created a whole way of doing philosophy itself. His advocacy of logic had as its main effect the acceptance in the Islamic world of the idea that the rules of logic and grammar are distinct. This had been a controversial issue, in that the grammarians and opponents of philosophy had tended to argue that logic was just Greek grammar being imposed on Arabic grammar, and so far less useful than using Arabic grammar to understand Arabic prose. The argument that logic is the underlying structure of all language and texts, and that it must be understood if we are to be able to understand that prose came to have a long and distinguished history in the classical period of Islamic philosophy.

At the centre of his Neoplatonic theory is the concept of emanation in the hierarchy of being. The First Being, God, is the source of the hierarchy and from it a second being emanates which is the First Intellect and the Second Being. In all, ten intellects emanate from the First Being.

---

[5] Al-Fārābī, *Attainment of happiness*, in M. Mahdi, *Alfarabi's philosophy of Plato and Aristotle* (Ithaca, NY, Cornell University Press, 1962), p. 43.

[6] Al-Fārābī, *Book of letters*, ed. M. Mahdi (Beirut, Dār al-Mashreq, 1970), p. 155. His point here could be regarded as the philosophical equivalent of the way in which the selection of correct *ḥadīth* was made, i.e. in terms of a justified chain of authorities leading down to the present time.

Emanation is an entirely intellectual process which results in the production of multiplicity out of unity, and provides a neat explanation for
the fact that a world which is created by a single being should exhibit
multiplicity. The First Intellect thinks about God (what better object of
thought can it have apart from itself?) and as a result produces a third
being which is the Second Intellect. The First Intellect also thinks about
its own essence and as a result produces the body and soul of the First
Heaven. The consequent sequences of emanated Intellects are linked
with the generation of other celestial things such as the Fixed Stars, the
planets, the sun and the moon. A particularly important role is played
by the Tenth Intellect, the intermediary between the celestial and the
terrestial worlds, between the higher and the lower worlds. This Intellect, which is the Aristotelian *nous poietikos*, the Active or Agent Intellect,
is responsible both for making human thought actual and making form
available to humanity and the sublunary world. What is interesting theologically about this theory is that God is distant from his creation, he only
has an indirect relationship with what he creates, and anything closer
would compromise his absolute unity. Another restriction which exists
is that our thinking can ascend no higher than to the level of the active
intellect, which as we can see from the description of the hierarchy of
being is not very high. So we cannot get closer to an adequate description
of what is higher than the active intellect, and in particular of God.

There are in fact four different kinds of intellect. These concepts became very significant tools in the conceptual resources of Islamic philosophy. The potential intellect is the ability to abstract the forms of an
object from its sensible nature. As the understanding of the form becomes more abstract, we move to the actual intellect, and when this is
perfected (only available to a few) the stage of the acquired intellect is
attained. This represents the level at which the intellect is fully actualized
and the individual human intellect is similar to the other immaterial intellect, the active intellect. It can now not only contemplate itself and the
intelligibles abstracted from material things, but also the active intellect
and the immaterial substances themselves, and this represents the limit
of human knowledge. Al-Fārābī calls this the stage of ultimate happiness
and compares it with immortality, but this is very different from personal
immortality, since for this sort of knowledge to be available to us we
probably need to abandon our bodies, at the same time abandoning the
basis of our personal identity.

The active intellect has an important political role. The perfect ruler
has a repertoire of qualities. He has the ability to rule since he is trained

for this role. He must perfect himself, be a good speaker and put his soul in contact with the Active Intellect, in other words, he must be a good politician. He is strong, with a good memory, respects the truth and despises material things. The ideal city is one which is directed to goodness and happiness, and it develops the appropriate virtues in the citizenry. The virtuous city is like the limbs of a healthy body in making it possible for people to live well. There are four kinds of corrupt city in which people are not encouraged to live virtuously and as a result suffer harm and punishment, a model derived from Plato. Happiness is attainable by the philosophers through their pursuit of intellectual knowledge, and is available to ordinary believers who are not capable of philosophy through their religious and social practices. The philosopher-king must also be a prophet, and uses his abilities to construct a political system in which the community as a whole will be able to participate in happiness and salvation. That means that each individual will be offered a route to salvation according to his capacity to travel on that route.

The ruler knows how to organize the state through his contact with the Active Intellect. The philosopher connects with the Active Intellect using his intellect alone, while the prophet uses his imagination, which is the source of revelation, inspiration and of course prophecy. Coming to knowledge through imagination means being able to express that knowledge in language which is accessible to the public at large, since he (and it is always a 'he' for al-Fārābī) can illustrate the nature of his message with vivid and persuasive images. Prophecy comes about through the interaction between the intellect and the imagination, and it produces in user-friendly ways the same truths available through philosophy. The highly developed imaginative skills of the prophet, which he has naturally as a result of being the person he is, means that he can receive an emanation from the Active Intellect. This is a good example of knowing the same thing in different ways. The prophet and the philosopher know the same thing, but they are obliged to express that knowledge differently, since the prophet has political skills not shared by the philosopher, who only has intellectual skills. Citizens in the imperfect states will find it impossible to perfect their thinking, but they will not necessarily be punished as a result. But if they live in ignorant cities, cities which do not understand the structure of the world, they will not survive as a consequence of their inability to perfect their intellectual abilities and so have no idea of what is happening. Citizens who live in the wicked cities, those who understand how they should act but reject that knowledge, will be punished in the afterlife by having their desires continued after death and continually frustrated. Since their desires are corrupt and essentially linked to the body, they will be permanently unsatisfiable, and so will eternally torment them. It is not clear how this would work, though, since without bodies how could physical pleasures linked with the body remain an issue for the inhabitants of the next world?

The argument that the state will be best run by an individual who not only has the relevant theoretical knowledge but also has the ability to make that knowledge comprehensible and acceptable to the widest possible audience became an important principle of Islamic political philosophy in the classical period.

In his metaphysics, al-Fārābī regarded existence as a predicate of essence, as opposed to an inherent quality of essence. This led to the distinction between two basic kinds of being, being which is necessary in itself since it cannot not be (i.e. God) and everything else, being which is necessary through the action of something else, but contingent in itself. This theory was developed in complex ways by ibn Sīnā, and in many ways has represented the party line of *falsafa*, ibn Rushd being a notable exception.

Al-Fārābī's thought was considerably extended and transformed by Abū 'Alī al-Ḥusain ibn Sīnā (Avicenna). He is without doubt one of the most significant philosophers produced in the Islamic world. He was born near Bukhara in 370/980 and showed a precocious fascination with learning of all kinds, something which was to characterize his very varied intellectual output for the rest of his life. His medical skill led to the local court, and a rather precarious political career as occasional vizier. Despite a tumultuous personal and political life, he produced a large number of logical, philosophical, medical, psychological, scientific and literary works by the time of his death in 429/1037.

There are some themes which run throughout Avicenna's thought. God is the principle of existence, and as pure intellect is the necessary source of all other existing things. The way in which the universe is produced is through emanation in accordance with the form of Neo-platonism so popular in Islamic philosophy, according to which there is a rational production of beings out of an ultimate cause. God is at the summit of the hierarchy of being, and the furthest that human be-ings can proceed along the hierarchy is towards the Active Intellect, the principle behind the logical organization of everything in our world and the last of the ten cosmic intellects that exist below God. This notion of the Active Intellect stems indirectly from Aristotle's concept of the *nous poietikos*, about which he produced little more than hints but which comes to have enormous significance in Neoplatonism and Islamic philosophy. Although the nature of our world appears to be contingent, if we appreciate the way in which causes lead to effects we will understand that once the cause is given, the effect proceeds inevitably and necessarily, yet only God is necessary in himself. We can grasp the nature of the Active Intellect by perfecting our rational abilities, and a prophet is able to do this perfectly since he has an entirely rational soul and is able to grasp the logical structure of reality.

Avicenna interprets Aristotle through Alexander of Aphrodisias in identifying the concept of the Active Intellect with the first cause of the universe. God's self-knowledge is eternal and results in a first intelligence which has as its object the necessity of God's existence, the necessity of its own existence as a result of its relationship with God, and its existence as possible in the sense that it is dependent upon God. From these thoughts arise other existents, until we reach the level of the Active Intellect which produces our world. As we descend down the hierarchy the intelligences diminish in power, and the Active Intellect is so far down the hierarchy that it cannot emanate eternal beings, by contrast with what is above it. Nonetheless, there is nothing really contingent in the universe, according to Avicenna. If something is possibly existent, then it must come to pass at some time; if something remains potentially existent but never comes about, then this is because it cannot come about. If a possibility is actualized, its existence is necessitated by its cause. It cannot not be. Indeed, its cause itself is necessitated by another cause, and so on, but not *ad infinitum*, since there is a being which is necessary through itself, God, who lies at the apex of the hierarchy of causes and effects. Once the existence of God is established by proof, everything else that exists flows from him necessarily, and so has to exist.

Logic for Avicenna is the main route to human perfection. The ignorant person who has no or little grasp of reasoning regards reality as a contingent flow of events. The imperfect thinker bases his thinking on language, while the route to perfection is through the purification of the concepts which are present in our linguistic concepts only imperfectly. Although languages differ, the underlying logical structure is the same in all of them, and it is the role of the philosopher to explore and refine these very general and abstract logical principles. We can acquire some knowledge through sense perception, but it is limited by its particularity. Avicenna gives an important role to imagination in epistemology, which permits us to produce images of things we have not experienced and so broadens the scope of our thought. The more advanced thinker needs to rise above the material nature of our images until he arrives at concepts that are free of physical features. Progressive refinement of our ideas leads to the point where the Active Intellect is able to work with us to produce the rational universals. All efforts by human beings to know can rise no further than the Active Intellect, which represents the basic structure of reality as emanated from God, the pure intellect. At this stage in the hierarchy of emanation, we reach a level of reality which is no longer powerful enough to generate an intelligence and soul. Rather, emanation generates from the Active Intellect a multiplicity of human beings and sublunary matter. Our souls emanate from the Active Intellect, and its illumination (*ishrāq*) of our souls makes possible the kinds of knowledge which can turn towards it. As we shall see in the last chapter, this idea was taken up by *ishrāqi* or Illuminationist philosophy to create an entirely new school of Islamic philosophy.

One of Avicenna's chief contributions to philosophy lies in what he does to the distinction between essence and existence, which he originally acquired from al-Fārābī's account of the distinction between being as necessary in itself and being as necessary through another. We cannot infer from the essence of anything that it must exist, with the sole exception of the essence of God. If all existence were only possible, it need never have actually come about and we should need something which led to existence rather than nothingness. Something must ultimately necessitate actual existence, yet that something cannot itself be merely possible since it would then require something necessary to bring it about if we are to avoid an infinite regress. Hence we arrive at God as the necessitating cause of the universe, the only necessary being in itself.

The soul has to be incorporeal, according to Avicenna, since thought itself is indivisible and cannot be held by something which is composite and divisible. In any case, thought can transcend material limitations so it can hardly be material itself. It is also immortal, and its link with the body, important though it is, is accidental. Since the soul is not composite, it is not subject to dissolution. The eternal soul can suffer penalties and rewards in a life after death as a result of the actions of the individual during this life. We have a choice between good and evil, and we are punished or rewarded in accordance with our actions in this world. Like most of the Islamic philosophers, Avicenna seems to adhere to a theory of the next life which can be understood by all people, regardless of their intellectual capacities. Those capable of intellectual thought will understand salvation in terms of rational improvement, and will not need to be motivated by the corporeal language of the afterlife in the Qur'an to motivate them appropriately. On the other hand, those who are not able to understand the intellectual possibility of a spiritual afterlife are provided in religion with a series of images which is capable of helping them understand that the consequences of their actions in this life have a scope which is not completely limited to this life. Such intellectually imperfect people are not to be encouraged to investigate the bases of their beliefs in the afterlife, since this will only result in confusion or even eventual lack of belief.

There has always been controversy regarding Avicenna's real philosophy, in that some have argued that along with the Peripatetic form of thought which he presented in his works based on Aristotle and Neoplatonism he also had a different form of philosophy, one based on a mystical approach to the nature of reality. He is thus sometimes seen as the originator of *ishrāqi* or Illuminationist philosophy, a form of philosophy which came to have a long and continuing history after the decline of Peripatetic philosophy in the Islamic world. This form of thought emphasizes religion and prophecy as the most important route to knowledge, and places reason in an inferior role. There is a text supposedly with the name 'Eastern philosophy' which is no longer extant, if it ever really existed, so it is difficult to know what the truth is on this issue. But it is certainly true that there are significant mystical aspects to much Islamic philosophy which needs to be acknowledged if we are to understand it as a whole. While his thought came to be regarded as inferior to that of Averroes in the West, in the Islamic world it played a large part in the creation of the Illuminationist philosophy which continues to be significant today, especially in the Persian world.

Avicenna came to have considerable influence on Western philosophy, and enormous influence on Western medicine, and his medical thought is still widely used in the Arab world today. Latin versions of some of his work started to appear in the late twelfth century and were extensively discussed by Aquinas and Albert the Great. Since Avicenna wrote so much on Aristotle, he was valued as an interpreter, although again Averroes was felt to be more accurate and less extravagant in his metaphysics. In the Islamic world Avicenna was severely criticized by al-Ghazālī in his *Tahāfut al-falāsifa* (Incoherence of the philosophers) and more gently criticized by Averroes in his response to al-Ghazālī's attack on Peripatetic thought. Al-Ghazālī was particularly incensed over the nature of Avicenna's views on three topics – the creation of the world out of nothing, God's knowledge of particulars, and corporeal immortality. It certainly is difficult to reconcile creation out of nothing with Avicenna's emanationist system. Given the latter, God seems to have little choice about creating the world, since it is an effect of his thinking about himself, an eternal event which does not take place within time. The account of creation in the Qur'ān is not clear on whether creation was out of nothing, but al-Ghazālī points out against Avicenna that if God is obliged to create the world in the way in which he does create it, then this goes against much of the understanding of creation in Islam. The question is whether God can do anything he wishes, both originally when the world is created and subsequently, through miraculously intervening in the system of nature. Avicenna's God seems to be unable to act freely in these respects, since what emerges from him is part of a logical and necessary system. The nature of the system already specifies what the system is going to be, something which al-Ghazālī argues is damaging to religion. Similarly, God's knowledge is confined to universals and unique events, since he can only be concerned with the formal aspects of reality, not their particular manifestations. Unique events are regarded as logical as opposed to contingent phenomena, since they represent a formal feature of material reality, and they appear to be the sole objects of divine knowledge about our world. It seems to follow from Avicenna's account that there are difficulties in the traditional religious understanding of God knowing everything which goes on in the world of generation and corruption, and this implies that there are then problems with the idea of him knowing how to reward and punish people. Finally, on Avicenna's account what survives death is the soul and not the body, which appears to contradict the Islamic view of the afterlife. Al-Ghazālī argued that Avicenna's conclusions are not only heretical but also unsatisfactory even given Avicenna's premises, and he set out to demolish the whole system of Islamic Peripatetic philosophy, based as it was on a form of Neoplatonism.

Abū Ḥamīd Muḥammad ibn Muḥammad al-Ghazālī was born in Tus in Persia in 450/1058 and had a typically tumultuous life for a member of the intellectual community at that time. The thinkers in this book rarely had stable existences, being part and parcel of the political life of the states in which they lived and so on a perpetual roller coaster as a result of the huge changes which often rocked the Islamic world. In addition, some thinkers were involved in a constant search for the truth, in the sense that they wanted to work out which approach to the truth was the most likely to get to the right end. Al-Ghazālī is perhaps the most difficult of the thinkers to classify, since he was at different times an enemy of *falsafa* (who nonetheless attacked *falsafa* using *falsafa*), an Ashʿarite prepared to use ideas unacceptable to the Ashʿariyya, and a

Ṣūfī who seemed not to require a shaykh, unlike every other Ṣūfī. He spent the first part of his life as head of the Nizamiyah college in Baghdad. He lectured there mainly on Islamic law and moved on to considering a variety of alternative theological interpretations of Islam, distinguishing between the acceptable and the unacceptable. A spiritual crisis led to his retirement from his career and his adoption of the life of a wandering Ṣūfī, which ended with his death in 505/1111.

Al-Ghazālī was an early adherent of the Ash'arite theological school, and its theory of occasionalism, ethical subjectivism and atomism. Their oponents, the Mu'tazilites, regarded human beings as the authors of their own actions, while the Ash'arites regard all action, both human and divine, as brought into being ultimately by God. The Mu'tazilites argued that the world and its creatures were created in order to represent divine justice, so God must do the best he can for us and must reward us in accordance with our deserts. Al-Ghazālī presented the Ash'arite response to these views, arguing that it detracts from the greatness and autonomy of God if the latter is obliged to follow and obey objective principles of justice. Surely God can do anything he wants, he can punish virtuous people and reward the wicked, he is under no obligation at all to his creatures. God has no purposes and his actions cannot be described using human notions like justice at all, so whatever he may do to his creatures cannot be called either just or unjust. While this debate took the form of a theological struggle in accordance with the principles of Islamic theology, it also embodies a great deal of philosophical sophistication, and often deals with the appropriate analysis of key ethical terms. Islamic theology analyzes the ways in which our main ethical language can be translated into language about God, if its 'deep structure' is to emerge.

It is interesting to remember that when al-Ghazālī's works were translated into Latin, his *Intentions of the philosophers* (Maqāṣid al-falāsifa) was such a reliable description of the views of the *falāsifa*, in particular al-Fārābī and ibn Sīnā, that he was often thought of as a *failasūf* himself. In this book he seeks to set out clearly the views of his opponents before demolishing them, in the subsequent *Incoherence of the philosophers*. In this latter book he sets out to overturn the main Neoplatonic and Aristotelian views of reality, in the form of twenty theses which he argues are invalid. The three most serious from an Islamic perspective are the theses that the world is eternal, that God cannot have knowledge of particulars, and that there is no such thing as physical resurrection.

What is interesting about al-Ghazālī's critique of philosophy here and in other places is his steadfast defence of Aristotelian logic as a principle of reasoning, and as a vital technique to be used in theology. Al-Ghazālī had a great influence on the Islamic world, and the form of philosophy which he criticized did fall out of favour in much of the Islamic world around the end of the sixth/twelfth century, while logic became a staple of Islamic theology. Some Islamic thinkers emerged who were so critical of philosophy that they condemned logic along with it (ibn Taymīyya is a good example), arguing that logic was irretrievably infected with philosophical ideas. There were others like ibn Sab'īn and al-Suhrawardī who also criticized Aristotelian logic and tried to replace it with other kinds of logic, yet these reactions to logic are not typical in Islamic culture, and one aspect of al-Ghazālī's influence was a sharp distinction between philosophy and logic.

In his later work, al-Ghazālī became disillusioned with theology as a route to the truth, and became committed to Ṣūfism. He argued that this is by far the best way to achieve salvation, a path which enables the Ṣūfīs to glimpse the world where God's decree is inscribed. Although al-Ghazālī's crisis of faith led him to abandon theoretical approaches to Islam which were not mystical, there is obviously a great deal of philosophy in his mysticism. Like the philosophers, he holds that the soul is the important part of the individual person, and that it is liberated from the body by death. The human soul is a spiritual substance totally unlike the body; it is divine and makes possible our knowledge of God. The body is the vehicle of the soul on its way to the next life, and if we restrain our anger, appetite and intellect we end up with the virtues of temperance, courage, wisdom and justice. We need to aim at the mean when operating with the body, and so transform ourselves through religion to imitate God, insofar as we can do this. Although Ṣūfism is often seen as a private and individual pursuit of a relationship with God, al-Ghazālī argues that the traditional aspects of Islamic life must be followed by the Ṣūfī if his pursuit of salvation is to be effective. As with the philosophers, there are two routes to God. One is the personal route to be undertaken by the Ṣūfī who has mastered the mystical path and who has undergone all the preparatory work which is necessary to achieve such an end. The other route is available to the ordinary believer, and it comprises an exacting obedience to the law and customs of religion, since this enables him to learn how to control himself and how to transform himself in such a way as to bring him as close to God as is possible.

Al-Ghazālī is not an easy thinker to categorize neatly, since he changed his mind over very important issues throughout his life. Some recent commentators such as Richard Frank have argued that he should not be seen as an enemy of the philosophers since so much of his work incorporated philosophical principles, even those of Avicenna. Others such as Leaman have suggested that while this is true, al-Ghazālī was only using the appropriate technical language in order to try to contradict the particular kinds of philosophy with which he disagreed. The important thing to grasp about al-Ghazālī, frequently known as the 'Proof of Islam' in the Islamic world, is that his arguments against philosophy are themselves philosophical, and that he is far too sophisticated to reject ideas just because they appear to contradict faith. The brilliance of his style and the suggestiveness of his writings led to their continuing popularity in the Islamic world for the last 1000 years, and in translation his ideas also entered the Christian and Jewish worlds. It is ironic that this considerable philosopher should be credited with ending Peripatetic philosophy in the Islamic world. Others would regard him as showing how limited in scope that philosophy was, and take him to have cleared the ground for the development of Ṣūfī and other forms of philosophical thought more attuned to the religious life.

Averroes is the Latin name of Abū'l Walīd ibn Aḥmad ibn Muḥammad ibn Rushd, who was born in 520/1126 in Cordoba, Spain. He was a public official, serving as both royal physician and judge, but his political career was often difficult, and by the time of his death in 595/1198 he had suffered banishment to North Africa. He is an outstanding representative of the great cultural achievements of Muslim Spain, and produced philosophical works which came to resonate through the West for many centuries after his death. Averroes' reputation rests to a large degree on his many commentaries on Aristotle, a task he was set by the caliph of Cordoba, presumably during a period when the pursuit of philosophy was officially sanctioned. Averroes wrote commentaries on most of Aristotle's works then extant in Arabic, and he often produced long, medium and short commentaries on the same work. These had different purposes. The long commentary was a detailed exposition of the text suitable for those skilled in philosophy, while the middle commentary dealt with the main ideas but did not precisely follow all the text. The short commentaries allowed Averroes to express what he thought were the implications of Aristotelianism for contemporary issues, and so were much freer in structure. One of the interesting aspects of Averroes' approach to these Aristotelian texts is his attempt to get away from the Neoplatonic modes of interpretation and seek the ideas of Aristotle himself, not an easy task since the post-Aristotelian commentators had had a great effect on how Aristotle was understood, and even how he had been translated into Arabic, in the Islamic world.

The idea that there are at least two routes to the truth, and that they both reach the same end, was misunderstood in the West, which understood Averroes through Latin and Hebrew translations as offering a 'double truth' theory, according to which something could be true in philosophy but false in religion at the same time. Averroes did think he could show that religion and philosophy are compatible, not contrary to each other. He was studied in Christian and Jewish Europe, and his commentaries in Latin were much used when people became concerned with trying to understand Aristotle. In the Jewish world his works were popular also, including his works on religion, since they contributed to understanding the precise relationship between faith and reason. By contrast, he rapidly disappeared in the Islamic world until the nineteenth century, when he came to be seen as the harbinger of an attempt to modernize Islam and its philosophy, and was taken up by the Islamic Renaissance movement.

The death of Averroes saw the end of Peripatetic (*falsafa*) thought in the Islamic world for many centuries, until its rediscovery during the Islamic Renaissance or *Nahda* of the nineteenth century. The thought of ibn Rushd came to have great importance in Jewish and Christian philosophical circles, initially because of his great skill as an interpreter of Aristotle. As we have seen, Aristotle was held to be the most important philosopher (the *shaykh al-ra'īs* in Arabic, or 'first master') in both Christian and Jewish philosophy, and Averroes was irreplaceable as a clear and consistent interpreter of Aristotle's views. The role of al-Andalus, Islamic Iberia, as a link between West and East was important here as well. In al-Andalus there existed three religious communities who lived in close proximity to each other and who of necessity had a good grasp of Arabic, which for a long time was the main language of scholarly activity and science, as well as of more prosaic activities. When Latin and Hebrew speakers wanted to know what Aristotle's theories were, they found it relatively easy to use translators from al-Andalus to transform the Arabic text of Averroes into Hebrew and Latin. The number of such translations which were commissioned shows how popular Averroes was as an interpreter, and how much demand there was for explanations of Aristotle's thought.

The return of Greek philosophy to the West represents an interesting paralleling of the original translations of Greek philosophy into Arabic in 'Abbāsid Baghdad in the ninth century. Then these translations were officially made, often via Syriac by Christians, while in the thirteenth century they were sponsored by Archbishop Raymond of Toledo and Frederick II of Sicily, often via Hebrew by Jews. Although the main direction of the translation movement was on the commentaries on Aristotle, these involved a good deal of Averroes' own philosophy, of course, and they led to the identification of Aristotle with particular controversial philosophical theses, such as the denial of the creation of the world out of nothing, the impossibility of individual existence after death and the relatively brisk dismissal of the role of theology and theologians.

The apparent views of Averroes quickly came to be condemned, and in 1270 and 1277 the bishop of Paris, Étienne Tempier, banned thirteen propositions which were identified with Averroes. The object of the criticism was Latin Averroism, the theory which came to develop as extreme fideism, the thesis that there are different logics involved in religion and philosophy, and that there is no difficulty in accepting that they contradict each other. This came to be known as the 'double truth' theory, which suggested that religion and philosophy could both be true, and yet result in contrary conclusions. Such a theory was held to be controversial, since it meant that religious truths could not be rationally justified, while philosophical truths are irrefutable.

Averroes continued to have his supporters and critics in the medieval period, and philosophers of the status of Aquinas, Albert and Bonaventure regarded him as important enough that they were obliged to deal with his views in their works. With the arrival of Greek texts in the European Renaissance one might have expected that the writings of Averroes would have fallen into obscurity, but the opposite was the case, since the renewed interest in the Greek Aristotle led to renewed interest in his interpreters, and in the Italian universities in the sixteenth centuries there was a revival of Averroism through the debates between Nifo (d. 1538) and Pomponazzi (d. 1525). The radical aspects of the thought of Averroes thus went on to play an important part in the philosophical curriculum of the West through the medieval and Renaissance periods, and provided the essential backdrop for the development of modern philosophy in the West.

Within the Jewish communities Averroes came to have an important place, in particular based on his accounts of the links between religion and reason. The translations which took place into Hebrew were often of his independent works as opposed to his commentaries, and so the discussions in Hebrew tended to be more accurate representations of Averroes' real philosophical views. Averroes continued to fashion the curriculum of the Jewish and Christian intellectual worlds long after he fell into obscurity in the Islamic world. The effect of his thought was to prepare the way for the complete separation of religion and philosophy, which allowed Western philosophy to develop into its characteristic form of modernity. Although the topic of this book is Islamic philosophy, it is worth bearing in mind that much Islamic philosophy was actually practised by non-Muslims. (Actually, many of the opponents of *falsafa* would argue that Islamic philosophy is carried out exclusively by non-Muslims!) The last philosopher whose work we shall consider in some detail is the Jewish thinker Mūsā b. Maimūn (Maimonides). He was born in Cordoba in 1135 CE and was obliged to leave when the Almohads drove the Jews and Christians out of the city. In 1159 he went to North Africa, but Almohad influence at Fez proved too great, and he finally travelled to Cairo, where he died in 1204. Like so many of the *falāsifa*, Maimonides was a famous physician and author of medical texts, but he is still notable for his systematization and codification of the Jewish law. Our interest here is in the tantalizingly complex *Guide of the perplexed*, which he wrote for readers who had some knowledge of philosophy but who did not see how it could be made compatible with Jewish religious doctrine and law. Although Maimonides presents his arguments within the context of Judaism and Jewish law, he is so deeply imbued with the methods and style of the *falāsifa* that it is important to include him in a discussion of some of their central arguments. Maimonides' thought was strongly influenced by Aristotle and al-Fārābī, and apparently hardly at all by his contemporary Averroes, and some of his arguments represent the culmination of particular themes in *falsafa*. Like many of his philosophical predecessors, he took an active part in the political events of his time, becoming head of the Jewish community in Egypt and having influence which spread far wider. It is important to note too that he was not without detractors within his own community, and philosophy was under just as much suspicion among orthodox Jews as it was among orthodox Muslims.

When one considers the work of these highly active individuals in both their public and their intellectual lives, one cannot but be impressed by their ability to produce so much excellent philosophical (and other scholarly) argument and commentary. When one considers the instability of the times, the danger in which they were sometimes placing themselves and the vocal opposition from the *'ulamā'* and the generally conservative Muslim and Jewish communities, their devotion to philosophy must have been considerable. After all, in the case of most of these thinkers their adherence to philosophy was an obstacle rather than an aid to their success in their communities. They could have achieved political influence in the state and intellectual influence within the fields of law, medicine and science, and theology without indulging in philosophical speculation which then lay them open to criticism and persecution. There are other thinkers whom we might have included from this period and who also produced interesting arguments, and where it is relevant their views will be briefly considered. In this book, though, we are largely concerned with al-Fārābī, Avicenna, al-Ghazālī, Averroes, Maimonides and of course Plato and Aristotle, because we can use them to follow through particular issues and arguments in a clear and coherent way.

What are these issues and arguments? There are a great number we might have considered, but we have limited ourselves to two broad themes. The first is to take up al-Ghazālī's challenge that the philosophers' adherence to three theses – that the world is eternal, that God cannot know individuals and that there is no bodily resurrection – constitutes opposition to Islam because they are entirely incompatible with basic religious doctrine. We shall see how these philosophical positions were built up by Aristotle, al-Fārābī and Avicenna, and how al-Ghazālī seeks to marshal philosophical arguments to disprove them and theological arguments to show they are equivalent to unbelief. Then we shall consider the counter-attacks of Averroes and the attempt to reconcile religion with Aristotelian metaphysics. Secondly, we shall concentrate on the conflict between reason and revelation in the area of moral philosophy, and especially over the issue of what constitutes human happiness. There exists in both these broad topics a very important hidden agenda, namely, the idea that the philosophers are not really being frank in their representation of their views, a point which al-Ghazālī and later commentators have pushed very firmly. This hidden agenda will be considered very carefully.

As far as the question of the *falāsifa*'s orthodoxy goes, it must be admitted that the absence of a priesthood in Islam meant that the question of which beliefs are heretical and which are acceptable could never be precisely settled. Belief in the divine character of the Qur'ān itself is a vital aspect of Muslim belief, and any belief or practice which is a candidate for acceptance by the community of Islam must be shown to be compatible with the Qur'ān, and sometimes this compatibility is very difficult to establish. This is hardly surprising given the very different societies which the Qur'ān eventually was called upon to regulate. Even looking for relevant sayings of the Prophet and his Companions to justify decisions became difficult without the large-scale manufacturing of such sayings to suit particular purposes. This involved passing off invented sayings as genuine sayings in order to establish the Islamic credentials of a practice or belief. A good deal of the 'wisdom' which was popular in the Middle East and which derived from non-Islamic religions and traditions became incorporated into acceptable Muslim thinking by the attribution of appropriate attitudes to the Prophet and his Companions. This free-for-all was eventually brought to an end by a strict selection from among the great mass of supposed *hadīth* to arrive at an orthodox corpus. This tidying-up process also involved restrictions on independent reasoning applied to scripture and on the relatively free use of interpretation. Yet the suspicion often existed that the orthodox views which thinkers might express were not really their own views, the latter involving all sorts of heretical and innovative principles which their adherents were too cautious to admit.

When one looks at the writings of theologians and philosophers one cannot but notice the frequent references they make to the necessity of concealing aspects of their approaches to doctrine in order both to escape the wrath of the powerful (either rulers, religious authorities or the masses) and to leave the masses secure in their uncomplicated faith. When one considers the extreme breadth of varieties of Islam, ranging from mystical Ṣūfīs, highly legalistic Sunnīs, Ismāʿilis, Zaidīs and so on it is indeed remarkable that they all chose to describe their beliefs as Muslim. It is often emphasized by Muslims how little persecution there was of heterodox sects and of the main religious minorities in the territory of Islam, and indeed by comparison with the history of much of Christian Europe this is true. Nonetheless, persecution did exist for both philosophers and theologians and was a very real factor in their thinking, making them recognize the desirability of caution in the expression and direction of their views. This caution is certainly present in their writings, yet the texts we shall be considering in detail here are not diminished in their philosophical acuity by this factor. The issue of discretion should not, it will be argued, be taken to negate the philosophical interest of what the *falāsifa* and their opponents say, provided that this is expressed in the form of arguments which can be assessed and analyzed.

This concentration on philosophical arguments is the reason for the inclusion of al-Ghazālī and Maimonides. The former certainly did not regard himself as a philosopher, yet did think it important to master philosophy before criticizing it and presented his criticisms in clear and challenging arguments. Although he opposed Greek philosophy and its development in Islam he was a passionate advocate of logic, claiming that Aristotelian syllogisms are already used and recommended in the Qur'ān, and even illustrating Aristotelian logic with examples from Islamic law.[7] He agrees with the philosophers that there are cases where concealment (*taqīya*) of the truth is no bad thing, that lying is not intrinsically wrong and may be employed if a praiseworthy end is unattainable by other means.[8] Although al-Ghazālī would no doubt have been horrified to find himself referred to as a philosopher, it is the interest and importance of his arguments which make it vital to include him in this book. A similar line of reasoning would justify Maimonides' place. Although not a Muslim, his arguments are excellent examples of *falsafa*. The topics he is concerned with are often the same as those of *falsafa* and he has a well-developed skill of summarizing neatly the philosophical debate up to his time. His arguments are interesting and mesh closely with those of the other thinkers discussed. He is very much part of the continuing debate which took place in the Islamic world in a philosophical form, a debate which more or less came to an end with the death of Averroes. This is not to say that there was no more philosophy but that interesting and novel arguments in Aristotelian form were no longer produced.

Commentators on Islamic philosophy have to avoid many pitfalls. One obstacle is the tendency to assess *falsafa* in terms of its afterlife in Latin in the medieval Christian world. Greek philosophy was initially introduced to that world via translations of Arabic texts into Hebrew and then into Latin, or directly from Arabic to Latin, and these translations formed an important part of the disputes and metaphysics of significant Christian thinkers. But often they were incompletely understood and used for argumentative purposes which were foreign to their origins. Sometimes there is an explicit or implicit assumption that Islamic philosophy is only important insofar as it throws light on Western Scholastic philosophy. This sort of approach is firmly rejected here.

Another pitfall is to over-emphasize the oblique view which the *falāsifa* had of Plato and Aristotle. As we have seen, they were obliged to study their works in translation and with the accretion of some Neoplatonic texts passing as Aristotelian. In addition, the philosophical curriculum which was passed on to them came from a wide variety of different and conflicting sources, with an approach to the interpretation of Aristotle very different from that which exists today. Some commentators

---

[7] Especially in his *The correct balance*, trans. R. McCarthy, *Freedom and fulfillment*, pp. 287–332.

[8] Al-Ghazālī, *Iḥyā' 'ulūm al-dīn* (The renaissance of the sciences of religion), ed. 'Irāqī (Cairo, 'Uthmānīyya Press, 1933), XXIV.

conclude from this that the *falāsifa* really failed to make contact with genuine philosophical controversies as the Greeks knew them, and that their thought is only interesting from the point of view of the history of ideas as opposed to philosophy itself. Those who accept this view would then be involved far more in an historical analysis of *falsafa* than in an analysis and evaluation of the arguments themselves. I shall criticize this approach and suggest that the arguments themselves are interesting and important, and that they do succeed in dealing with crucial issues in Greek philosophy. The addition of Islamic issues to Greek philosophy makes for a fascinating combination and is well worth philosophical as well as historical attention.

But, it is important to avoid yet another pitfall, which is to exaggerate the importance of Islamic philosophy to such an extent that it is seen as the catalyst for much modern Western thought. Although *falsafa* is well worth studying, it is not philosophically very creative. The philosophical distinctions it took from the Greeks were not transformed radically to construct entirely new systems of thought. Yet these distinctions were intriguingly combined with issues in Islamic theology and medieval religious life via subtle arguments, and some of these are the subject of this book. No doubt the arguments presented here by me have their own pitfalls, but hopefully they will avoid those criticized above.

A good example of how philosophical terms came to be created in Islam occurs in the case of the term which came to represent 'being', in Arabic '*wujūd*', or 'existence'. The verbal root *wjd* means 'to find' (*wajada*) and is one of the main words used to represent 'being' in Arabic attempts to replicate Greek ontology, with the present passive *yūjadu*, and the past passive *wujida*, leading to the nominal form *mawjūd*. *Al-mawjūd* means 'what is found' or 'what exists', and a derivative, *wujūd*, is the abstract noun which ended up being used to represent existence. *Wujūd* is often used to represent the copula, the English word 'is' where this is used as a predicate, and it is also used to represent existence. This ambiguity was spotted right at the start of the use of this term for these purposes by al-Fārābī, who points out that the statement *Zayd yūjadu 'ādilan* (Zayd is just) can be understood purely syntactically without having any implication that Zayd actually exists (*Ḥurūf* p. 126). By contrast, in his *Commentary on the De Interpretatione* he refers to the use of *wujūd* as an attribute to make a claim that something actually exists. But he is generally clear that existence is not part of the essence of a thing, and it is not implied by its essence either. Existence is never anything more than an accident.

Al-Fārābī uses the expressions *muṭlaq* and *wujūdī* to describe Aristotle's notion of the assertoric proposition in his *Prior Analytics*, where *wujūd* obviously represents 'belonging'.

By the time of ibn Sīnā, a crucial distinction was explicitly made between *wujūd* and *māhiyya*, where the former represents being in the sense of existence and the latter essence or quiddity. He spoke of God as the *wājib al-wujūd*, the only being whose essence is to exist, by contrast with everything else which is contingent. The realm of existence can be divided up into the *wājib al-wujūd bi-dhātihī*, necessary being in itself, and everything else which follows from it. The idea that there are essences or concepts which then need something to bring them into existence was adopted enthusiastically by many of the *mutakallimūn*, and they discussed the particular kind of existence which is appropriate to God, a very different kind than that which is applicable to his creatures. In this vein al-Ghazālī describes God as 'Being without qualities' (*al-wujūd bi-la māhiyya*) (*TF* 251). He was able to fit the account of being provided by ibn Sīnā into his Ashʿarite and occasionalist metaphysics, since ibn Sīnā accepts that something is needed to move a thing from being nothing more than an idea to becoming an actual existent, and this role is that traditionally assigned to God.

Manuals of logic from the fourth/tenth century regarded *wujūd* as possessing an essence that the mind can comprehend without apprehension. This point is developed at great length by al-Suhrawardī, who argues that the immediacy of existence can be linked via presence (*ḥuḍūr*) and represent unmediated knowledge of reality.

This point is developed by ibn Rushd, who is more explicit on the function of *wujūd* as indicating a truth claim. Existence may be understood as attributing a predicate to a subject, an accident being applied to the substance which serves as the subject of the statement (*TT* 224). He formalized a powerful line of opposition to ibn Sīnā's views on being, however, since ibn Rushd argued that existence has priority over essence. Ibn Rushd accepted the logical distinction between existence and essence, but criticized its application to ontology. It is not just a matter of existence being brought to an essence which allows us to talk of the essence as being actualized, since the real existence of the essence is part of the meaning of the name, and so is a condition of our use of the essence in the first place. If the existence of a thing depended on the addition of an accident to it, then precisely the same would be the case for existence itself, leading to an infinite regress. Al-Suhrawardī took this to show that essence is prior, since if existence were a predicate of essence, essence has to exist itself before any further question of existence can be raised. In his *ishrāqi* approach, existence is nothing more than an idea, and one can describe reality in terms of lights with different intensities.

Mullā Ṣadrā rejected this argument and replaced it with *aṣālat al-wujūd*, the priority of existence. He argued that existence is accidental to essence in the sense that existence is not a part of essence. But there is no problem in understanding how existence can itself exist as more than a thought, since existence is an essential feature of actuality itself, and so no regress is involved. A development of the concept is provided by Mullā Ṣadrā, who uses the term *wujūdiyya*. He argues that the *wujūd* in everything is real, except for the abstract notion of being where this is an entirely mental abstraction. It provides scope for making a more abstract reference to *wujūd*, as in the expression *mawjūdiyyat al-wujūd*, but he maintains the distinction between the *wujūd* which is a mental abstraction and the *wujūd* which is real. The former tends to be identified with the notion of universality, and when *wujūd* is used in its widest sense Mullā Ṣadrā claims that it is used *bi-l-tashkīk*, not in a univocal manner. Everything which exists has something in common, since otherwise we should say that they do not exist, and what they have in common is not exactly the same attribute, but something which they share analogously. By contrast with al-Suhrawardī, what everything shares is some degree of existence, rather than some degree of light. Like his predecessors he distinguishes between the copulative use of *wujūd* (*al-wujūd al-rābiṭ*) and real being (*al-wujūd al-ḥaqq*). In the case of the former, what is connected by *wujūd* are ideas in the mind, not necessarily anything real. What is it, then, that the different uses of *wujūd* have in common, which manages to distinguish them from claims concerning non-existence? The answer for Mullā Ṣadrā is that all uses of *wujūd* imply either mental or real existence.

He argues that existence is the basic notion of metaphysics, not essence. He accepts that we can think of a concept existing in reality, and only existing in our minds, but this does not show that existence is merely an attribute which is tacked on to the concept's essence in the case that it actually exists. When something exists and yet we think of it as not existing we are thinking of the same thing, our name refers to the same object, and so existence comes first, and its precise characterization later. Even things which only exist in our minds are existing things, and we then need to say what they are like.

In the second part of this book, an important issue in both Islamic theology and philosophy will be discussed, namely, whether an action is right because God says it is right or whether God says it is right because it is right. This controversy provides a good opportunity to outline some of the features of the different views of the reason – revelation relationship in Islamic philosophy, and to explore the implications for political philosophy. There will also be an account of approaches to the interpretation of Islamic philosophy which take a different direction to that of this book. In the first part the agenda has been very much established by the attacks of al-Ghazālī on Islamic philosophy, in particular:

In the three questions . . . they were opposed to [the belief of] all Muslims, viz. in their affirming (1) that men's bodies will not be assembled on the Last Day, but only disembodied spirits will be rewarded and punished, and the rewards and punishments will be spiritual, not corporal . . . they falsely denied the corporal rewards and punishments and blasphemed the revealed Law in their stated views. (2) The second question is their declaration: 'God Most High knows universals, but not particulars.' This also is out-and-out unbelief . . . (3) The third question is their maintaining the eternity of the world, past and future. No Muslim has ever professed any of their views on these questions.[9]

In the first part we shall see what arguments the Islamic philosophers could put up to disprove al-Ghazālī's subtle arguments in these, and other, areas of importance.

[9] Al-Ghazālī, *Munqidh*, trans. McCarthy, pp. 76–7.

PART I

Al-Ghazālī's attack on philosophy

CHAPTER I

How did God create the world?

Religious texts which are designed to serve as the very basis of faith rarely incorporate philosophically or scientifically exact statements concerning the creation of the world, and Islam is no exception here. The Qur'ān makes several quite definite claims about the nature of the creator of the world and of the manner of its creation, yet these statements do not point unambiguously in just one direction. In the Qur'ānic description of God there is no doubt according to the Ash'arites that he is represented as superior to all his creatures, that he is the only God and that there is nothing in the universe upon which he is dependent. He is self-sufficient and has no need of human beings; he could do away with us and replace the world with something else without as a result ceasing to be himself. He need not have created the world, and now that it is created he could ignore it if he wanted to. We are told that God did create the world, that he is the origin of the heavens and the earth, that he created night and day, the sun, the moon and all the planets. He brings about the spring which reawakens nature and gives to gardens their beauty. Fortunately, for human beings, God designed nature and all his creation for our benefit, although he need not have done so, and all he 'requires' in return is prayer and adoration. Many theologians would want to add to these claims the clear assertion which they find in Islam that there was a time when God was and the world was not, and a later time when God was and the world was too. This rather unexciting view was the cause of great controversy between philosophers and theologians, and also within those groups themselves.

Let us first look briefly at how some of the problems concerning the nature of creation arose. We are told, for instance, that creation took six days. We might want to know whether anything existed before the world was created and out of which it was created. We might wonder whether time started with the first of those six days or whether it already existed before God created the world. If one looks carefully at the Qur'ānic text itself there seems to be no definite answer to these sorts of problems. The language which is used there is not precise enough to come down on one side or another with any certainty when discussing creation. There are interpretations which suggest that God created the world in a free manner out of nothing. One of the Arabic terms frequently used for creation, *khāliq*, means 'to bring about' or 'to produce', and there are examples of its being used in a specifically divine sense to describe how God creates both the form *and* the matter of existence. In the orthodox Ash'arite commentary of al-Rāzī, for instance, for us even to talk about determining (*taqdīr*) or creating and producing (*takhlīq*) something is to speak loosely or metaphorically. God is regarded as having a qualitatively distinct intelligence from ours, and he does not even have to go through a process of reasoning to work out what he is going to bring about, nor have something already in existence for him to use as material for his construction. He can just do it. In a strict sense, then, only God can properly be said to bring into being. But even al-Rāzī has to admit that there is an interesting ambiguity in the meaning of *khāliq*, since in some Qur'ānic references it can mean either *muqaddir* (who determines) or *mūjid* (who brings into existence). If the creator merely determines the character of the universe then the suggestion could well be that he was working with previously existent matter which he at some point organized in a certain way. There are indeed some Qur'ānic passages which could be taken to point to the existence of something before the creation of the world. There is a suggestion, for example, that before the creation, heaven and earth were nothing but smoke. In the Arberry interpretation of the Qur'ān passage XLI,10–12 we are told: 'Then He lifted Himself to heaven when it was smoke, and said to it and to the earth, "Come willingly, or unwillingly!" They said, "We come willingly." So he determined them as seven heavens.'[1] One could take this text to imply that the smoke itself was created by God. But Averroes takes it in another sense:

if the apparent meaning of Scripture is searched, it will be evident from the verses which give us information about the bringing into existence of the world that its form really is originated, but that being itself and time extend continuously at both extremes, i.e. without interruption . . . Thus the theologians too in their statements about the world do not conform to the apparent meaning of Scripture but interpret it allegorically. For it is not stated in Scripture that God was existing with absolutely nothing else: a text to this effect is nowhere to be found. (*FM* 56–7)

---

[1] Quotations from the Qur'ān will, unless otherwise specified, be from A. J. Arberry, *The Qur'ān interpreted* (Oxford, Oxford University Press, 1964).

Even texts which might seem to point obviously in the direction of creation being *ex nihilo* can, with a little effort, be interpreted otherwise. For example, there is the interesting passage where Muhammad is attacking unbelievers who accuse him of authorship of the Qur'ān and so deny its divine provenance, where he says: 'Let them bring a discourse like it, if they speak truly. Or were they created out of nothing? Or are they creators? Or did they create the heavens and earth?' (LII,34–5). The Arabic expression *min ghayri shay'in* could indeed mean 'from nothing', and that reading would cohere quite well with the subsequent rhetorical question. It would then imply that the heavens and earth were created from nothing on the Qur'ānic view. Yet this is far from being the only interpretation of that passage. The Arabic could also mean 'from nothing' not in the sense of 'out of nothing' but in the sense of 'by nothing' or without purpose or aim, and such a reading would be neutral with respect to the nature of what if anything preceded creation. It is worth noting, too, that there are passages which could point to a different account of creation than the *ex nihilo* doctrine, in particular 'And it is He who created the heavens and the earth in six days, and his throne was upon the waters' (XI,9), a verse readily seized upon by Averroes to 'imply that there was a being before this present being, namely the throne and the water, and a time before this time, i.e. the one which is joined to the form of this being, namely the number of the movement of the celestial sphere' (*FM* 56–7).

Why were the *falāsifa* so eager to snatch every hint in the Qur'ān that creation might not be *ex nihilo*? What does it matter whether time is finite and commenced with the creation of the universe? If creation *ex nihilo* is in many ways the most obvious reading that the relevant Qur'ānic texts can be given, why did apparently orthodox Muslims (or at least writers who tried to pass themselves off as orthodox Muslims) suggest that what seems to be the uncomplicated religious view is unsatisfactory? Certainly this point was taken up with alacrity by thinkers in other religions. In the first of the twelve errors which Giles of Rome found in Averroes, the Christian claims that the Muslim thinker must be condemned 'Because he reviled all law, as is clear from Book II of the *Metaphysics* and also from Book XI, where he reviles the laws of the Christians ... and also the law of the Saracens, because they maintain the creation of the universe and that something can be produced out of nothing.'[2] As we shall see, Maimonides also explicitly claims that Judaism insists on creation

---

[2] Giles of Rome, *Errores philosophorum*, ed. J. Koch and trans. J. Riedl (Milwaukee, WI, Marchette University Press, 1944); in R. Mandonnet, *Siger de Brabant* (Louvain, 1908), pp. 8–10.

ex nihilo.[3] But it is not clear that Islam requires creation *ex nihilo* as in these other religions. There is no doctrine of the precise age of the world in Islam and it might seem quite acceptable, although hardly common, to adhere to some other account of its creation such that perhaps it has always existed. And yet, as we have already seen al-Ghazālī felt that Islam was so strongly committed to the thesis of the world's creation out of nothing that philosophers who held different views were not just mistaken but had defined themselves as unbelievers and so were not Muslims at all.[4]

Given that so much religious opinion in all three religions of Islam, Judaism and Christianity was in favour of creation *ex nihilo*, why did the *falāsifa* set out to present a different model of the world's generation? One possible explanation is that they just rather slavishly followed Aristotle on this topic. Aristotle came to the issue after a considerable period of controversy in Greek philosophy with radically different opinions being offered by different philosophers. Some of the arguments which the *falāsifa* give in opposition to the creation *ex nihilo* doctrine are indeed Aristotelian, while others are Neoplatonic or even theological. It is worth having a look at the model which the *falāsifa* constructed of the relationship between God and the world to see why they could not accept the *ex nihilo* doctrine and yet tried to encompass orthodox Islamic doctrines at the same time.

Al-Fārābī and Avicenna constructed the main framework of this philosophical analysis of God and the world which ran into so much theological opposition. They start off by claiming that God is the only uncaused thing in the universe. Everything other than God in the universe is brought about by some cause external to itself. One of the ways in which they distinguish between things that exist is to talk about entities which have existence as part of their essence and those which do not. Something which can only exist if it is brought into existence by something else is clearly contingent and dependent upon something else. As Avicenna put it: 'the existence of something which is dependent upon something else which actually brings it into existence is not impossible in itself, for if it was it would never come into existence. It is not necessary either, since if it was it would not be dependent upon something else, and we have to conclude that it is possible in itself.'[5] Avicenna adds: 'What is necessary is

---

[3] *GP* II,13, p. 281.
[4] Especially in his *al-Munqidh min al-Dalāl*.
[5] Al-Fārābī, *Philosophische Abhandlungen*, ed. F. Dieterici (Leiden, Brill, 1890), p. 67, but in fact by Avicenna.

what cannot be assumed not to exist without a contradiction. The possible, by contrast, can be assumed not to exist, or to exist, without any sort of contradiction at all.'[6] This distinction between necessity and contingency is designed to contrast God, the creator of everything in the world, and what he has created. If God had himself been created then there would exist something even more powerful than God. If we could think of God not existing then his existence might be regarded as some kind of accident, sharing the status of the objects which we see in the world and which we can quite easily imagine not to exist. In calling God necessary and his creation contingent the suggestion is that we are presented with a theological system which contrasts an independent and self-sufficient deity with his product, a contingent and dependent universe.

But we should be careful about accepting this suggestion. For Avicenna immediately complicates his initial distinction between contingency and necessity to talk about two types of necessity. The first type, which we have already examined, is where 'a contradiction is involved if it is assumed to be non-existent'. If we assume, for the sake of the argument, that God does not exist, then we are involved in a contradiction, since existence is so much a part of the definition or meaning of God that denying his existence is rather like questioning whether a rectangle has four sides. Nothing is a rectangle if it does not have four sides; similarly, nothing is God if it does not exist. Avicenna's other kind of necessity is more complicated. Something 'is necessary, provided a certain entity other than it is given . . . while considered in its essence it is possible, considered in actual relation to that other being, it is necessary, and without the relation to that other being, it is impossible'.[7] Avicenna is talking here about a type of being which relies upon something else to bring it into existence, but given that cause, it exists necessarily. This is an unusual distinction to make. The standard approach would be to distinguish possible beings which can, but do not, exist and possible beings which can, and do, exist, and a necessary being is that which cannot not exist by contrast with both types of possible beings. Avicenna is not interested in the standard approach at all. Indeed, he would claim that what has been called 'the standard approach' is rather misleading. He argues that a possible being is only possible if it *must* exist, while accepting of course its contingency upon the causal power of something else. He claims that those things which are necessary through the influence of

[6] Ibn Sīnā, *Najāt: Kitāb al-najāt*, ed. M. Kurdi (Cairo, Saʿadah Press, 1938), p. 224.
[7] *Ibid.*

something else are exactly what he means by the things which are possible in themselves.

His reasoning takes this form. A thing which is contingent and which is regarded separately from its cause either can or cannot exist. If one says that it cannot exist, then one is claiming that it is impossible, that it involves some sort of contradiction. If one claims that it can exist, then it must either exist or not exist. If it does not exist, it would be impossible. Avicenna returns to this point time and time again. In a chapter entitled 'What is not necessary does not exist' he argues:

> Thus it is now clear that everything necessary of existence by another thing is possible of existence by itself. And this is reversible, so that everything possible of existence by itself, if its existence has happened, is necessary of existence by another thing; because inevitably it must either truly have an actual existence or not truly have an actual existence – but it cannot not truly have an actual existence, for in that case it would be impossible of existence.[8]

When Avicenna talks about the status of a thing which is not necessary in itself he comments: 'The thing, when looked at in terms of its essence, is possible but when examined in terms of its links with its cause, is necessary. Without that nexus it is then impossible. But if we think of the essence of the thing without linking it with anything else, the thing itself becomes seen as possible in itself.'[9]

It might seem that Avicenna is contradicting himself here when he considers the results of thinking of the relationship between an entity and its causes no longer holding. His argument is quite plausible, though. He is suggesting that it is possible to think of something like one's coat without thinking of how it was made and where the materials etc. came from. But it is not possible to think of that coat as having no relation whatsoever to what preceded it in existence. Every contingent thing is related to something else which brings it about; the only thing which is not thus related and which can be thought of as completely independent is God who is necessary in himself. Insofar as it goes, then, Avicenna's distinction does not involve a contradiction.

It is clear that for Avicenna a contingent thing can only exist if it is brought into existence by something else, and we would get an infinite regress of such causes were there not in existence a thing which is necessary in itself and which therefore does not require a causal push into

---

[8] *Ibid.*, p. 226; trans. G. Hourani, 'Ibn Sīnā on necessary and possible existence', *Philosophical Forum*, 6 (1974), pp. 74–86.

[9] Ibn Sīnā, *Najāt*, ed. Kurdi, p. 226.

existence. Now, many views of God and his creation would interpret this relation as one of God considering which of the possible states of affairs he could bring into existence if he is to fulfil his aims in constructing the world. God can select any possible state of affairs as desirable and then bring it into existence in the world. But this is not Avicenna's view at all. Contingent things are obliged to wait before they exist in a kind of metaphysical limbo which is entirely independent of God's will. All God can do is determine whether contingent things will exist or not; he cannot affect their possibility. This has interesting consequences. Avicenna distinguishes between possible material and possible immaterial substances. The former are essentially as they are before God's causal powers get to work on them; were they to be otherwise, on Avicenna's familiar argument, they would not be possible because 'whatever enters existence can be either possible or impossible before it exists. Whatever cannot exist will never exist, and whatever can exist has a possibility which exists before it is actualized . . . And so matter exists before everything what comes into existence.'[10] God's control over even existence is severely circumscribed with regard to the possible immaterial substances which are dependent upon him for their existence and not necessary in themselves, but for whom there was no time when they were not in existence. They are necessary but only necessary through another thing, God, and they exist in tandem with him. In so far as the contents of the material world go, though, God is confined to willing the possible to exist. He cannot will the possible to be existent *and* possible. He is rather in the position of the customer in a restaurant who has no choice as to what he can order. He can and indeed must order the fixed menu, and he has no control over the selection which is set before him.

So far we have been talking about three types of being. These are: (i) that which is necessarily existent in itself; (ii) that which is necessarily existent by reason of another but possibly existent by reason of itself; and (iii) that which is possibly existent by reason of itself without being necessarily existent by reason of another. As we have seen, members of the third class become rather difficult to distinguish from members of the second class. There is a class of things that are necessary without having a cause of their being necessary and another class of things which are necessary through a cause, this cause being a member of a former class. Examples of beings which are necessarily existent by reason of

---

[10] *Ibid.*

something else are 'combustion', which is 'necessarily existent . . . once contact is taken to exist between fire and matter which can be burned', and 'four' which is 'necessarily existent . . . when we assume two plus two'.[11] These examples suggest that the distinction between the kinds of being which we have called (ii) and (iii) above is rather artificial. One of the ways in which Avicenna characterizes necessity is in terms of 'indicating something which has to exist'.[12] The necessarily existent in itself is that which has certainty of existence by reason of itself, while the necessarily existent through another would be that which has certainty of existence through another. So in the end there is no real difference between necessary existence through another and actual existence for anything other than God. We might put Avicenna's argument in this way. So long as something is only possible, there is nothing in existence which can move it from non-existence to existence. The possibly existent can only become actually existent if something decides to shift it from the substitutes' bench to the playing area, as it were. Whenever that something is present and sets a series of events in train, the consequent existence of the possible being is inevitable. It will certainly exist and thus is necessary. So when the possibly existent actually exists, its existence is necessary, and when it does not exist, its existence is impossible. All that Avicenna can mean by talking about a class of things which are possibly existent without being necessarily existent is that, if we abstract from all external conditions, the class of possibly existent things can be *conceived* since they are always possibly existent.[13] If we are to divide up the actual existents we need only two categories, that of the necessarily existent by reason of itself, where an impossibility results if we assume it not to exist by reason of itself, and the necessarily existent by reason of another, where an impossibility or contradiction also results if we assume it not to exist, but this time only because it is assumed that something else exists.

To try to become clearer concerning the philosophical motives for this conflation of necessity and possibility we need to look at some aspects of the work of Aristotle. He pointed out that in ascribing a certain power or ability to a thing it is necessary to determine the limits of this power. We do not say that a thing can lift weight as such, but that it can lift a certain weight or range of weights. If we say, then, that something is capable of existing and of not existing, we are bound to add the length

---

[11] *Ibid.*, p. 225.

[12] Ibn Sīnā, *Shifā': Ilāhiyyāt* (Healing: Metaphysics), ed. G. Anawati and S. Zayed (Cairo, Uthmānīyya Press, 1960). p. 36.

[13] See *ibid.*, p. 38; and *Najāt*, ed. Kurdi, pp. 226, 238.

of time in each case. If the time in question is infinite (and Aristotle does indeed argue that time is at least potentially infinite), then we are committed to saying that something can exist for an infinite time and also not exist for another infinite time, and this, he claims, is impossible. In a slightly different approach, Aristotle sometimes views potentiality as a sort of natural tendency. There is certainly something rather odd about saying that something has a natural tendency which is never fulfilled, even during an infinite period of time. Aristotle does indeed present an argument to suggest that what never happens is impossible.

This Aristotelian approach has been taken up by a commentator on his philosophy, Jaako Hintikka, and called rather appropriately the 'principle of plenitude'.[14] Hintikka argues that for Aristotle something is called necessary if it always was and always will be so and he interprets the sense of possibility relevant here as equivalent to saying that what is possible has happened or will happen at some time. A familiar logical notion is that of worlds which represent alternative arrangements to our existing world and which philosophers call logically possible. Clearly, Aristotle's apparent view that every possibility will in due course be realized runs counter to such an approach.

Aristotle's arguments for his thesis are not convincing. For example, he claims: 'It is not allowable that it is true to say "this is possible, but it will not be"' (*Met.* 1047b 3f.), and he reasons in this way. What is possible can conceivably occur. Imagine it occurring then but assume it will not occur; so imagining it to happen contradicts our assuming it will not happen. He gives the rather misleading example of saying we can do an impossible task but never will. He produces a more plausible argument when distinguishing between something like a cloak and things which like the stars exist for ever and are for ever active (*De Int.* 19a 9–18). Since the stars exist for ever, for the whole of time, possibilities cannot remain for ever unactualized. The sun and stars, if they could stop, would, given the whole of time, indeed stop. So the dual possibility of being and not being does not apply to what is for ever active. Aristotle gives another example when he suggests that if something were at all times sitting, it would be incapable of standing, and that which always exists is incapable of perishing (*De Caelo* 281b 3–25). His argument is not applied to the transient things of this world like cloaks but only to everlasting things and their eternal qualities. Yet it is not obvious why his analysis should not be extended to transient things. For although

[14] J. Hintikka, *Time and necessity: studies in Aristotle's theory of modality* (Oxford, Oxford University Press, 1973), ch. 5.

a cloak which has been eaten by a goat does not continue to possess the capacity to be burnt, it does for ever possess the negative property of not being burnt. Aristotle does accept that things can continue to possess negative properties after they have ceased to exist (*Cat.* 13b 26–35: *De Int.* 16b 11–15). If in the whole of time it will not be burnt, there should, on Aristotle's reasoning, be no time left at which a capacity to be burnt could be actualized, and so the cloak should be incapable of being burnt. It must be admitted that Aristotle carefully limits his principle of plenitude to eternal things – 'In everlasting things, there is no difference between being possible and being the case' (*Phys.* 293b 30) – and yet it is very interesting for our discussion of the notions of possibility and necessity that it is feasible to think of his arguments being extended to things which are not everlasting. Maimonides is quite clear on the distinction which Aristotle wants to make:

When a species is said to be possible, it is necessary that it exists in reality in certain individuals of this species, for if it never existed in any individual, it would be impossible for the species, and what right would one have for saying that it is possible? If, for example, we say that writing is a thing possible for the human race, it is necessary then that there be people who write at a certain time, for if one believed that there is never any man who writes, that would be saying that writing is impossible for the human race. It is not the same when possibility is applied to individuals, for if we say that it is possible that this child writes or does not write, it does not follow from this possibility that the child must necessarily write at one particular moment. Therefore, the claim that a species is possible is not, strictly speaking, to place the species in the category of possibility but rather to claim that it is in some ways necessary.[15]

We shall see later the significance of this approach when we come to look at Maimonides' analysis of the topic of the creation of the world.

Avicenna's account of the nature of beings results in a good deal of necessity seeping into the world of transient things, with the principle of plenitude being extended to cover everything other than God. Now, the connection between the doctrine of necessity and the model of the creation of the world takes a particular form in Avicenna, one which originally stems from Plotinus. The notion of creation as emanation is not always described in the same way by Avicenna, but it is possible on the whole to give an account of its essential features. God is identified as the necessary existent and is one and simple. This necessary existent or being does not produce other things as though intending them to come into

---

[15] Letter to Samuel ibn Tibbon, cited in S. Munk 'Commentary' *Le guide des Egares* (Paris, A. Franck, 1861), p. 39.

existence, however, for then he would be acting for something lower than himself and would thereby introduce multiplicity into the divine essence. Rather, the first effect, a pure intelligence, necessarily proceeds from his self-reflection. This first intelligence which results from God's coming to know himself is an example of a being which is necessary through another, the necessary existent, but which unlike its originator is only possible in itself. It is the introduction of this intelligence that introduces multiplicity into the system which is extended once it considers three facts of existence. Firstly, it considers God's existence as necessary in itself. Then, it considers its own existence as a necessitated being. Lastly, it recognizes that its own existence is only possible and very different from the existence of its creator and originator. These three acts of knowing bring about the existence of just three things, maintaining the principle that from one only one proceeds and can proceed. The existence of another intellect, a soul and a sphere (the sphere of the heavens) are necessitated. Then we get a series of triads which explain the creation of yet more beings. The second intelligence replicates a similar process of thought as the first and so leads to the production of a third intellect, another soul and a sphere, this time the sphere of the fixed stars. The process continues via the thoughts of the successive intellects and results in the spheres of the planets, the sun and the moon, each with its intellect, soul and body, only coming to an end with the sublunary world, the world of generation and corruption in which we live. The tenth or last intelligence is the agent intellect, which does not have a soul and the body of a sphere, but rather produces human souls and the four elements of our world. We shall see later the significance of the agent intellect in Islamic philosophy.

Avicenna had the problem of reconciling an eternally existing world and an eternally existing God without having the perfect simplicity and unity of God destroyed by contact with the multiplicity of material things. His strategy was to interpose many levels of spiritual substances, the intelligences, between God and the world of generation and corruption to insulate the divine unity from multiplicity. This model of the development of the universe is hardly close to the traditional religious view. There is a big difference between producing something out of nothing and producing something by emanation from one's thinking. In the latter case there is a resemblance between the agent and the product, which is not to be found at all in the former case. Avicenna asserts that the necessary existent emanates the world via its emanation of the first intelligence, and that choice or deliberation has no part to play in its decision. After all, God's will is identical to the knowledge of the best universal world order. Once the process of emanation has been set in train there is no place for God's intervention in the course of nature. Indeed, while the One of Neoplatonic thought and the necessary being in Avicenna's model can exist without the products of its thought, all that this means is that it can be conceived to exist by itself, i.e. that it is transcendent. Yet how can this be reconciled with the existence of the immaterial beings as necessary and eternal, with the fact that the intelligible world which has emanated from the One cannot not exist nor can it exist in a different form – it is necessarily produced by the One and produced in such a way that it must have a certain form? As al-Fārābī puts it:

> The first exists in and by itself, and it is part of its essence that it can lead to the existence of what is outside it. So that essence from which existence emanates onto other things is part of its definition . . . from which the existence of something else is produced. This cannot be separated into two separate things, one of them being something it brings about in itself, the other being that which brings about the existence of something else.[16]

So there are things which God brings into existence which cannot possibly not exist and which cannot be other than they are. The gap between God and his creation starts to look as artificial as the gap between beings which are necessarily existent by reason of another and beings which are possible in themselves and not necessitated by anything else.

This is a very different picture of creation and of God's relation to the universe than that implicit in the Qur'ān. To take an example which comes this time not from a verse relating to the creation of the world but rather dealing with the world's possible destruction, we are told that: 'All things perish, except His face' (XXVIII,88). The idea that God can, if he wants, bring his creation to an end is an important expression of the power that God has over the world, something of a theme of the Qur'ān. At one point it says: 'On the day when We shall roll up heaven as a scroll is rolled for the writings; as We originated the first creation, so We shall bring it back again – a promise binding on Us; so We shall do' (XXI,104). Yet the heavens and the world are regarded as eternal by the *falāsifa*. They proceed necessarily from the divine essence and eternally persist in their continuous motion. Avicenna is aware of this problem and provides an orthodox interpretation of XXVIII,88 when he says: 'He dominates, i.e. he has the power to bring about non-being and to deprive of existence those

---

[16] Al-Fārābī, *Al-siyāsā al-madaniya* (The political régime), (Hyderabad, Dā'irah al-Ma'ārif, 1927), p. 18.

essences which in themselves deserve annihilation. Everything vanishes except he.'[17] It might be possible to argue that in this verse 'all things' refer to the contents of the universe rather than the universe itself, so that it is taken to mean that only what is found in the realm of generation and corruption goes to destruction. However, this would not cover the verse which refers to the rolling up of the heavens. It might then be argued that it is part of the essence of the necessary and eternal things that they go to destruction, and that eternal things can be destroyed if motion is brought to an end, since on an Aristotelian view of time it is only motion which makes time possible. If there is no longer any sense in talking about time then there would no longer be any point in talking about eternity. On such a view 'eternal' would mean something like 'existing until the end of time'. But this would be a difficult view for an Aristotelian to put forward, given the Aristotelian arguments for the infinity of time.

As one might expect, then, Avicenna is hardly enthusiastic about this line of argument. He claims quite confidently that there is no great problem for his approach coming from XXVIII,88:

The existence of something which is contingent on a cause outside itself is not impossible, for if it were it could not possibly exist. Nor is it necessary, for then it could not be contingent on something else for its existence. The existence of such a thing is possible in itself. With respect to its cause, it is necessary, and with respect to the absence of the cause it is impossible. In itself it has no capacity except to be ultimately destroyed, but with respect to its cause it is necessary – 'All things perish, except his Face.'[18]

The Qur'ānic verse is then taken to distinguish between God and those things which are caused to exist by God. God will not be destroyed, but he could destroy everything else in the universe. Yet the sense which Avicenna gives to this claim is the rather weak explanation that nothing could exist were God not to exist also, that without God the possible things which only require some agent to bring them to existence would not be actualized and so in that sense could be thought of as impossible and destroyed. This seems a rather special sense of destruction. Since God is the 'principle of existence' of those things which are necessary through another, i.e. through him, he at first sight should have no difficulty in bringing their existence to an end. It might seem that all that God would need to do to make everything go to destruction is to will such an event. Yet for Avicenna it follows from the nature of God and

---

[17] Al-Fārābī, *Philosophische Abhandlungen*, ed. Dieterici, p. 83, but in fact by Avicenna.
[18] *Ibid.*, p. 67, but in fact by Avicenna.

the nature of the possible things in the universe that they will be arranged in a certain optimum way; God could not just decide arbitrarily
to change things around. It would be to go against his nature. On this
sort of view the Qur'ānic passage which explains that everything goes
to destruction except God could either be interpreted as a metaphori-
cal way of expressing God's uniqueness and self-sufficiency and not be
regarded as literally true at all. Or it could be taken as the claim that
were it to be a desirable state of affairs for the world to cease to exist,
then God would have pre-arranged such a state of affairs. As we shall
see in the following section, for us to talk about something ceasing to
exist is regarded by the *falāsifa* as rather more accurately described as its
changing into something else: 'from this point of view the philosophers
do not regard it as impossible that the world should become non-existent
in the sense of its changing into another form ... But what they regard
as impossible is that a thing should disappear into absolute nothingness'
(*TT* 86). Yet even if it is possible to accommodate Qur'ānic references
to the destruction of the world within Islamic philosophy it remains true
that in the philosophical account of creation God does not seem to have
much work to do. God can only create what is possible, and there are
beings which are possible and conceivable independently of the act of
creation, and so of God. This is neatly put by al-Shahrastānī (d. 547/1153)
thus:

The essential qualities of substances and accidents belong to them in themselves,
not because of any connection with the creator. He only enters ... in connection with existence because he tipped the scales in favour of existence. What a
thing is essentially precedes its existence, i.e. the basic qualities which make it
a particular thing. What a thing has through omnipotence is its existence and
actual instantiation.[19]

Once God has tipped the scales in favour of existence, what has he left
to do? If the possible things emanate from him necessarily, at however
remote a stage, what control has he over them, what knowledge has he
of them, what choice does he have in selecting one thing over another
for existence? The difficulties involved in answering these questions in
a manner acceptable to Islam suggests that a very different, albeit not
necessarily irreconcilable, model of the connection between God and his
creation is being presented.

[19] Al-Shahrastānī, *Kitāb nihāyat al iqdām fi 'ilm al kalām* (The 'Summa Philosophiae' of al-Shahrastāni),
ed. and trans. A. Guillaume (London, Oxford University Press, 1934), p. 155.

AVERROES V. AL-GHAZĀLĪ ON THE CREATION OF THE WORLD

By far the most brilliant of the opponents of *falsafa* was al-Ghazālī. Studying his writings is a pleasure because of both his clear and polished style and his skill and fervour in argument. He took considerable pains to master expertly the reasoning which had led the philosophers to what he saw as erroneous and theologically dubious conclusions. What gives his arguments their importance is that he attacked the philosophers on their own ground, arguing philosophically that their main theses were invalid on logical grounds. For example, in his book *The incoherence of the philosophers* he sets out twenty propositions which he attempts to disprove, seventeen of which constitute innovation or heterodoxy (in his opinion), and three of which actually reveal what he calls unbelief, an even stronger charge. These three propositions concern the denial of the resurrection of the body, the fact of God's knowledge of particulars, plus the doctrine of the eternity of the world. What is important, though, is not his charge that the *falāsifa* present un-Islamic views, but that they go awry in their arguments:

It is in the metaphysical sciences that most of the philosophers' errors are found. Owing to the fact that they could not carry out apodeictic demonstration according to the conditions they had postulated in logic, they differed a great deal about metaphysical questions. Aristotle's doctrine on these matters, as transmitted by al-Fārābī and ibn Sīnā, approximates the teachings of the Islamic philosophers.[20]

The philosophical doctrine which al-Ghazālī spends a great deal of time discussing in *The incoherence of the philosophers* is that of the eternity of the world. He argues both that the *falāsifa* are incapable of demonstrating that the world is eternal and that there is no way of reconciling belief in (the Muslim) God with adherence to the world's eternity. In charging those who adhere to the eternity doctrine with unbelief he was making a very strong claim, namely, that that doctrine is so inconsistent with Islam that no one can accept it and remain genuinely part of the community of Islam. Al-Ghazālī is especially careful in making this claim: he was very critical of the practice of some writers in his time as well as of his predecessors of making wild and unjustified accusations of unbelief against opinions and individuals that merely differed from their own on rather peripheral issues.[21] The line of argument which runs right through

[20] Al-Ghazālī, *Munqidh*, trans. R. McCarthy, p. 76.
[21] See al-Ghazālī, *Faysal al-tafriqa bayn al-Islām wa l-zandaqa* (The clear criterion for distinguishing between Islam and godlessness), trans. R. McCarthy, *Freedom and fulfillment*, pp. 145–74.

al-Ghazālī's attack on the *falāsifa* is that belief in God is equivalent to belief that God's existence makes a real difference to the way things are in the world. He claims that there is a serious drawback in the theories of the philosophers in that they seem to want to allow God only a subsidiary role in the eternally organized and determined universe which they defend. He brings the same sort of charge against them for their apparent denial of resurrection and God's knowledge of particulars – these two denials also remove God and his power and knowledge from the world in a way that is obviously problematic for a Muslim. As we have seen so far, the *falāsifa* are not averse to appending their philosophical claims to passages from the Qur'ān, which one might think would be embarrassing given their adherence to theories which are, at least superficially, unsympathetic to the meaning of such religious passages. Al-Ghazālī is hinting that the *falāsifa* use these religious verses as a sort of camouflage for their real views, pretending that their doctrines are quite in accordance with religion when they know that they are quite otherwise. This approach to the *falāsifa* has been highly influential in interpreting their work even today, and al-Ghazālī has posed a methodological question to which we shall return throughout this book. It must be emphasized at the outset that al-Ghazālī is asking a vitally important question about the actual arguments of the *falāsifa*, namely, what difference does the introduction of God into a philosophical theory make? If it makes no difference at all, then surely it is just an attempt to mislead readers when religious vocabulary and Qur'ānic passages are used as though they fitted into philosophical arguments when quite plainly they do not.

The interchange between al-Ghazālī and Averroes is interesting for the subtle argument it often involves and the close relationship which the argument always bears to specific controversial issues. An intriguing feature of the discussion is that Averroes (in his *Incoherence of the incoherence*) is in effect fighting with one hand tied behind his back, since he is often critical of the approach to philosophy which al-Ghazālī criticizes, that of al-Fārābī and Avicenna. Averroes was especially critical of aspects of Avicenna's approach to modal concepts such as possibility and necessity. He argued against the combination of the 'possible in itself' and 'necessary through another', which he saw as a mistaken doctrine. He suggests that we should differentiate clearly between the possible and the necessary (*TT* 146), and argued that Avicenna's position is too heavily influenced by the theologians. Averroes also distanced himself to a degree from what he could perceive as non-Aristotelian (i.e. Neoplatonic) philosophical concepts in an attempt to return to the 'real' Aristotle for his philosophical inspiration. It must be admitted, though, that he did use a good deal of both Avicennan and Neoplatonic theory in his defence of philosophy, and this was inevitable given the fact that the burden of al-Ghazālī's attack lies heavily on those aspects of philosophical thinking in Islam.

When it comes to considering the creation of the world, al-Ghazālī was repelled by the philosophical conception of the universe as eternal and brought about by emanation, with an eternal matter continually taking different forms. He accepts the view which he regards as traditional that the world was created by God out of completely nothing a finite time ago, and that both the matter and the form of the world were brought into being by God in this original act. It is worth pointing out perhaps that the Neoplatonic model of the relation between God and the world embodies all kinds of features which might well be *prima facie* attractive to mystics. For example, the large number of striking analogies to express the relationship between God and his creation, the stress on the generosity of the One and its self-reflection, the emergence of beings which in turn generate other beings and indeed eventually everything, and especially the power which is ascribed to *thought* as such, all these are principles dear to much mystical thinking. It is difficult to believe that al-Ghazālī, with his well-known fascination for mysticism, was not initially attracted to philosophy as a rational basis for his religious beliefs. When he came to the view that philosophy was a false god he rejected it with all the fervour of an apostate who still sees what is compelling in the old set of beliefs. His *The incoherence of the philosophers* is on the surface a cold and technical work, yet under the surface it is possible to detect the passion with which he abandons an immensely attractive way of looking at the world. Al-Ghazālī is driven to represent the arguments of the philosophers in close detail, replying himself to the criticisms which others might make of their main points before he presents the argument which he regards as the coup de grâce. His almost obsessive concern with accurately describing the arguments of his opponents is evidence of the love-hate relationship which he has with philosophy. It is often regarded as ironic that one of his books, *The intentions of the philosophers*, which sets out clearly the main doctrines of *falsafa*, should have given Christian Scholasticism the impression that he was a *failasūf* himself. It might well be argued that this 'mistake' is highly revealing.

The starting point of al-Ghazālī's approach to the *falāsifa* is to bring out how difficult it is to reconcile with Islam the central tenets of their view of God and the world. A view which emphasizes that from one can only come one, that has at its apex an entity whose deliberations are limited to his own essence and who can only metaphorically be described as having a will or choice in his actions is not only dubiously compatible with Islam but also, al-Ghazālī argues, philosophically questionable. He insists that only an argument which stresses creation in the Islamic sense can allow for the existence of an effective Islamic God who actively determines what, where, how and when contingent states of affairs take place. He is not necessitated in his creating but considers choices; no general principles direct his choosing in one direction rather than another.

Al-Ghazālī clearly has a very different conception of God and the universe than the *falāsifa*. He defends his ideas carefully and slowly, developing a piecemeal critique of *falsafa* which I shall attempt to discuss and assess in some of its detail. The First Discussion of his *The incoherence of the philosophers* discusses four proofs which he considers to be the best of those presented by the philosophers in defence of the eternity of the world. The First Proof deals with some of the problems in making sense of the notion that the world came into existence suddenly. On the *falāsifa*'s understanding of Aristotle, every change which takes place must be determined to occur by some cause which is external to it. This is the case not just for physical objects but for states of mind as well. So presumably if God wills a change to take place, some external cause must have led him to that decision. If the world as a whole had come into existence rather than existed eternally this would present a difficulty. There would then have been nothing outside God's mind to influence him into making a decision about the existence of the world, since nothing but God yet existed. Now, we know from our experience that the world is already existing and so we can conclude that this sort of problem did not prevent it from existing. In that case the world must surely have been in existence all the time, an assertion which once it is accepted sidesteps neatly the problem of having to explain how the first change which created the world came about. Given the model of creation through emanation, the world continually emanates from the One and it is of the nature of the One to produce what it thus produces and how it thus produces. The main difficulty which the philosophers see is in explaining the first change, the creation of the world, on the creation *ex nihilo* doctrine. If God at one time existed without anything else, before he created the world, what could have persuaded him to create the world in the first place? There was nothing around in existence to affect him and he could have remained perfectly constant and unmoved. We know, though, that there is a world and we believe that God created

it, and we can only make sense of this fact if we admit that his creation
is eternal.

Al-Ghazālī is aware that he has to defend the possibility of the world
coming into existence at a certain time. He repeats the Ash'arite view
that God could easily have willed eternally that the world should come
into existence at a certain time in the future if he wanted to. After all,
according to the Qur'ān, all that God has to say is 'Be, and it is' (III,42).
Why could he not postdate, as it were, the existence of the universe? The
world could then come into existence at a particular time in the future.
The traditional objection to such a possibility by the philosophers is that
there must be some reason why someone who wills something which he is
capable of performing at a particular time desists from the performance.
If he wants X and can get X, why should he wait a certain length of time
after the performance *could* be carried out to satisfy his want? Surely
there cannot be any obstacle which impedes an omnipotent God from
carrying out his purpose? As al-Fārābī put it:

What delays his making it is the obstacle to his making it, and the non-success
which he thinks and knows will occur, if he makes the thing at that time is the
obstacle which prevents his making it . . . If there is no cause of non-success, its
non-existence is not preferable to its existence, and why did it not happen? . . . if
he were personally the sole cause of the success, the success of the action should
not be retarded in time, but both should happen together, and therefore when
the agent is sufficient in himself alone for something to come into existence from
him, it follows that the existence of the thing is not later than the existence of
the agent.[22]

The Ash'arite response to this sort of objection is to press the analogy
between natural and conventional norms and to suggest that God could
make the creation of the world contingent on certain conditions being
satisfied in the future, in the same way that a man can divorce his wife in
Islam as from a particular time in the future. Averroes' objection to this
example is that it is invalid to relate natural and conventional causality
closely in this way. It is no doubt true that we can determine the legal
nature of the future given the legal validity of certain procedures, yet
we cannot delay natural events until a future time in the same way.
This objection to al-Ghazālī is hardly apposite since, as we shall see
later, he adheres to a theory of causality which identifies it with God's
commands, and he would probably agree that the analogy of natural and

---

[22] Al-Fārābī's *The fuṣūl al-madanī of al-Fārābī* (Aphorisms of the statesman). ed. and trans. D. Dunlop,
University of Cambridge Oriental Publications, 5 (Cambridge, Cambridge University Press,
1961), p. 66.

conventional causality does not work when applied to human beings, but would be highly appropriate when applied to God, the aim of the analogy in the first place. Perhaps a stronger objection that Averroes might have used would be to ask what *motive* God could have for delaying the creation of the world. After all, there is nothing in existence with him to influence him and one might have thought that if he was interested in creating the world he would just create it and not spend a period of time at rest after having willed the world to be created. This is certainly the point of al-Fārābī's argument above. After all, the use of a legal device as a result of which a man can divorce his wife in the future has as its purpose some practical effect. For example, a wife may be warned that if she does something objectionable in the future then she will from that time immediately be divorced. What possible practical consequences could God's postdated creation of the world have? There is surely no context available in which he would need to threaten or warn anyone or anything, since there is before the creation, on al-Ghazālī's view, absolutely no one and nothing except God himself.

Al-Ghazālī challenges the claim that even the divine will cannot produce a delayed effect. Why *must* there be an obstacle to explain such a phenomenon? What justification have philosophers in ruling it out completely? He argues for the possibility of such a delayed effect by presenting an intriguing account of how the divine will might well work. If we return to the previous point, that the philosophers are dubious about the possibility of a delayed effect since there seems to be no conceivable motive for the delay, we can see that there is also a problem with the creation of the world at one particular time rather than at another particular time. If God did create the world at a certain time, then he decided to create it at that time and not at another time, assuming that he was not acting haphazardly. Yet before anything exists except God what reason could God have for creating the world at one particular time at all? There exists nothing to motivate him in this respect except his thoughts, and why should he select one time in preference to another time? Al-Ghazālī is impatient with this sort of objection to the creation of the world at one finite time:

as to your affirmation that you cannot imagine this [a will causing a delayed effect] do you know it by the necessity of thought or through deduction? You can claim neither the one nor the other. Your comparison with our will is a bad analogy, which resembles that employed on the question of God's knowledge. Now, God's knowledge is different from ours in several ways which we acknowledge. Therefore it is not absurd to admit a difference in the will . . . How will you refute those who say that rational proof has led to establishing in God a quality the nature of which is to differentiate between two similar things? Besides, we do not even with respect to our human will concede that this cannot be imagined. Suppose two similar dates in front of a man who has a strong desire for them but who is unable to take them both. Surely he will take one of them through a quality in him the nature of which is to differentiate between two similar things . . . Everyone, therefore, who studies, in the human and the divine, the real working of the act of choice, must necessarily admit a quality the nature of which is to differentiate between two similar things. (*TT* 21)

Averroes replies sharply to this argument:

But this is an error. For, when one supposes such a thing, and a willer whom necessity prompts to eat or to take the date, then it is by no means a matter of distinguishing between two similar things when, in this condition, he takes one of the two dates . . . His will attaches itself therefore merely to the distinction between the fact of taking one of them and the fact of leaving them altogether; it attaches itself by no means to the act of taking one definite date and distinguishing this act from the act of leaving the other . . . he gives preference to the act of taking over the act of leaving. (*TT* 23)

This response is effective. After all, the importance of the choice in such a case does not consist in the quality of one date as against the other, but the fact that there is a clear choice between taking at least one of the dates and remaining hungry. There is then an obvious reason for selecting either of the dates, but not for selecting one rather than the other. Al-Ghazālī wants to establish the point that it is the will which makes choices among equivalent things and distinguishes what is otherwise identical even in the case of human beings. This sort of example will not make his point. It is quite easy to redescribe his example to ensure that there is a choice and a reason for making the choice, too, which is far from arbitrary.

Al-Ghazālī broadens his argument to suggest that it shows that there could be alterations to the structure of the universe which would be neither better nor worse, and so there is no specific reason for God's creation of one particular type of universe rather than another. He considers the objection to creation which asks what could have motivated the creator to create the world at one time rather than another. As we have seen, he replies that although there was nothing about the time when the universe was created which demanded that creation must take place at that time (which would detract from God's power), nevertheless an act of pure will on the part of the creator chose that time. Al-Ghazālī appreciates that the philosophers who defend eternity may well argue that will consists in the selection of the preferable of two alternatives, and when things are similar in every respect, no property can distinguish one from the other. Why, then, could al-Ghazālī not argue successfully that the fact that the universe has one form rather than another is evidence of such an act of pure will? After all, God could presumably have created the universe without roses in it. He obviously decided at some stage to create the universe *with* roses, but not a great deal hangs on this decision. Is this not evidence for the pure act of choice which al-Ghazālī is looking for? These sorts of examples will not really do since the philosophers could argue that some apparently arbitrary features of the universe such as its size and shape, for example, are optimal and so were preferred over alternatives, if we want to speak in the language of creation by God. An argument can be presented to suggest that those properties of the universe are better than different properties, and so such an example cannot be used to suggest that God's arbitrary choice is possible.

Al-Ghazālī does actually discuss two phenomena variations in which apparently manifest no difference that might serve as a basis for the choice of one from among several alternatives. These are the differences in the directions of the movements of the spheres, and the selection of a pair of definite points in the outer sphere to serve as poles around which the heavens revolve. With respect to the latter, he argues that since all parts of the sphere are of the same character, nothing could render any one pair of opposite points preferable to another as a location of the poles. This would suggest that even within the principles of Aristotle's description of the world it is necessary to talk about a decision having been taken which was entirely arbitrary and not determined by the merits of the alternatives. As far as the direction of the heavens is concerned, why should we accept that the movement of one of the celestial spheres to the west and the others to the east represent the (only) optimal arrangement? Al-Ghazālī argues that the same effects would surely be achieved in a universe that moves in the reverse direction, with the highest sphere moving to the east rather than to the west. In that case the present arrangement of these movements is entirely arbitrary. If this is plausible, even the philosophers must agree that there are instances in the universe of the instantiation of one alternative rather than another quite similar state of affairs, and so they should not object to creation by arguing that nothing could prefer one moment for creation over another. Exactly the same determining factor which selected the location of the poles and the direction of the movements of the spheres could similarly have selected a time for creation.

Averroes' reply to this objection is rather lame (and like many of his less satisfactory arguments quite long). He suggests that a scientist would be able to say precisely why the world has its specific features and why it would not work properly, or as well, as an integrated system were the changes which al-Ghazālī considers conceivable to take place. Indeed, he even refers to two Qur'ānic verses (XVIII,103–4 and VI,75) which stress the importance of seeing the world as a divinely constructed unit, organized in the wisest and best possible manner. Averroes basically suggests that al-Ghazālī has set up a problem which a competent scientist, working on appropriately Aristotelian premisses, could quite easily answer. But al-Ghazālī has identified a very significant weakness in Aristotelian conceptions of the universe which Averroes' bluster fails to disguise. Happily, though, Averroes can also argue, this time more plausibly, that where it is a question of God considering whether to create or not to create the world there is not a question of a choice between similar alternatives, but rather the possibility of creating life and all that goes with it as against not acting at all. In so far as indifferent alternatives occurred in the construction of the world, then God might be assumed to have done the divine equivalent of tossing a coin to decide which alternative to accept. Again, if it is a better state of affairs for a world such as ours to exist rather than not to exist, then presumably the longer it exists the better. This would give weight to the arguments that God created the world from eternity, that it came into being with him.

Al-Ghazālī produces a second objection to the proofs concerning the eternity of the world. The philosophers admit that an eternal being can cause temporal beings; after all, that is how God brings things about in the world. Their argument for the existence of a first mover is based on the problems in conceiving of an infinite chain of causes which would otherwise have to be regarded as responsible for the phenomena with which we are familiar. The chain of causes, going from more specific to more general causal explanations, must end somewhere if it is not to be infinite. At the end of this causal chain there is a being necessary in itself, uncaused by anything prior to it and eternal. As we have seen, the model of creation which is employed is that of emanation, so that there is a continual creation and activity. Al-Ghazālī's point is that if the philosophers accept that there is such a cause for each state of affairs that takes place in time, are they not then compelled to admit at the same time that there is such a cause for the world as a whole? In other words, why do they reject the idea that God brings into existence the entire world as a whole at any time he wishes? Averroes claims that al-Ghazālī achieves this conclusion by a sleight of hand. The eternal being does not directly cause any temporal event. Every such event has an *accidental* cause which occurs in an infinite series of preceding temporal events. But the entire eternal series is caused *essentially* by an eternal being acting upon the whole. Such a being is an essential cause in the sense that it brings about its effects simultaneously with its own existence, which is just the opposite of the temporal priority which holds in the case of accidental causes. The eternal being is not, then, a cause of temporal beings directly, but only in so far as they are members of the whole series of beings. This is intended to show that God does not act directly in time. The distinction which Averroes makes here between accidental and essential causes may seem rather artificial, but it has an interesting and persuasive Aristotelian basis. Essential or substantival change is, according to Aristotle, very different from qualitative or quantitative change. A piece of bronze is essentially changed into a statue of Apollo when it is finished, and the change is completely instantaneous. It occupies no time at all. This is obviously an appropriate model upon which to base God's creation of the world; his work is rather like that of completing a sculpture in that an entirely novel substance is brought into existence, and there was no period over which this change stretched. It just happened, and did not happen in time.

Al-Ghazālī skilfully sets about attacking the way in which the philosophical account of creation has difficulties with the phenomenon of change. The eternal being on that account requires some medium to affect the temporal realm of generation and corruption. The most distant heaven was selected since as a whole it is in eternal circular movement, yet its particular movements are changing all the time and so are temporal. Al-Ghazālī's comment on this theory is sharp and to the point:

Is this circular movement temporal or eternal? If it is eternal, how does it become the principle for temporal things? And if it is temporal, it will need another temporal being and we shall have an infinite regress. And when you say that it partially resembles the eternal, partially the temporal, for it resembles the eternal in so far as it is permanent and the temporal in so far as it arises anew, we answer: Is it the principle of temporal things, because of its permanence, or because of its arising anew? In the former case, how can a temporal proceed from something because of its permanence? And in the latter case, what arises anew will need a cause for its arising anew, and we have an infinite regress. (*T T* 36)

Averroes makes a brief rejoinder which leaves us still in the dark as to how a movement which remains at all times the same can bring about changes in the world. Al-Ghazālī wants to attack the philosophers on this point not just to reveal how shaky some of their arguments are but also to show how they fail to account for the influence of a personal God on the events of our material world. These events are members of an 'accidental' chain if the philosophers are correct, and thus very remotely connected with God.

The Second Proof of the philosophers concerns the nature of time. Al-Ghazālī is interested here in attacking the use which the *falāsifa* make of Aristotle's notion of time. For Aristotle, time is not an absolute independent framework in which all events can be identified. He connects the notion of time very closely to change. Time is regarded as the number of motion with respect to before and after; in other words, time is one movement measuring other movements by comparing the number of times the one takes place while the others take place. He is interested in the way in which we make the temporal judgments before and after, earlier and later, among events, and how our criteria for assessing periods of time involve comparing the changes we are concerned with in terms of other changes we use as standards or measures. And of course for Aristotle the fact that there are changes in the world is just a fact which cannot be denied. At the very basis of our temporal judgments lies the regularity and reliability of the movement of the heavenly bodies. Why is it relevant to al-Ghazālī and the philosophers to determine the question of the finitude or eternity of time? What is the significance of the answer to this question for the nature of the existence of the world? On Aristotelian premises, the existence of time presupposes the existence of movement and so of a moving being. Since time is the measure of movement, if it can be shown that time is eternal, it would follow that a moving being, i.e. the world, is eternal. And indeed Aristotle argued that there must be eternal and continuous change.

Al-Ghazālī applies the same sort of technique as when dealing with the First Proof. He tries to adhere to Aristotelian principles while at the same time arguing that they do not inevitably lead to the conclusions which the philosophers draw from them. He bluntly claims that the issue is whether time and a moving world are both eternal or whether time and a moving world are both finite. If time is closely related to movement in the way the philosophers argue, this might appear helpful to someone like al-Ghazālī who is going to argue that when God created the first movement, he at the same time brought about time. The first moment of time existed when God set the universe in motion. Before this point God existed with nothing else:

Time is generated and created, and before it there was no time at all. The meaning of our words that God is prior to the world and to time is: He existed without the world and without time, then he existed and with him there was the world and there was time ... the world is like a singular person; if we should say, for instance, God existed without Jesus, then he existed with Jesus – these words contain nothing but, first, the existence of an essence and the non-existence of an essence, then, the existence of two essences, and there is no need to assume here a third essence, namely time, although imagination cannot desist from assuming it. But we should not heed the errors of the imagination. (*TT* 38)

He thus argues that before the creation of the world God existed, but not in time, and if we wonder what it means to say that *before* the creation there was no time, if we wonder how we can use temporal terms to refer to a non-temporal period, then al-Ghazālī suggests that we are being misled by imagination. It is not clear, though, why he thinks imagination is involved here. The opponent of his view would presumably argue that there exists a *conceptual* connection between the notion of change and the notion of time such that we cannot make sense of talking about the one without implicitly mentioning the other. Al-Ghazālī suggests that time just pops up in people's minds when they are thinking about change as though it were an idea merely *associated* with change.

With his usual knack for criticizing the crucial Aristotelian premiss, al-Ghazālī is challenging Aristotle's claim that the world is eternal since no moment could be the first moment of the world's existence. Aristotle argues in this way:

We say that change is the actuality of the changeable thing in so far as it is changeable. It is necessary therefore that for each change there are things capable of being changed ... Further these things necessarily either come to be – at some time they do not exist [al-Ghazālī's view] – or they are eternal. If therefore each of the changeable things came to be before that change another change must have come to be, according to which the thing capable of being changed or changing came to be. The supposition that these things existed always but unchanged appears unreasonable immediately, but even more unreasonable if one goes on to investigate the consequences. For if, among the things that are changeable and capable of producing change, there will at some time be something first producing change and something changing, while at another time there is nothing but something resting, then this thing must have previously been changing. For there was some cause of rest, rest being a privation of change. Therefore before this first change there will be a previous change. (*Phys.* 251 a 9–28)

Aristotle's argument is that there cannot be a beginning or end of time in that a 'now' is not a period of time but a limit which brings one time period to an end and starts another. There is thus time on both sides of it. There could not be a first 'now' with no time before it, nor a last 'now' with no time after it, and so no beginning or ending of time. The existence of time is dependent upon someone measuring changes. For an event to occur at some time it is necessary that it stands in a determinate relation to the present.

For Aristotle the world is eternal and uncreated, and he takes this to mean that if one were to measure a period of time which covered all events in the world's history, that period would be infinite. Aristotle regards such a measurement as impossible, since although we can measure some of the events of history, there will always be more events to be measured than we can accomplish. One cannot measure the time elapsed in the entire previous history of the world. How can we tell, then, that the world is eternal? Were we to be able to measure the world, then presumably we could say that we had arrived at an eternal measurement, and so could justifiably claim that we had discovered that the world is eternal. For the world to be eternal, it must have existed at all times, or, there was no time at which the world did not exist. Yet since time is the measure of change, and the motion of the heavens provides the standard measure of change, were there to be no world and so no change, neither would there be any time. Thus we can arrive at the conclusion that the world is eternal by putting together the indubitable evidence of our senses and the valid rules of logical reasoning, namely, that there is change in the world and there could not logically be a first change.

Al-Ghazālī tries to test this theory of the eternity of the world in a stronger way than just trying to present examples of language which are temporal and yet, he argues, do not presuppose the presence of time. He goes on to bring in the nature of space. He claims that there is a useful analogy to be drawn between space and time, pointing out that if the philosophers admit that space is finite since it is a property of body which is finite they should also accept that time is finite, since it too is a property of finite movement. He suggests that the proof of the impossibility of an infinite extension applies just as clearly to space as to time. As Averroes puts it: 'al-Ghazālī treats the quantity which has no position and does not form a totality, i.e. time and motion, as the quantity which possesses position and totality, i.e. body. He makes the impossibility of endlessness in the latter a proof of its impossibility in the former' (*TT* 43–4).

Al-Ghazālī has asked a very interesting question, again, at least initially, from within an Aristotelian system of thought. Time is regarded as
a measure of change and one measures a particular change by selecting
a motion which is uniform and by using it as a standard against which
the time of a given change is measured. The best measure of change
for Aristotle is regular circular motion such as the eternal motion of
the heavenly bodies. However, a body in motion clearly passes over a
magnitude of space and so if time is infinite and time is measured by
motion, why does not the infinity of time imply the existence of an in-
finitely extended magnitude? A basic distinction between space and time
in Aristotle is that the latter is dependent for its existence on a soul that
is measuring changes, whereas this is not the case for the former. The
sort of reply which Averroes produces to this challenge is to appeal to
what Aristotelians regard as just facts or obvious. A major argument for
the finitude of space is that were it otherwise the observable and regular properties of the heavens and the theory of natural motions would
become impossible. An infinite space would also presumably involve an
infinite chain of causes of a given thing, and so we would not be able to
know the explanation of that thing, since the mind cannot grasp all the
contents of an infinite series. We are limited beings and not gods, and we
cannot grasp that which is without limits. Yet we can know the causes of
a thing, we can produce explanations as to why things happen as they
do in the world, and so they must be finite. If the properties which made
up a substance were infinite in number then we could not know the substance. Yet we can know what substances are and so they only contain
a finite number of properties in their definitions. We cannot understand
the world unless it is a finite place which contains equally finite things,
and it is clear that we do understand the world. Averroes is reduced in
his wordy response to al-Ghazālī's attacks to repeating these Aristotelian
principles and arguments.

The Third Proof which al-Ghazālī considers is by far his shortest
discussion and a very interesting one. He sets out to attack the theory of
potentiality, which was so popular among the *falāsifa*, and its links with the
notion of an ungenerated universe. The argument starts by claiming that
the existence of the world before it actually existed, were there to be such
a state of affairs, was always possible. It must have been always possible
since now it is actual. Indeed, since it has always been possible it must
always have been actual too, and so the world is eternal and not finite.
This seems a rather strange argument, and one way of unravelling it is
to agree with Van Den Bergh that an unstated assumption which makes

the argument plausible is that the world as a whole is ungenerated.[23] Everything ungenerated is eternal, since by definition it can never go out of or come into existence. The world is possible and we know that it exists at some time, and it follows that if it exists at some time it must have existed at every time, as it is ungenerated. This interpretation of the philosophical argument is implausible. For one thing, al-Ghazālī might well be expected to spot such a suspect hidden assumption and challenge it. The 'hidden assumption', or rather the principle which is in this argument accepted and not defended is the principle of plenitude which attempts to establish a conceptual connection between the eternally possible and the actual. In his comments on this proof al-Ghazālī takes the notion of possibility in a logical sense, so that the realms of possibility and actuality need not be the same. This accounts for the fact that Averroes and al-Ghazālī make statements which fail to engage with each other at all – they are using different notions of possibility. Averroes suggests that:

The man who assumes that before the existence of the world there was one unique, never-ceasing possibility must concede that the world is eternal. The man who affirms, like al-Ghazālī in his answer, that before the world there was an infinite number of possibilities of worlds, has certainly to admit that before this world there was another world and before this second world a third and so on ad infinitum, as is the case with human beings, and especially when it is assumed that the perishing of the earlier is the necessary condition for the existence of the later. (*TT* 58)

But what al-Ghazālī would mean by saying that before the world was created all sorts of possibilities of world could be conceived is that it is perfectly possible to think about all these alternative worlds. What Averroes means by such a claim is that if these worlds are genuinely possible, then something must (eventually) necessitate their existence, and so they must have existed in a sort of series before our world was created, rather in the way that previous generations of human beings have led to our generation. What is ironic in this discussion is that al-Ghazālī seems to be using a contrast between possibility and actuality which was originally established by Aristotle, while Averroes is identifying those notions in a way which seems close to the thinking of some of the Ash'arite thinkers in holding that possibility is coextensive with reality, that the possible is what has come to be.

The Fourth Proof extends in much more detail the arguments for the eternity of the world that rely upon some version of the principle of

---

[23] S. Van Den Bergh (trans.), *Averroes' Tahāfut al-tahāfut* (London, Luzac, 1978), 'Notes', p. 43.

plenitude. The Aristotelian argument upheld to some degree by the *falāsifa* is that while the world as a totality is ungenerated and uncorrupted, the parts of the world are in continual flux. Change is only possible if matter acquires different forms and thus new things are brought about. Matter must always exist, it is the necessary substrate of all change and so it cannot itself be subject to change and merely *possible*. It must itself be necessary (although not necessary in itself – that description is reserved for God) and cannot require other matter to affect it causally in order for it to exist, since otherwise there would be an infinite regress. As Averroes approvingly adds to al-Ghazālī's formulation of the philosophers' arguments:

The summary . . . is that everything that becomes is possible before it becomes, and that possibility needs something for its subsistence, namely, the substratum which receives that which is possible . . . Since it is impossible that the possibility prior to the thing's becoming should be absolutely without substratum, or that the agent should be its substratum or the thing possible . . . there only remains as a vehicle for possibility the recipient of the possible, i.e. matter. Matter, insofar as it is matter, does not become; for if it did it would need other matter and we should have an infinite regress. Matter only becomes in so far as it is combined with form. (*TT* 59–60)

A vital aspect of Aristotle's notion of matter is that of a substratum or subject in the analysis of change. He argued that there must be a persistent element in change. In many cases of change where something grows or moves we ordinarily identify a subject undergoing the change. We talk about the same subject changing from one state to another. Where there is substantival change, where one substance goes out of existence (a pint of beer) and another comes into existence (the growth of a person), Aristotle claims that the generation of one substance involves the destruction of another. What persists in this sort of case is not a particular subject of a given form, as with a moving ball changing from being in one place to being somewhere else, but the matter that was elsewhere. Previously it was in the beer, and now it is transferred into human growth. There are three main aspects of any change: a substratum, a form and a privation. The substratum is the subject that is changing, the form is the end towards which the change is directed, and the privation shows that the form was not present at the beginning of the change. Had the privation been present then there could not have been any change in the first place. The relation between the beginning and the end of a change is that of contraries or opposites so that, for example, any change in the colour of something from white has to be either to black or to some compound of white and black.

Al-Ghazālī's aim is to attack the attempt to establish the existence of an eternal matter whose whole rationale is the impossibility of something coming from nothing. He seeks to defend the notion of something coming from nothing when God so decides. The first objection which al-Ghazālī presents is very much based upon his use of a logical rather than 'Aristotelian' notion of possibility:

The objection is that the possibility of which they speak is a judgment of the intellect, and anything whose existence the intellect supposes, provided no obstacle presents itself to the supposition, we call possible and, if there is such an obstacle, we call it impossible and, if we suppose that it cannot be supposed not to be, we call it necessary. These are rational judgments which need no real existent which they might qualify. (*T T* 60).

His first suggestion is that if possibility presupposes a substratum then so does impossibility, yet 'impossibility has no real existence, and there is no matter in which it occurs and to which it could be related' (*T T* 60). A perfect example of the way in which al-Ghazālī and Averroes fail to come into contact on this issue emerges with the latter's reply to this attack. He entirely agrees with al-Ghazālī:

Indeed the impossible demands a substratum just as much as the possible does, and this is clear from the fact that the impossible is the opposite of the possible and opposite contraries undoubtedly require a substratum. For impossibility is the negation of possibility, and if possibility needs a substratum, impossibility which is the negation of this possibility requires a substratum too, e.g. we say that ... the presence of opposites at the same time in the same substratum is impossible ... i.e. in reality. (*T T* 60–1)

Averroes is clearly understanding by 'possibility' and 'impossibility' something very different from al-Ghazālī. The latter divorces these modal notions from 'real existence' while the *falāsifa* as we have seen closely connect them.

A similar problem affects al-Ghazālī's next objection to the philosophers' theory of possibility. He argues that if possibility presupposes the existence of matter, it would be impossible to conceive of certain properties, like colour for example, as being possible when they are unrelated to matter. That is, we can think of *red* without necessarily thinking of red *things*. This is a familiar form of philosophical argument which is based upon a thought experiment which establishes the presence or absence of a conceptual connection between ideas. If it is possible to conceive of a colour without at the same time conceiving of a coloured thing then, al-Ghazālī suggests, this shows that there is no essential connection between properties and their material substrate, 'And this shows that the intellect in order to decide whether something is possible need not admit an existing thing to which the possibility can be related' (*TT* 61). Averroes replies by arguing that non-existence cannot become existence without passing through a middle stage, this intermediary being represented by matter. Matter must always be present as a substratum for change: 'Therefore there must necessarily be a substratum which is the recipient for the possibility and which is the vehicle of the change and the becoming, and it is this of which it is said that it becomes and alters and changes from non-existence to existence' (*TT* 62). He is arguing that if some state of affairs is possible, then it can come into existence, and if it is to come into existence it must come from somewhere and change in the manner described by Aristotle. Al-Ghazālī, with his thought experiment to show that we can think of things as possible without being actual, tries to show that we can thus conceive of things independently of their instantiation in the world. Then how can it be claimed that the notion of possibility depends upon or presupposes the notion of actuality or existence, in this case the eternal existence of matter as a substratum? Averroes suggests that what is important about the notion of possibility is that it identifies states of affairs which are potentially *actual*. He is being faithful here to the broad interpretation of the principle of plenitude, that: 'It is not allowable that it is true to say "this is possible, but it will not be" ' (*Met.* 1047b 3). If there can be no colours which are not actualized, if there can be no empty spaces, then trying to conceive of such states of affairs is pointless philosophically. That is why Averroes replies to al-Ghazālī by describing in detail the Aristotelian account of change, in particular the significance of the substratum, which appears on the face of it to be a completely irrelevant move in the argument. His point is that the significance of talking about *possible* states of affairs is in terms of their eventual transformation into *actual* states of affairs, and to understand the process of change we must follow the logic of Aristotle's account.

Many commentators who deal with the First Discussion of the *Incoherence of the incoherence* leave the text at this stage and go on to consider the nature of the argument between the two thinkers. But there remains an important section in which al-Ghazālī rehearses some of the counter-arguments which the philosophers might produce to overturn his attacks. And indeed, they are not dissimilar in many cases from the arguments which Averroes does produce. One of the compelling aspects of al-Ghazālī's approach, and one of the most annoying for Averroes, is that not only does he present the philosophers' arguments well, but he also argues cleverly that they do not work and then presents accurately the sorts of counter-objection they will produce to defend indirectly their original positions. He does this at the end of the First Discussion where he runs through plausible counter-arguments to his proofs of the independence of possibility from matter. Then he appropriately discusses the importance of the difference between his view of the notion of possibility and that of his opponents. As we have seen, this difference is at the essence of the rather bloodless nature of the dispute. He sets out to argue that the philosophers ought to accept the use of modal concepts which he employs:

And the answer is: To reduce possibility, necessity and impossibility to rational concepts is correct and as for the assertion that the concepts of reason form its knowledge, and knowledge implies a thing known, let them be answered: it cannot be said that receptivity of colour and animality and the other concepts, which are fixed in the mind according to the philosophers . . . have no objects. Still these objects have no real existence in the external world and the philosophers are certainly right in saying that universals exist only in the mind, not in the external world, and that in the external world there are only particular individuals, which are apprehended by the senses, not by reason . . . now, in the same way, it can be said that possibility is a form which exists in the mind, not in the exterior world, and if this is not impossible for other concepts, there is no impossibility in what we have said. (*TT* 64–5)

This clever move suggests that just as universals are subjective and 'in our minds', so is the notion of possibility. If this is true, then the philosophical connection between possibility and actuality will be well and truly severed. Averroes suggests that al-Ghazālī has misunderstood what is meant by saying that universals are subjective: 'The theory of the philosophers that universals exist only in the mind, not in the external world, only means that the universals exist actually only in the mind, and not in the external world, for the meaning is that they exist potentially, not actually in the external world' (*TT* 65). His point is that it is possible to *use* universals in the external world, and so they exist potentially, without having to accept that there *are* universals in the external world. Universals do not actually exist in the world since they are not the sort of concept which can be said to be instantiated as separate, individual entities. Although we can pick out red things in the world, the universal 'red' does not consist in (just) those things but is generally applicable to any appropriately coloured thing which might confront us at any time. We can quite easily talk about tables and chairs existing, and about red tables and chairs existing, but when we talk about 'red' existing it is not clear what we mean. Al-Ghazālī argues that what we might mean by talking about 'red' existing is that we can form an idea in our minds about that colour without at the same time necessarily bothering about what objects if any in the world have that property. So 'red' is an idea in the mind and not an aspect of the external world.

Now, Averroes agrees that we cannot talk about 'red' existing in the same way that red tables exist, since the latter is a question of the existence of particular things, while the former relates to the status of universals, or to the properties of those particular things. The fact that we can use such universals suggests to Averroes that they must succeed in abstracting features of the external world which actually do exist: 'it cannot be doubted that the judgments of the mind have value only in regard to the nature of things outside the soul. If there were outside the soul nothing possible or impossible, the judgment of the mind that things are possible or impossible would be of as much value as no judgment at all, and there would be no difference between reason and illusion' (*T T* 67). Like universals, possibility has an external existence in the sense that we can use that notion in identifying phenomena, and so it exists potentially in the external world. Averroes seeks in this way to refute al-Ghazālī by showing that notions like possibility are not just 'in our minds' but rather have a foot in both the camp of our minds *and* the camp of the external world. Averroes refuses to accept that either modal notions or universals are merely formal concepts, with no corresponding, albeit irreducibly individual, objects in the real world. Towards the end of the First Discussion, the argument quite clearly is stripped for perhaps the first time to the basic issue which so importantly separates the philosophers from al-Ghazālī, and that issue is the notion of possibility.

Averroes thinks he can dispose of the theological objections to the notion of the eternity of the world by similarly reducing the controversy to one which is about the way in which certain key terms are taken. In one of his more popular works, the *Decisive treatise on the harmony of religion and philosophy*, he describes the dispute thus:

Concerning the question whether the world is pre-eternal or came into existence, the disagreement between the Ash'arite theologians and the ancient philosophers is in my view almost resolvable into a disagreement about naming ... For they agree that there are three classes of being: two extremes and one intermediate between the extremes. One extreme is a being which is brought into existence from something other than itself and by something ... and ... its existence is preceded by time ... All alike, ancients and Ash'arites, agree in naming this class of beings 'originated'. The opposite extreme to this is a being which is not made from or by anything and not preceded by time: and here too all members of both schools agree in naming it 'pre-eternal'. This being is apprehended by demonstration; it is God . . .

The class of being which is between these two extremes is that which is not made from anything and not preceded by time, but which is brought into existence by something, i.e. by an agent. This is the world as a whole . . . the theologians admit that time does not precede it, or rather this is a necessary consequence for them since time according to them is something which accompanies motion and bodies [so the theologians are all taken to be Aristotelians!]. They also agree with the ancients in the view that future time is infinite and likewise future being [so they did not according to Averroes accept the Qur'ān's prediction of everything except God going to annihilation]. They only disagree about past time and past being: the theologians hold that it is finite . . . while Aristotle and his school hold that it is infinite. (*FM* 55–6)

Averroes suggests that the dispute, for all its heat, is nothing more than a storm in a teacup. It is just a matter of each party thinking that time more closely resembles either what is generated or what is pre-eternal. And in his view 'in truth it is neither really originated nor really pre-eternal, since the really originated is necessarily perishable and the really pre-eternal has no cause' (*FM* 56). Averroes is certainly taking liberties with the views of most of the Ash'arites, but he does have a point in suggesting that if the theologians will go along with an Aristotelian theory of time's dependence upon movement, then it is possible to defuse to a degree the whole controversy. If time is parasitic upon the concept of motion and so is inconceivable without the existence of the universe, then time can be seen as eternal if the universe has always been in production. Before this continual production, this creation, there was nothing out of which the universe could be created. So the universe was created out of nothing and was not preceded by time. But is this attempt at separating the question of creation *ex nihilo* from the question of the eternity of the world a success? Averroes thinks he can accept creation *ex nihilo* without abandoning the eternity of the universe. Creation in time can be regarded as the contrary of creation from eternity; creation *ex nihilo* need not be identified with creation in time at all.

There are indications that this approach has more general support. In a more popular work, al-Fārābī upholds Aristotle's position that the world as a whole is not subject to generation and destruction, reconciling this position with the doctrine of creation by suggesting that Aristotle's doctrines of movement and time do not exclude the possibility that the world as a whole together with time were created from nothing by a

God who is the world's final and efficient cause. He even claims that Aristotle in his *Theology* (in reality part of the *Enneads* of Plotinus) has made it clear that he believes that God created the world *ex nihilo*.[24] Yet intriguingly in that work the world, including its matter, is represented as emanating from the essence of God, as one would expect given its authorship. Wolfson comments on this apparent confusion and thinks it reveals a significant clue to an appropriate understanding of the sense of creation *ex nihilo*. He claims that: 'The fact that al-Fārābī ascribes to that work the view that matter was created ex nihilo undoubtedly means that in his opinion creation ex nihilo meant the same as creation from the essence of God.'[25] It is interesting that Aristotle actually claimed that the *ex nihilo nihil* principle (nothing can come from nothing) was as old as philosophy itself and the 'common assumption' of all those who wrote on nature (*Phys.* 187a 27–9; *Met.* 1062b 24–5). By contrast, al-Fārābī argues in his *Agreement of the opinions of the philosophers Plato and Aristotle* that Plato and Aristotle were agreed on the doctrine of creation *ex nihilo* unlike pagan, Jewish and Magian philosophers. This is not just an uninteresting confusion based on the ignorance of the real authorship of the *Theology of Aristotle*. It points to the fact that the expression '*ex nihilo*' or 'from the not existent' has two senses. It could mean 'nothing' in the sense of 'not a something'. On the other hand, it could be identified with 'matter', and indeed was by Plotinus who identified it with 'something'.

Plotinus developed a new theory of the origin of the world which appeared alongside the older theories of Plato and Aristotle. The world was no longer regarded as being created from a pre-existent matter which was itself coeternal with God (Plato), nor was it regarded as being in its completeness coeternal with God (Aristotle); it is now seen as being eternally generated or emanated from the essence of God. This new view attempts to interpret the belief in creation *ex nihilo* as the temporal generation of the world from the essence of God. This is not just an example of philosophical nit-picking, but of considerable importance in challenging the idea that al-Ghazālī is eager to defend, namely, that there is a wide gulf between the proposition that the world was created *ex nihilo* and the proposition that time is eternal. But, as we have seen, the claim that the world was created after complete non-existence is not equivalent to the claim that the world was created *ex nihilo*. The former claim

---

[24] Al-Fārābī, *Philosophische Abhandlungen*, ed. F. Dieterici, p. 23.

[25] H. Wolfson. 'The meaning of *ex nihilo* in the Church Fathers, Arabic and Hebrew Philosophy, and St Thomas', in *Medieval studies in honor of J. D. M. Ford* (Cambridge, MA, Harvard University Press, 1948), pp. 355–70; pp. 356–7.

implies that before creation there had been non-existence, while the latter may be interpreted to signify the continuous creation of existence out of non-existence or the eternal forming of matter. Such a view of creation *ex nihilo* is far from being incompatible with the theory of the eternity of time.

It rather seems, then, that because the philosophers and al-Ghazālī use a different notion of what creation '*ex nihilo*' comes down to, their arguments fail to clash just as they avoided each other when discussing arguments involving the notion of possibility. Like so much philosophical dispute it is a matter of both sides presenting different analyzes of the key concepts upon which their reasoning is based and leaving it to the reader to decide which analysis makes better sense in the context. Al-Ghazālī is trying to re-establish the role of a personal, powerful and omniscient God which he feels cannot be reconciled with the basic metaphysical and logical theses which the philosophers accept and defend. In so far as he tries to do this while trying to maintain an Aristotelian, or aspects of an Aristotelian, system he must be judged to have failed. When he accuses the philosophers of having reduced God's role in the world to one of relative impotence it is always open to them to reply with Averroes that 'impotence is not inability to do the impossible, but inability to do what can be done' (*T T* 52). But al-Ghazālī definitely succeeds in demonstrating how limited a role the philosophers' God retains once he is put alongside a deterministic and eternal world, and how different this role is from that explicitly described by Islam. On the other hand, bearing in mind Averroes' point above, perhaps that is the only role which can be made philosophically respectable.

MAIMONIDES AND THE PROBLEM OF CREATION

Some writers regard Maimonides as a specifically *Jewish* thinker, whose arguments and theories are designed to be theological rather than philosophical. In other words, he is regarded as primarily engaged in defending the tenets of religion and only incidentally as a philosopher trying to establish truths which may well be independent of religion. I shall argue, however, that Maimonides is indeed a *failasūf* well within the tradition of *falsafa* and that he has some very interesting comments to make upon the sorts of arguments which the *falāsifa* produced and upon their applications. When we started to discuss the issue of creation and how traditional interpretations of God's creation of the world *ex nihilo* could be reconciled with Aristotelian arguments in favour of the world's eternity, we concentrated upon the sorts of modal distinctions which al-Fārābī, Avicenna and Averroes made. While Maimonides uses much the same technical vocabulary as his predecessors he alters it in various ways. He agrees that God is the only thing necessarily existent in himself while everything else is possible and requires a cause outside itself in order to exist. He also accepts that the universe is controlled by necessary causes yet tries to avoid the model of emanation which sees the universe as derived from a cause connected necessarily and eternally with its immaterial part. One of the themes of Maimonides' thought is the stress on the gap which exists between God and his creation, and the emanationist system in effect reduces that gap by arguing that the things of this world and the things of the divine world merge into each other, however indirectly. Maimonides indeed objects to that system by using one of the basic Neoplatonic problems, namely, how to reconcile two kinds of creature, God and mortal beings, when they have nothing in common with each other.[26] The model of emanation is designed to show how things which have nothing in common with each other do at the same time have interconnections. The intermediaries are represented by those entities which al-Fārābī and Avicenna called necessary through another and which seem to determine God's actions and decisions without giving him the opportunity to choose to do anything at all he might like. Maimonides is in fact operating with a slimmed-down version of metaphysics as compared with the *falāsifa*. Following Aristotle closely, al-Fārābī's *Catalogue of sciences* divides the subject of metaphysics into: (i) the science which studies being insofar as it is being; (ii) the science which investigates the basic principles of the individual sciences; and (iii) the science which investigates the supersensible beings. In his *Treatise on logic*, Maimonides omits any suggestion that metaphysics should be concerned with the ontological problems of (i).[27] Of course, he would acknowledge that distinctions can be made between different kinds of supersensible beings, such as God and the angels, but he would not regard them as important distinctions. The basic distinction he is concerned with is that between created and uncreated beings.

Maimonides argues consistently that there is no possible demonstrative proof for the immutability and necessity of the laws which regulate this universe. He challenges the *falāsifa* to present evidence which *proves*

[26] A structural feature of Neoplatonism with which all religious philosophers had to struggle.
[27] Maimonides *Treatise on logic*, ed. and trans. I. Efros, Proceedings, American Academy for Jewish Research (AAJR), VIII (New York, AAJR, 1938).

that the laws we are familiar with are the only possible laws which could apply to the world, evidence which is more solid than just pointing to the fact that these are in fact the laws which prevail now. We are immediately reminded of the argument between Averroes and al-Ghazālī over the Second Proof. By a rigorous proof or demonstration Maimonides means, like Aristotle, a reasoning which starts from true and certain premisses and proceeds by syllogistic rules of valid reasoning to a conclusion which is as indubitable as the premisses. A syllogism is just an argument in which, certain things having been assumed, something other than those assumptions follow necessarily. Maimonides does not doubt that these laws are necessary in the sense that they have been necessitated by God's will, but he denies that they are necessary in the sense that they necessitate God's will to select them in the first place. This enables him to try to accommodate Aristotle in what passes for a theologically acceptable manner:

He [Aristotle] said that the first matter is subject to neither generation nor passing-away and began to draw inferences in favor of this thesis from the things subject to generation and passing-away and to make clear that it was impossible that the first matter was generated. And this is correct. For we do not maintain that the first matter is generated as man is generated from the seed or that it passes away into dust. But we maintain that God has brought it into existence from nothing and that after being brought into existence, it was as it is now – I mean everything is generated from it, and everything generated from it passes away into it; it does not exist devoid of form; generation and corruption terminate in it; it is not subject to generation as are the things generated from it, nor to passing-away as are the things that pass away into it, but is created from nothing. And its Creator may, if He wishes to do so, render it entirely and absolutely nonexistent. (*GP* II,17,296–7)

It is one thing to argue that the laws which regulate the world are well devised and are not arbitrarily altered by their creator, but quite another to claim that these laws are the only possible ones:

For we, the community of the followers of Moses our Master and Abraham our Father, may peace be on them, believe that the world was generated in such and such manner and came to be in a certain state, which came after another state. Aristotle, on the other hand, begins to contradict us and to bring forward against us proofs based on the nature of what exists, a nature that has attained stability, is perfect, and has achieved actuality. As for us, we declare against him that this nature, after it has achieved stability and perfection, does not resemble in anything the state it was in while in the state of being generated, and that it was brought into existence from absolute nonexistence. (*GP* II,17,296)

Interestingly, though, Maimonides does not claim that the philosophers are wrong in their adherence to the eternity of the world. He argues in this section of the *Guide of the perplexed* that, while he is in a position to demonstrate the possibility of creation *ex nihilo*, he cannot demonstrate its truth, nor can the philosophers demonstrate the eternity and the necessity of the world.[28]

Maimonides shares to a large extent the approach to *falsafa* adopted by al-Ghazālī. They both contrast in detail the model of emanation with the traditional notion of God as a free and omnipotent agent who considers a variety of possible creations and then effects one of them. Basic to their views of religion is a creator by design, a creator who freely wills the world's organization in the sense that that organization can be changed if God wants to and so must come *after* him in time. Maimonides is not convinced of the possibility of the reconciliation between the claim that the world was created by design and yet is eternally actual, since he argues that the latter claim entails a divine will being obliged to determine from all eternity and so not really being autonomous:

For the meaning of the assertion, as maintained by Aristotle, that this being proceeds necessarily from its cause, and is perpetual in virtue of the latter's perpetuity – that cause being the deity – is identical with the meaning of their assertion that the world derives from the act of the deity or exists in virtue of His purpose, will, free choice, and particularization, but that it has always been and will always be as it is – just as the sunrise is indubitably the agent of the day, though neither of them precedes the other in point of time. But this is not the meaning of purpose, as we propose to conceive it. For we wish to signify by the term that it – I mean the world – does not necessarily proceed from Him, may He be exalted, as an effect necessarily proceeds from its cause without being able to be separated from it. (*GP* II,21,315)

We saw in the previous section that there is not necessarily an incompatibility between creation *ex nihilo* and the doctrine of the eternity and necessity of the universe, but Maimonides is determined to reject the forms of emanationism which would make these two positions cohere. He accepts that the proofs for the existence of God do not depend on the assertion of creation (*GP* II,2,252), that there can be no philosophical demonstration of creation and that biblical passages which refer to creation need not be regarded literally (*GP* II,25,327–30). Yet creation is a fundamental principle of the Jewish religion, equal in importance to the principle of God's unity (*GP* II,13,281). The principle of creation is so

---

[28] The sort of 'possibility' he has in mind here is obviously different from that involved in the principle of plenitude – it has no necessary connection with actuality.

central because of the close connection between the nature of the world and the possibility of miracles:

If we accept the eternity of the universe as taught by Aristotle, that everything in the universe is the result of fixed laws, that nature does not change and that there is nothing supernatural, we should necessarily be in opposition to the foundation of our religion, we should disbelieve all miracles and signs, and certainly reject all hopes and fears derived from scripture, *unless miracles are to be explained figuratively* [my emphasis].[29]

There does indeed seem to be no place for miracles as ordinarily understood in the Aristotelian universe given its necessary and necessitated structure. Maimonides' argument is that if God is to be provided with some metaphysical room in which to operate as he wishes then the principle of creation *ex nihilo* must be accepted.

Or does he rather try to conceal his true views on this issue? Maimonides quite explicitly refers to his *Guide of the perplexed* as having been written in a particularly difficult to penetrate manner, so that those who would be in danger of damage to their faith by their imperfect apprehension of the views contained in it remain untroubled. One of the techniques Maimonides uses to make it difficult to grasp his real position is contradiction. He employs contradictions in several different ways, one of which is to discuss a difficult subject whose truth may be dangerous to the faith of the ordinary people (and perhaps also to the welfare of the philosopher) and so must remain concealed. One way of concealing the point is for the writer to make a claim which contradicts something else he has said, and it is vital that the contradiction remains undetected by the ordinary reader while at the same time alerting the wise to the device of concealment and the need to unravel the writer's real meaning. According to Leo Strauss, Maimonides pretends to adhere to a God who has created the world out of his free will, who can intervene in it, who has knowledge of his creatures and sometimes actually answers their prayers. His genuine view is that there is no such thing as free will for God who cannot act in the world nor have knowledge of material sublunary entities. Maimonides' account of creation is couched very much in terms of the seventh reason for contradiction, i.e.

In speaking about very obscure matters it is necessary to conceal some parts and to disclose others. Sometimes in the case of certain dicta this necessity requires that the discussion proceed on the basis of a certain premise, whereas

[29] Maimonides, *Treatise on resurrection*, ed. and trans. J. Finkel, Proceedings, American Academy for Jewish Research, IX (New York, AAJR, 1939), p. 31; see also, *GP* II,25,329.

in another place necessity requires that the discussion proceed on the basis of another premise contradicting the first one. In such cases the vulgar must in no way be aware of the contradiction; the author accordingly uses some device to conceal it by all means (*GP* Introduction,18).

And indeed, there are passages where Maimonides contradicts his claims which seem to establish his adherence to orthodox religious interpretation of creation. For example, he suggests that the theory of the world's eternity should be assumed in his proofs of the unity, existence and disembodied nature of God in order 'not [to] cause the true opinion . . . to be supported by a foundation which everyone can shake and wish to destroy, while other men think that it has never been constructed' (*GP* I, 71,182). The foundation which he mentions here as especially dubious is presumably that the world came into existence after a state of nonexistence. Of course, he makes clear that he thinks the Aristotelian view of creation cannot be demonstrated and that it can only be used to establish other desirable conclusions. Yet his proofs relating to God suggest that our knowledge of God depends on the premiss of eternity (*GP* II, Introduction,239–40).

Not only does Maimonides in places seem surprisingly sympathetic to Aristotelian views of eternity, he also sometimes seems to adhere to an Aristotelian view of the necessity of creation. In Maimonides' account of the spheres as the source of all earthly motion, even 'free' acts of man are determined by purely physical factors. The sphere causes the external factors which determine the purposes of the human soul. Thus even the motion caused by the soul is ultimately brought about by the sphere. Now, Maimonides claims that he is an opponent of Aristotelian arguments which hold that all things exist by divine necessity, believing rather in divine purposes as the cause of everything (*GP* II,19,303; II,21,316–17). He insists that 'all that exists has been brought into existence . . . by God through his volition' (*GP* II,13,284). Yet he also argues that there are serious difficulties in talking about God having a will and wishes and that applying the term 'purpose' to describe the purposes of God and human beings is to use that term equivocally (*GP* III,20,483; II,18,301; II,21,315). Indeed, Maimonides does seem to leave the possibility of reconciling divine necessity with the divine will open. In explaining the Aristotelian notion of the necessary derivation of the world from God, he comments that 'this necessity is somewhat like the necessity of the derivation of an intellectum from an intellect' (*GP* II,20,313). Of course, for God 'knowledge of things is not derived from them . . . On the contrary, the things . . . follow upon his knowledge which preceded and established them as they are . . . He also knows the totality of what necessarily derives from all his acts' (*GP* III,21,485). This could be taken to suggest that when Maimonides talks about God willing certain states of affairs to take place and then bringing them about, the latter does not really have the power to make choices in the way in which we (seem to) make choices. These 'choices' might just be the way in which Maimonides chooses to describe what God, being God, is obliged to do.

A clue to Maimonides' position on creation might be discovered by exploring the relationship that he suggests exists between different positions on the question of creation and on the topic of prophecy. When the discussion of prophecy in the *Guide of the perplexed* begins, he comments that 'The opinions of people concerning prophecy are like their opinions concerning the eternity of the world or its creation in time' (*GP* II,32,360). The opinions which relate to creation and eternity are these:

1C The opinion . . . of all who believe in the Law of Moses . . . that the world as a whole . . . after having been purely and absolutely nonexistent . . . through [the divine] will and volition [has been] brought into existence out of nothing.

2C The . . . opinion . . . that there exists a certain matter that is eternal as the deity is eternal . . . He is the cause of its existence; and . . . He creates in it whatever He wishes. Thus He sometimes forms out of it a heaven and an earth, and sometimes He forms out of it something else.

3C The . . . opinion . . . of Aristotle, his followers, and the commentators of his books . . . He thinks that this being as a whole, such as it is, has never ceased to be and will never do so; that the permanent thing not subject to generation and passing-away, namely, the heaven, likewise does not cease to be; . . . and . . . that the thing subject to generation and passing-away, namely, that which is beneath the sphere of the moon, does not cease to be. (*GP* II,13,281–4)

The three views concerning prophecy which Maimonides mentions are these:

1P The first opinion – that of the multitude of those among the Pagans who considered prophecy as true and also believed by some of the common people professing our Law – is that God . . . chooses whom he wishes among men, turns him into a prophet . . . According to them it makes no difference whether this individual is a man of knowledge or ignorant, aged or young. However, they also posit as a condition his having a . . . sound morality.

2P The second opinion is that of the philosophers. It affirms that prophecy is a certain perfection in the nature of man. This perfection is not achieved . . . except after a training that makes that which exists in the potentiality of the species pass into actuality . . . According to this opinion, it is not possible for an ignoramus to turn into a prophet . . . Things are rather as follows: When, in the case of a superior individual who is perfect with respect to his rational and moral faculties, his imaginative faculty is in its most perfect state and when he has been prepared, . . . he will necessarily become a prophet . . . According to this opinion it is not possible that an individual should be fit for prophecy and prepared for it and not become a prophet.

3P The third opinion is the opinion of our Law and the foundation of our doctrine. It is identical with the philosophic opinion except in one thing. For we believe that it may happen that one who is fit for prophecy and prepared for it should not become a prophet, namely, on account of the divine will. To my mind this is like all the miracles and takes the same course as they. For it is a natural thing that everyone who according to his natural disposition is fit for prophecy and who has been trained in his education and study should become a prophet. (*GP* II,32,360–1)

The first opinion, then, is that prophecy is a miraculous event brought about by the direct will of God, the second is that it is a purely natural phenomenon and the third is that God can miraculously withhold prophecy if he wishes.

Maimonides rather weakens his claim that the two sets of three opinions are in some way related by adding 'I mean that just as people . . . have . . . three opinions concerning the eternity of the world or its creation in time, so are there also three opinions concerning prophecy' (*GP* II,32,360). Yet most commentators have assumed that he meant the connection between the two sets of opinions to be more than just numerical. Great controversy has taken place over exactly what Maimonides intended the comparison to show, if anything. Certain resemblances between the two sets of claims are tempting, though. The belief in creation *ex nihilo*, which we have called 1C above, is regarded by him as the orthodox religious view, while 3C is taken to be Aristotle's view that the world proceeds from the first cause in an eternal, necessary and immutable manner, leaving no room for divine free will. Plato is credited with a view which lies between these two positions, namely, that the form of the world is created and the matter is eternal. Matter must be eternal since the generation of something from absolutely nothing is held to be impossible. God created the world by imposing a form on matter which had existed, with him, from all eternity. As we have already seen, Maimonides sharpens ontological distinctions which he regards as serving no directly logical purpose – hence the disappearance of the class of entities which lies between God and his creation. Similarly, with theories of creation, he claims to perceive no real difference between the Aristotelian and the Platonic views (a position he shares with many *mutakallimūn*) since both 'believe in eternity; and there is, in our opinion, no difference between those who believe that heaven must of necessity be generated from a thing and pass away into a thing or the belief of Aristotle who believed that it is not subject to generation and corruption' (*GP*II,13,285). This is surely not quite correct. The Platonic view is compatible, after all, with the view of creation as being *ex nihilo* given the interpretation of matter as equivalent to 'nothing', as we saw in the previous section. However, Maimonides rejected the account of creation which could support that interpretation of 'nothing'. Yet the only act which God cannot perform on the Platonic view is to create matter out of nothing, but once the matter is there he can carry out all of the theologically required actions, just as though he had created the world out of absolutely nothing. Maimonides even seems to allow that the Platonic view is acceptable from a religious point of view, as opposed to Aristotelian accounts of the world's eternity (*GP* II,25,330). Were we to accept that his real view is to be attained by searching for contradictions, it would seem here that his real view is that God created the world out of pre-existent matter, which might be thought to be hardly a very exciting theory that needs to be concealed.

There are important aspects of the Platonic view which should make us hesitate before agreeing that Maimonides could quite happily accept it. The notion that matter is eternal is linked by Plato to the doctrine that evil is due to matter (*Timaeus* 147 and *Statesman* 268–74). This suggests that God's power to direct affairs in the world is limited. Averroes was prepared to accept this:

Those evil events which inevitably affect the individual cannot be said not to have come from God . . . he cannot do absolutely anything at all, for the corruptible cannot be eternal, nor can the eternal be corruptible. In the same way that the angles of a triangle cannot be equal to four right angles, and in the same way that colour cannot be heard, so it is an offence against human reason to reject such propositions.[30]

In this passage Averroes links limitations in God's power to bring about the best with logically impossible propositions, a strong claim indeed. This brings out quite clearly an important implication of Platonic views of matter and creation, namely, that God's sphere of action is limited

---

[30] Averroes, *Summary (Jami') of Aristotle's 'Metaphysics'*, in *Rasā'il ibn Rushd* (Hyderabad, Dā'irah al-Maʿārif, 1947), p. 171.

by the *nature* of matter. The eternity of such matter is only theologically acceptable if the matter is completely unformed and so does not in any way limit form, which is far from the Platonic view.

It might seem rather strange to relate views on creation and prophecy to each other; what sorts of connection could possibly hold between these different concepts? To appreciate the significance of this comparison it is necessary to look a little more closely at the sort of notion of prophecy which Maimonides is using. The source for his analysis of prophecy is quite clearly al-Fārābī. According to the latter, philosophy is both logically and temporally prior to religion. As we saw in the introduction, al-Fārābī believed that he represented a stage in the development of a long tradition of philosophical reasoning which preceded Islam by a long time, so that Islam would have to be regarded as temporally subordinate to philosophy. Religion is logically subordinate to philosophy because it consists of theoretical claims (e.g. that there is such a phenomenon as bodily resurrection) for which it provides no demonstrative grounds for acceptance at all. Also, the laws which religions establish are designed to apply to a specific group of people at a particular time, and so are not the same as the very general, indeed universal, ethical principles which moral and political philosophy discuss. These religious laws can only represent examples of norms which embody knowledge of the ends of human beings as such in their realization of their ends, namely, happiness. These laws will be presented in figurative and compelling language with no explicit reference at all to their philosophical grounding in the knowledge of human nature which the legislator should employ in constructing them. This might seem peculiar, to frame legislation in such a way as to make it represent accurately ethical norms but at the same time to conceal this fact from the community. The reasoning behind this approach is that a philosophically sophisticated system of norms might well fail to be grasped by the masses, with dire consequences, and even if it is understood the masses may fail to feel suitably motivated to obey the laws without some additional reason for such obedience. The legislator is essentially a *popularizer* who translates his philosophical awareness of how people ought to live, what happiness really is, into a system of persuasive stories or pictures which show them how to act in ways which are really in their own interests. These stories contain images of kings and prophets who existed in the past and who behaved virtuously and who were opposed by evil men. In this way the important rules of how people in the community are to behave are put over persuasively to the masses, where philosophical and theological argument would totally fail to move them and would probably result in the weakening of the general belief in religion.

The perfect or ideal philosophical legislator, who in theory originally set up the state, has a complete grasp of both theoretical knowledge of the very general ends which all human beings have and practical knowledge of the types of institutions which will foster these ends in the state. As we have seen, though, this will not be enough to enthuse the community concerning those institutions and those ends; there is also a need to create images which teach the people to behave in appropriate ways. These images must embody philosophical concepts and yet be acceptable right across the community, to the ignorant as well as to the wise. Maimonides closely follows this analysis of prophecy as actualizing a person's rational and imaginative faculties. The divine overflow from the Active Intellect (a concept we shall examine in greater detail in the chapter dealing with immortality) to the rational faculty produces theoretical perfection, while to the imaginative faculty it results in practical perfection, including both the production of the rules necessary for ethically desirable behaviour and the ability to disseminate this information in an acceptable and persuasive manner to others who are not recipients of the divine overflow (*GP* II,36). God's part in this process seems rather restricted, especially when we are told to acknowledge the necessary mediation of the Active Intellect between God and human beings. In addition, before the prospective prophet can hope for revelation, he must first perfect his intellect. While theoretical perfection is a necessary condition of prophecy, it clearly is not sufficient. Moral qualities are also required. The prophet is a person who is not satisfied with the knowledge he can acquire by the use of reason alone but also tries to discover the nature of the most important things in the universe, appraisal of which necessarily involves the application of his imagination. He may well then go on to enter the public world of his community to persuade people to think and behave in certain ways.

Moses is an exceptional prophet for Maimonides, the only really political legislator, and like al-Fārābī's philosopher-king he could suspend existing laws and establish new ones. Maimonides claims that the term 'prophet' is properly used to describe Moses and only applicable to other people in an 'amphibolous' or analogical sense. Moses' prophecy is not mediated by angels, Maimonides' term for the personal imaginative faculty. This does not mean that he received a direct prophetic gift from God and did not require mediation by the Active Intelligence. Moses' prophecy was entirely intellectual and did not require imagination. Nonetheless, it is important to recognize that Moses' character and disposition to receive prophecy are both unique and natural. He attained the highest possible degree of perfection that is natural to the human species, and which must necessarily be realized in at least one individual (*GP* II,35,367–9). Since he was succeeded by lesser prophets there was a need to write down the law which then required interpretation by poorer intellects. The sort of prophecy with which Maimonides is concerned in the *Guide of the perplexed* is natural prophecy, the sort of prophecy which Aristotle discusses in his *On divination in sleep* and likens to veridical dreams. Aristotle is reluctant to accept that these dreams are sent by God since they come to all sorts of people, not necessarily the best and the wisest, and he suggests that they just arise in such people when the normal senses are dormant. Once one accepts, as al-Fārābī does, a model of the whole of existence which includes God and consists of a continuum of emanations starting from God and filtering through a hierarchy of intelligences to reach the Active Intellect, the source of forms in our world, then the nature of the potential recipients of prophecy determines whether they will get it or not. Indeed, since it is also suggested that this system has *always* been in operation, presumably it is laid down from all eternity who will get what amount of prophecy. There is no longer any room for individual divine actions. Although to some extent Maimonides distanced himself from the emanation model, and while he does indeed sometimes talk about the divine will having a part to play in disposing human intellects to prophecy, he does not seem to have in mind God deciding through a case-by-case thought process on whom to bestow his gracious gift of prophecy, but rather he points to the arrangement of the universe as characterized by God's wisdom, in a naturalistic manner.

Let us return to Maimonides' reference to the comparison between opinions concerning creation and prophecy and lay out a sort of table:

Creation		*Prophecy*		*Adherents*
1 C	*Ex nihilo*	1 P	*Ex nihilo*	The vulgar
2 C	From eternal matter	2 P	Prophecy is a natural quality	The philosophers
3 C	Eternal existence	3 P	2P + possibility of miraculous prevention	The Jews = opinion of the law

As one might imagine, a great number of permutations of these different opinions has been carried out by commentators and interpreters of Maimonides, with very varied conclusions.[31] Not only do interpreters need to look for resemblances between these opinions, but even contradictions are grist to the mill given that Maimonides did refer to the use that contradictions might play in concealing the truth from those whose faith might suffer as a result, and surely these topics are precisely such theologically sensitive areas. Although it is difficult to find an interpretation of the two sets of opinions which is totally satisfying, Maimonides is quite right to relate them in the sense that they both represent different opinions on how something or some property came about. One might well expect that the sort of answer that is provided to explain the generation of the world would also fit the explanation of prophecy. For example, if one thought that the world was created *ex nihilo* then one might well also adhere to 1 P. These connections are rather weak, though, and it is difficult to believe that Maimonides really expected them to show very much, if anything at all. He may just have been laying out different opinions and pointing to relations they might share with other opinions *to some degree* similar. To suggest that Maimonides in his comparison of these opinions is inviting readers to indulge in rather arbitrary and ad hoc connections between different theoretical positions is to fail to take seriously his commitment to demonstrative reasoning as the only valid form of argument. It will be recalled that he comments on Aristotle's theory of eternity that it is neither demonstratively established nor held to be so established by Aristotle himself (*GP* II,15; II,19). Whatever form of argument is involved in the comparison between the opinions on prophecy and creation, it is hardly demonstrative and unassailable as proper reasoning ought to be.

I would like to compare the form of proof appropriate to creation with that applicable to prophecy by first discussing in detail a particular argument which Maimonides presents to suggest that the world was created by God. Maimonides employs the traditional theological argument from determination which finds reasons for saying that the world could have been determined to have features different from those which it in fact does have, and so its creator was not obliged to form it in a

---

[31] See, for example, W. Harvey, 'A third approach to Maimonides' puzzle', *Harvard Theological Review*, 74 (1981), pp. 287–301; L. Kaplan, 'Maimonides on the miraculous element in prophecy', *Harvard Theological Review*, 70 (1977), pp. 233–56; H. Davidson 'Maimonides' secret position on creation', in I. Twersky (ed.), *Studies in medieval Jewish history and literature* (Cambridge, MA, Harvard University Press, 1979), pp. 16–40.

particular manner. We have seen already how al-Ghazālī used this sort of argument to throw doubt on the Aristotelian claim that the world had to be constructed in the way it was constructed (in his discussion of the Second Proof reproduced by Averroes at *TT* 51). The reasoning behind Maimonides' adaptation of the argument is this: if there exists in the universe things which are not absolutely necessary to the nature of the universe, so that it is conceivable that there might have been other different things, then this suggests that the existence of an agent who by decision of his free will has brought about this particular variety can be established. For example, some theologians used the argument derived from the variations in the motions of the spheres against the philosophers, accepting for the sake of the argument that the circularity of motion which is common to all spheres may be an essential property of the nature of the substance of the spheres, but challenging the philosophers with the problem of explaining why there are then variations in the motions of the spheres which are said to be essential to the nature of the substance of the spheres. The theologians suggest that such variations are evidence of a selection having taken place from among several alternatives, which implies that there is an agent who freely has picked one among the many possibilities of a world (*GP* II,4).

In the running warfare between theology and philosophy, the former argued that a large number of features of the universe which the philosophers regard as necessary are instead only possible. As we have seen in the Averroes/al-Ghazālī confrontation, the philosophers respond by arguing that those features of the world which the *kalām* calls possible are necessary, and the theologians fail to recognize the validity of philosophical proofs to this end. Yet there are features in the world which both philosophers and theologians can agree are only possible and might well have been different, like the particular shapes of things, their size and position and their properties. Accordingly al-Ghazālī does not just use the argument derived from the variation of the motion of the spheres, but also makes much of the fact that certain things in the world are white while others are black, that some things move while others rest, and that particular shapes rather than others are found in the world. The fact that there are in the world things which could have been otherwise proves on his view that there must be a determining cause which acts freely. Maimonides complicates his version of the argument by distinguishing between three types of variation in the motions of the spheres. Firstly, there is a difference in the direction of the motions of the spheres, since some rotate from east to west while others rotate in the opposite direction (*GP* II,19,305–6). He argues that there is no necessity for that sort of diversity. Similarly, with the differences between the velocity of the motion of the spheres and in the courses of the motions of the planets, he rejected the explanation of their necessity in terms of theories of epicycles and eccentric spheres and so could find no satisfactory explanation of these differences by examining the phenomena alone. The only remaining explanation is that God brought these phenomena about and established those variations. Maimonides also uses examples which show that some particular accidents in the structure of the universe are not necessary. For instance, while each of the seven planets has several spheres, the fixed stars are all contained in one sphere. The stars and spheres are attached to each other and yet differ from each other because the former are at rest and opaque while the latter are in motion and transparent. Lastly, the stars in the eighth sphere are of different sizes and distances from each other. None of these facts is necessary given the nature of heavenly bodies themselves – they could have been different. Thus, Maimonides concludes, the only explanation of such phenomena is the influence of a free will which determined the selection of one in preference to the others.

It is important to emphasize that despite the complexity of Maimonides' examples and arguments, he does not think he has *proved* anything by his points. He cannot demonstrate the truth of his conclusion since his initial premises are themselves not certain, and perhaps not true. All he can do is argue for the plausibility of his point of view, and refute other contrary views – a typical dialectical procedure. Indeed, Maimonides claims that Aristotle himself did not think that the issues of the eternity of the world and the nature of its creation were capable of determinate and demonstrative proof. Maimonides does argue, though, that his view of the creation of the world by an agent acting freely is the most likely given the evidence of the nature of the world and Aristotle's principle that eternity implies necessity. Were the world to be an eternal entity, it would be necessarily organized in a particular way, and there would be no room for free choice. But if it had been organized necessarily in just such a way we could not conceive of all the varieties and deviations from uniformity which we find in the world. We can accept the possibility of such contingent features of the world being changed and so they cannot be necessary. They were created at a finite time in the past by an agent acting freely (*GP* II,19).

Maimonides uses a similar type of argument to establish the creator's free will when he discusses the nature of the celestial spheres. The Aristotelian theory regarded the celestial spheres as consisting of differing matter as opposed to the sublunary objects. This is because the natural motion of the spheres is circular, whereas the sublunary objects follow a rectilinear path. Another and different kind of matter in the universe is that which belongs to the stars, which also accordingly have a distinct type of motion. Now, it is the nature of matter to accept whatever form is appropriate to it; it is determined to have that particular form. If the spheres consist of a common matter, as they must since they possess a common motion, then the matter of each sphere is as likely to receive the form of any sphere as it is to receive the form of a particular sphere. Similarly, the stars are all made up of a common material substance and could receive any sort of form which is appropriate to that sort of matter. Were the world to be run entirely on the lines of a natural process, one would expect that the matter of the spheres and of the stars would copy the matter of the sublunar world in constantly changing form. That is, one would expect things with matter in common to receive all the different forms which they are capable of receiving. Why, then, are the stars and spheres only affected by one particular type of organization or form? The explanation which Maimonides offers is that a conscious and free agent has determined that each sphere will continually pass through a particular circular motion and each star will continually radiate a particular light.

It is worth dwelling for a moment on Maimonides' way of arguing in these passages. He is not employing *kalām* techniques which sometimes presuppose the truths of religion. He tries to present purely rational arguments which can support the idea of God's free will, and thus defend the belief in creation. It is possible, then, to show how miracles and prophecy came about, for: 'Know that with a belief in the creation of the world in time, all the miracles become possible and the Law becomes possible, and all questions that may be asked on this subject, vanish' (*GP* II,25,329). He sets out to challenge the view that necessity controls the activities of the universe as a whole, at the same time accepting that Aristotle has proved that necessity characterizes all events (even our own) in the sublunar world. The fact that Aristotle is not successful in showing that necessity can explain the features of the heavenly world provides Maimonides with the opportunity to argue that those features are only explicable given a freely acting creator, who in turn brings about miracles and prophecy. Creation *ex nihilo* must be accepted if God's autonomy is to be possible.

Yet, as we have seen, it would be an over-simplification of Maimonides' very diverse arguments and suggestions in the *Guide of the perplexed* to feel totally satisfied that this conclusion represents his unambiguous view. He might mean by it that since God's autonomy is *not* possible, perhaps because he accepts the view that the world is eternal, then creation *ex nihilo* should be rejected. If we accept his argument at *GP* II,25 cited above that, with belief in creation *ex nihilo*, miracles themselves become unproblematic, then we might think at least that we can understand the miraculous prevention of prophecy as the extraordinary witholding of a natural characteristic from people, as in the prevention of King Jeroboam from moving his hands and of King Aram's soldiers from seeing (*GP* II,32,39). A miracle prevents prophecy in a person naturally fit to prophesy as a miracle prevents sight or motion in a person naturally fit to see or move. Yet we must be careful here. Is the notion of natural prophecy which Maimonides derives from al-Fārābī not very different in its theological implications from natural capacities such as motion or sight? After all, the notion of prophetic experience for Maimonides is an internal psychological process only contingently related to external reality. Where angels are said to be present in prophetical visions or dreams, then this is not a pointer to an objective element in those experiences; on the contrary, it suggests that such experience is entirely imaginative. The prophet is not just a good and wise person, but must in addition have great imaginative powers. The references to angels might be seen as direct reference to the internal nature of the creative experience: 'Accordingly, Midrash Qoheleth has the following text: When man sleeps, his soul speaks to the angel, and the angel to the cherub. Thereby they have stated plainly to him who understands and cognizes intellectually that the imaginative faculty is likewise called an angel and that the intellect is called a cherub' (*GP* II,6,264–5). This goes against the view that biblical texts with references to angels should be taken literally, and yet religious orthodoxy insists that such spiritual causes do actually have effects upon the world. Maimonides' view, that prophets create pictures and tales in order to make appropriate religious points, is very different. In possibly accepting that God can prevent this exercise of prophetic imagination by miraculous intervention Maimonides may be making a gesture in the direction of preserving God's autonomy. Yet at the same time he is importing a notion of prophecy which is far removed from the religious norm. It is not clear, either, that he regards the arguments that establish this notion of prophecy as not demonstrative in nature, which is his description of the arguments concerning creation.

There are many ways to approach Maimonides. A very popular approach over the years since his death is to wonder what he actually believed. Here we are more concerned with seeing how he sharpened and made more extreme the philosophical theories expounded by his predecessors. He developed to its furthest degree the theory of prophecy devised by al-Fārābī in order to explore its novel implications. He extended the form of argument used by al-Ghazālī to challenge Aristotelian accounts of the structure of the world as necessary by using Aristotelian principles themselves and not theological presuppositions. He argued very much in the tradition of al-Ghazālī that the emanative system could not be reconciled with the notion of a freely creating deity, and that references by the philosophers to God having precisely those properties are empty unless they provide him with the metaphysical space in which to act and will.

CREATION AND THE CONTROVERSY OVER
THE NATURE OF CAUSALITY

One of the advantages of the Aristotelian distinction of actuality and potentiality is that it conceives of change as a continuous process instead of a sudden re-creation of new states of being after previous states of being. In adhering to a metaphysics of atoms and accidents which are continually being re-created by God, the Islamic theologians had to reject Aristotle's distinction between actuality and potentiality and his account of causality. For Aristotle, causation occurs when an actual being actualizes some potency. Since the theologians were using a system of atoms and accidents they could accept no such action of one being upon another. Any change in being could not be due to the atoms since they do not endure through time. Change would then occur only when God re-created the atoms in new states of being at each successive instant. This theological account brings out the reason for the controversy in Islamic philosophy concerning the nature of the causal link between God and the world, and the religious significance of the notion of the causal relation as such, especially in so far as it applies to the sublunary world. The significance lies in the relationship between human and natural causality and creation. The causality of agent must involve creation, in the sense of bringing about a certain state of affairs. Since God is an omnipotent agent and so responsible for the creation of everything in the world, how, then, can we understand the human act as really a human act, something for which we are responsible? This problem was much discussed in the *kalām*, and al-Ash'arī had the problem very much in mind when he tried to describe human causality in such a way as to reconcile God as the sole and unique creator of all states of affairs with the reality of human causal power. His attempted solution was to describe our causality as an accident which is created by God. Human beings are created by God and there is no aspect of us which is not entirely dependent upon his creativity, yet God does not perform the human act even though he is the creator of our causal power. God cannot be the efficient cause since he has already created as an accident our causal power and it is as a result of this power that we bring things about in the world.

It is important to appreciate that the Ash'arites did not deny that the existence of causes can be inferred from the existence of effects, nor did they deny that there are causal relations between events. They were concerned rather to refute the thesis that the causal power of a thing is a necessary consequence of the thing's nature or essence. Aristotle's thesis of the simultaneity of cause and effect (*Met.* 1014a 20ff.) was used by Avicenna to support arguments in favour of the world's eternity, which itself involves the notion of the eternal agent producing the world by the necessity of his eternal essence. This model of beings coming about necessarily through the causal efficacy of their originators, only ending with the First Cause or God, was strongly opposed by the Ash'arites. It is important to be clear on what Avicenna meant by 'coming about necessarily'. It is not just that every contingent thing must have a cause, but also that its existence is necessitated by that cause. Indeed, once all the causal conditions are fulfilled, it follows necessarily that the effect follows. Only something which obstructs the effects could be used to explain the non-appearance of the effect. We have already seen what use Averroes made of this point when challenging the theologians to explain why, on their account, an immortal omnipotent deity *waited* before carrying out the creation. The Ash'arites argue that God wills the existence of the world but delays the instantiation of this wish for a period of time. Given the way in which the philosophers take the notion of cause, such a view of the possible gap between cause and effect is incoherent.

Al-Ghazālī was an enthusiastic proponent of this Ash'arite view in opposing the Aristotelian claim that empirical knowledge is necessarily connected to the causal relations between objects and events. His strategy is to deny that there is anything *necessary* in the relation between cause and effect: 'According to us, the connection between what is usually believed to be a cause and what is believed to be an effect is not a necessary connection; either of two things has its own individuality and is not the other, and neither the affirmation, negation, existence and non-existence of the other' (*TT* 316). Al-Ghazālī demands from the philosophers a proof of sufficient rigour to establish the logical nature of the relationship between cause and effect. He does not in any way challenge the belief that some events in the world bring about other events, and that our experience of such facts provides us with good grounds for believing that we can make sense of what is going on in the world. All he challenges is the thesis that the causal nexus is necessary. Causal relations are only as they are because of God's organization of events in the world. Al-Ghazālī uses a number of examples to make his point. One involves a piece of cotton put in touch with a flame. He claims that there is no logical flaw in one's reasoning were one to deny that the cotton *must* catch fire:

We regard it as possible that the contact might occur without the burning taking place, and also that the cotton might be changed into ashes without any contact with fire, although the philosophers deny this possibility. The discussion of this matter has three points. The first is that our opponent claims that the agent of the burning is the fire alone; this is a natural, not a voluntary agent, and cannot abstain from what is in its nature when it is brought into contact with a receptive substratum. (*TT* 316)

On an Aristotelian account, if there is material which is capable of burning (its receptive substratum being disposed to burn) and a flame with the purpose and formal essence of bringing about burning, then we are dealing with entirely natural phenomena which must lead us to the conclusion that the cotton will, indeed must, burn. Interestingly, as with his objections to the theory of the world's eternity, al-Ghazālī suggests that on Aristotelian principles themselves the philosophical position on the necessity of causality falls down. For Aristotle argued that matter is of itself incapable of movement, that it is passive until energized by some prime mover (through appropriate intermediaries), so that the claim that physical objects have essences which of themselves make necessary certain processes in nature seems inconsistent with the philosophical view of the nature of matter.

Averroes is in no doubt concerning the serious implications of al-Ghazālī's view:

Denial of cause implies the denial of knowledge, and denial of knowledge implies that nothing in this world can be really known, and that what is supposed to be known is nothing but opinion, that neither proof nor definition exist, and that the essential attributes which compose definitions are void. The man who denies the necessity of any item of knowledge must admit that even this, his own affirmation, is not necessary knowledge. (*T T* 319)

Two claims are made in this passage. The weaker claim is that were al-Ghazālī correct, there could be no such thing as knowledge. Were we to abandon the search for causes, then all enquiry would come to an end. However, we shall see that al-Ghazālī is not in favour of abandoning the search for causes. The stronger objection is that if al-Ghazālī were right then he refutes himself, since his proposition will have no sense. The connection between a concept of a thing and its causal properties is not just accidental, but it is rather a question of meaning. A concept of a thing has as part of its meaning various causal properties, and denying the necessary nature of this relation is to reject the meaning of the term itself. Indeed, we often only count a particular thing as a member of a certain class of objects if it shares basic causal properties with those other objects. For instance, a pencil with which it is impossible to write because it has no lead might well be denied the name 'pencil' given its lack of the causal power generally associated with pencils. This objection produced by Averroes is an interesting one and we shall return to it later.

Al-Ghazālī claims that the only justification there is for believing in a causal nexus is experience, and we are very limited in what we are entitled to assert as a result of such experience: 'Indeed, the philosophers have no other proof than the observation of the occurrence of the burning, when there is contact with fire, but observation proves only a simultaneity, not a causation, and, in reality, there is no other cause but God' (*T T* 317). He gives a picturesque example to support this point. Suppose that someone is blind and has never heard people talk about the difference between night and day. Such a person might well imagine, were sight to be made available to him or her, that the opening of the eyelids caused the appearance of the visible objects before that person. Yet once the night comes on it will be appreciated that in fact it was the light from the sun which is a necessary condition of seeing objects:

The true philosophers were therefore unanimously of the opinion that the accidents and events which occur when there is a contact of bodies... proceed from the bestower of forms who is an angel or a plurality of angels, so that even they said that the impression of the visible forms on the eye occurs through the bestower of forms, and that the rising of the sun, and the soundness of the pupil, and the existence of the visible object are only the preparations and dispositions which enable the substratum to receive the forms; and this theory they apply to all events. And this refutes the claim of those who profess that fire is the agent of burning, bread the agent of satiety, medicine the agent of health and so on. (*TT* 317–18)

Al-Ghazālī argues that, although we can talk as though some things cause others to change, in reality there is a power which does not exist in the things themselves but ultimately in God and which makes possible the transformation which we can see in the world. He is perfectly prepared to deal with the obvious philosophical objection to his account, namely, that if God has complete power to control and fashion every temporal event, what sorts of constant conjunctions or regularities in the world can we rely upon? What prevents our experiences and expectations from being chaotic and haphazard?

The Ash'arite response to these questions is that our impressions of the uniformity of nature are nothing more than a habit or custom arbitrarily established by the divine will. The contingent atoms and accidents which constitute our world are nothing more than creations *ex nihilo*, combined to form bodies and maintained in temporally finite spaces of existence by divine action. These combinations give us the impression of uniformity actually implanted in the phenomena themselves, yet exceptions or the creation of miracles are easily conceivable. Can this way of looking at causal properties do justice to our experience in the sort of way that Avicenna's discussion of knowledge does? For Avicenna, when the proper conditions of knowledge obtain, we attain through our senses indubitable knowledge of particulars external to us. A necessary condition is the natural causal power of the object to influence the appropriate sense organ. One might wonder how al-Ghazālī could accept the certainty of such knowledge when he denies any causal power to the things which are said to affect our senses. The answer is that a benevolent God has no desire to deceive us and so has organized nature in such a way that when he brings about conditions like those in Avicenna's account, but without the causal properties in natural things, he creates simultaneously in us indubitable knowledge of the object. On one side of the epistemological fence we have knowledge in the form of potential knowers and on the other side exist particular things, and there is no causal link between them. Instead of there being a natural connection there is a supernatural connection.

Al-Ghazālī argues quite convincingly that it is possible to reconcile the philosophical thesis that things have essences with doubts concerning the immutability of these essences:

The second answer . . . is to agree that in fire there is created a nature which burns two similar pieces of cotton which are brought into contact with it and does not differentiate between them, when they are alike in every respect. But still we regard it as possible that a prophet should be thrown into the fire and not burn, either through a change in the quality of the fire or through a change in the quality of the prophet, and that either through God or through the angels there should arise a quality in the fire which limited its heat to its own body, so that it did not go beyond it, but remained confined to it, keeping, however, to the form and reality of the fire, without its heat and influence extending beyond it; or that there should arise in the body of the person an attribute, which did not stop the body from being flesh and bone, but still defended it against the action of the fire. For we can see a man rub himself with talc and sit down in a lighted oven and not suffer from it; and if one had not seen it, one would deny it, and the denial of our opponents that it lies in God's power to confer on the fire or to the body an attribute which prevents it from being burnt is like the denial of one who has not seen the talc and its effect. For strange and marvellous things are in the power of God, many of which we have not seen, and why should we deny their possibility and regard them as impossible? (*TT* 326–7)

Matter can receive any form, and so any of these events in the world must be conceivable. We could then look for a new causal determinant of the change in what previously was normal behaviour for the material objects involved. Al-Ghazālī is quite prepared to admit that if there is no relevant difference between two pieces of cotton, then a fire which will ignite one will also ignite the other. Nonetheless, it is always open to God to affect the nature of cotton in such a way that it will not catch fire.[32] This sort of explanation clashes sharply with that provided by Avicenna. For the latter, as we have seen, those things which exist and yet which are not necessary in themselves are brought about necessarily by something else. The world emanates from God in a continually necessitating and necessitated chain of states of affairs, with perfect regularity

---

[32] Terminology is important here. Al-Ghazālī moves away from the use of the philosophical term *ṭabīʿa*, which has the sense of the fixed and Aristotelian natures that are a part of the philosophical notion of causality, and instead uses the term *khalqa* or creation, which explicitly establishes a relation to a creator. Still al-Ghazālī appears to have no problem with the idea of natural acts (*fiʿl ṭabīʿī*) in other contexts, e.g. *K. al-tawḥīd* (Book of divine unity), *Iḥyāʾ ʿulūm al-dīn* ed. ʿIrāqī, IV, pp. 219–20.

and immutability of the natural order guaranteed by the eternity and permanence of that which makes everything else necessary, i.e. God. The mutability which al-Ghazālī's analysis imports in principle into the constitution of the world is clearly designed to contrast with the natural uniformity of a deterministic Avicennan system.

A significant motive for al-Ghazālī's attack on natural necessity is his desire to leave room for miracles in the scheme of things in the world. He claims that it is possible for God to bring about miracles whereby the moon will split, a staff will become a serpent and the dead will be revived:

There is no denying this, except through a lack of understanding and an un-familiarity with higher things and oblivion of the secrets of God in the created world and in nature. And he who has examined the many wonders of the sci-ences does not consider in any way impossible for God's power what is told of the wonders of the prophets. (*TT* 328)

We ought to consider whether Avicenna and the philosophers must deny the possibility of the sorts of miraculous events which al-Ghazālī mentions here in order to remain consistent with their arguments. Given the definition of a miracle as an interruption of the course of nature, then it does seem difficult for the philosophers to accept miracles into their view of the world. After all, whatever exists is necessary of existence, and cannot be supposed not to exist without the occurrence of an impossi-bility. Yet the Qur'ān refers, as al-Ghazālī points out, to the transfor-mation of Moses' staff into a serpent, the resurrection of the dead and the splitting of the moon to herald the final judgment. The philoso-phers could either deny these accounts or interpret them as showing that prophets have extraordinarily developed psychic powers (and so are glorified magicians), or regard them as allegorical and not supposed to be taken by the wise as historically accurate. As far as Avicenna is con-cerned, ability to forecast accurately future events is interpreted as an entirely *natural* process. The emanation of causal laws from the heavenly intelligences upon the souls of their respective spheres are transformed into material phenomena and can produce ideas in souls which outline what events will occur in the future. Once the imaginative potential of some people attains remarkable control over the external senses and so is no longer distracted by them, it is ready to receive an emanation of these ideas from the heavenly souls. Prophetic miracles, then, do not interrupt the course of nature, but rather are evidence of the great power and imaginative capacity of the prophet.

A different sort of miracle results from the perfection not of the imag-ination but of the intellect. Some people are extremely quick-witted in their ability to run through valid reasoning processes when presented with incomplete premises. They can formulate demonstrative proofs to answer problems in the fastest possible time. With no more than perhaps the middle term of a syllogism, or just the major and minor premises, they can reconstruct the proof, and even derive others from it in rapid succession. All that such people require is a hint and they can go off by themselves thinking logically and acquiring a comprehensive knowledge of the world. They can even extend their understanding of the principles governing this world to those controlling the heavens, and they can even acquire knowledge of all the intelligible things (*TT* 313–14). It is worth adding that although these people do not require teachers, they do require the emanative overflow of the Active Intelligence, the provider of forms to all things in the sublunar sphere, before they can proceed to amplify their knowledge and reasoning to all that is knowable.

A last type of 'miracle' which Avicenna mentions is not really a miracle at all. There are occurrences which appear to violate necessary causal connections in nature but do not really do so. He has in mind here phenomena like sending thunderbolts to punish the wicked, with accompanying tempests and earthquakes. These events are certainly surprising and insufficiently understood by people, yet they proceed by entirely normal, albeit rather dramatic, causal processes.

Averroes is rather hesitant in his description of miracles. He starts off by claiming that the ancient philosophers deliberately omitted to mention miracles, not because they failed to acknowledge their reality but because they recognized that belief in miracles is among the fundamental principles establishing religious laws (*TT* 314). Miracles are divine events which contribute to the attainment of virtue and are themselves beyond comprehension. He is rather scathing about Avicenna's naturalistic view of miracles:

As to what al-Ghazālī relates of the causes of this [miracles] as they are according to the philosophers, I do not know anyone who asserts this but Avicenna. And if such facts are verified and it is possible that a body could be changed qualitatively through something which is neither a body or a bodily potency, then the reasons he mentions for this are possible: but not everything which in its nature is possible can be done by man, for what is possible to man is well known. Most things which are possible in themselves are impossible for man, and what is true of the prophet, that he can interrupt the ordinary course of nature, is impossible for man, but possible in itself; and because of this one need not assume that things logically impossible are possible for the prophets, and if you observe those miracles whose existence is confirmed, you will find that they are of this kind. The clearest of miracles is the Venerable Book of Allah, the existence of which is not an interruption of the course of nature assumed by tradition, like the changing of a rod into a serpent, but its miraculous nature is established by way of perception and consideration for every man who has been or who will be till the day of resurrection. (*TT* 315)

Averroes claims that Avicenna over-extends the causal range of the prophet's soul, taking in not just activities which ordinary people cannot do but even activities which are logically impossible. This criticism is hardly fair and gives rise to the suggestion that Averroes is employing the technique of *taqīya* or concealment here, concealing his real view that miracles are entirely natural events which are not consciously brought about by human beings of a certain moral perfection but just happen to people, with no prior moral and intellectual preparation being necessary. In the passage just quoted Averroes might be taken to imply that if prophets can really carry out the miracles ascribed to them then they are not human beings. His selection of the Qur'ān as the best sort of miracle could be taken to mean that it is designed to enable all people to attain virtue and happiness in the most effective way. He seems hesitant about accepting the normal interpretation of miracles as interruptions in the course of nature brought about through exceptional natural power as presented by Avicenna. He is far more attached to the Aristotelian principle that the sorts of miracles which involve qualitative change through non-material agents may well be logically impossible. And indeed it is worth emphasizing that Islam as a religion does not make much use of miracles. Muḥammad does not claim to have performed miracles himself:

none denies our signs but the evildoers. They say 'Why have signs not been sent down upon him from his Lord?' Say: 'The signs are only with God, and I am only a plain warner.' (XXIX,49)

The unbelievers say, 'Why has a sign not been sent down upon him from his Lord?' Say: 'God leads astray whosoever he will and He guides to Him all who are penitent.' (XIII,27)

At XVII,92–6 the Qur'ān is particularly contemptuous of the idea that God should have sent miracles with Muḥammad to explain the Book and to 'validate' it. Later on in that sura, at 103–4, there is a reference to Pharaoh's reaction to Moses' nine clear signs of his divine mission as an accusation that the prophet was bewitched! This suggests that the evidence for the veracity of the Qur'ān is internal rather than external, stemming from the work itself rather than from additional 'tricks' which are then described as miracles.

In his defence of the possibility of miracles, al-Ghazālī by no means wants to assert that God can do anything at all. He delineates quite precisely what is impossible for God, even an omnipotent God. He cannot perform that which is logically impossible, nor can he transform a being of one genus into another:

We say that for one thing to become another is irrational. If, for instance, the black could be transformed into power, the black would either remain or not, and if it does not exist any more, it is not changed but simply does not exist any more and something else exists . . . and when we say that water becomes air through being heated, we mean by it that the matter which has received the form of water is deprived of this form and takes another, and the matter is common to them, but the attribute changes. (*TT* 329–30)

Al-Ghazālī's adherence to Aristotelian terminology here is designed to prepare the way for an attack upon the analysis of causality provided by Avicenna. In Avicenna's *Metaphysics*, he distinguishes the efficient cause from the other Aristotelian causes as the only type capable of bringing about an existence other than itself. An agent's efficient cause is an essential attribute, it is part of the agent's nature and is necessarily involved in the activities of the agent. There are two types of efficient cause, one accidental and one essential. The former is described as being prior to the effect in time, while the latter both produces and sustains the effect in existence. Given the model of the universe as emanation, God is the essential efficient cause of the world which is his necessary effect. There is no question of choice in the matter, since God, being God, has to produce this sort of world, and given the necessarily stipulated law-like structure of the world, there appears to be no room for miracles. Al-Ghazālī has successfully isolated the central philosophical thesis which is the key to what he regards as the philosophers' error. The idea that action is logically entailed by something's nature is vital to Avicenna's entire metaphysical system. Al-Ghazālī opposes it by arguing that nothing can really be an agent unless it has a will. Only inanimate objects can be said to behave in one way rather than another as a result of the necessity of their essence. To suggest as Avicenna does that God's actions are constrained by his essence is tantamount to suggesting that God is inanimate. (Al-Ghazālī is convinced that this is indeed an assumption which the *falāsifa* make, albeit surreptitiously.)

How does al-Ghazālī reconcile his claim that 'in the case of two things which have no connection with each other and which are then related in existence, it is not necessary that from positing the negation of the one, the negation of the other will follow'[33] with his belief in the validity

---

[33] Al-Ghazālī, *Al-iqtiṣād fī al-iʿtiqād* (The golden mean in belief), ed. I. Çubukçu and H. Atay (Ankara, 1962), p. 99.

of scientific knowledge? Both al-Ghazālī and Avicenna entirely agree
that constant conjunction is not the same as causal connection, that we
cannot validly move from *post hoc* to *propter hoc*. The fact that events are
frequently related in an apparently law-governed manner is not enough
in itself to show that that connection is a causal one. It could just be the
continual repetition at certain times and in certain places of two otherwise
unconnected states of affairs. Al-Ghazālī follows Avicenna's account of
the nature and types of demonstrative reasoning very closely.[34] He agrees
that if a syllogism is to be demonstrative then its premisses must be certain
and its conclusion valid. When empirical premisses are considered they
can be divided into those which consist of truths arrived at immediately
by the senses, where our sense faculties are sound, the object of perception
is in an appropriate position and there is no obstacle present, and those
which provide us with justified knowledge of regular events in the past,
thereby enabling us to claim that it is certain that such regularities will
continue in the future. Al-Ghazālī almost quotes an Avicennan (and
Aristotelian) image of a 'hidden syllogistic power' (*qūwa qiyāsīya khafīya*)
embedded in the world, since were the order of nature to be a matter
of chance, it would not have been able to continue as regularly as it
has done most of the time.[35] The use of this comparison with reasoning
is designed to suggest that basically the workings of the natural world
are just as formally laid out and inevitable as the structure of a logical
reasoning process. Avicenna of course claims that such uniformity is due
to the inherent nature of objects and events in the world. Their essences
determine the various necessary connections which such objects and
events have with each other. Al-Ghazālī agrees that on the whole there
are such connections, but the explanation for the connection itself is not
correctly analyzed on Aristotelian lines. He argues that the trouble with
Aristotelianism is that it seeks to explain the essence of what brings about
change, whereas all it really does is describe that change. For example,
from a theological point it is not decapitation which brings about death,
nor eating satiety, nor fire burning, but God is the ultimate agent of
all these events. This was very much the burden of his argument in *The
incoherence of the philosophers*, that it is rational to expect decapitation to lead
to death, but that does not show that it is decapitation by itself which
brings about that death. In fact, by looking at the sequence of events
themselves we could not say whether they had come about through

[34] M. Marmura, 'al-Ghazālī's attitude to the secular sciences and logic', in *Essays on Islamic Philosophy
    and Science*, ed. G. Hourani (Albany, State University of New York Press, 1975), pp. 101–11.
[35] Ibn Sīnā, *al-Shifā'; Logic V; Demonstration*, ed. A. Afifi (Cairo, Dār Ma'ārif 1955), pp. 95, 96, 223.

some sort of causal necessity, through the direct will of God, or through God's habitual actions. All Aristotelianism does is talk about what can be observed to be the connection between causes and effects, but we have to look deeper if we are to understand the nature of the connection itself.[36]

Al-Ghazālī's shrewd point is that he is offering a different analysis of the way in which the connection takes place, not of the connection itself. (Indeed, Aristotle also makes clear that his discussion of the four causes is really a discussion of four forms of explanation.) Nature is organized in such a way that it is possible for us to make certain judgments about it and predictions from it, yet we must never get away from the fact that that organization is not inherent in nature but rather comes from God.

Let us return to al-Ghazālī's argument that there is no real sense in which inanimate objects can be called 'agents'. An 'agent' is really a being that lives, wills and knows, in which case decapitation by sword can result in death without the sword or indeed the decapitation being the agent of death. The only real agent, then, is God. Al-Ghazālī's point here, and indeed throughout his critique of Avicenna, is that it is perfectly possible, indeed easy, to adopt Avicenna's basic starting point and then draw totally different conclusions. It is perfectly possible, that is, to accept that there are connections between states of affairs and that we can use these connections to make reliable judgments about the external world, yet it is always open to al-Ghazālī to translate judgments which mention the causality of such connections in terms of personal connecting on the part of God. But beyond showing that this can be done, does it have any point? The attempt to limit the use of 'agent' to animate beings is only persuasive once one has accepted the whole enterprise of translating causal language into language referring to God's actions.

Averroes does not, needless to say, have any sympathy with al-Ghazālī's thesis. He bitterly attacks al-Ghazālī over the way he uses the term 'habit' to explain our expectations of the regular connection between cause and effect. Averroes argues convincingly that this term is ambiguous because three different things might be meant by it. It could either be the habit of God in determining the normal course of things, the habit of things themselves in following their normal course, or our own habit in passing judgments upon things. He argues that it is not possible for God to have this habit, since 'habit' is definable as a 'trait acquired by the agent and necessitating the recurrence of his activity in the generality of cases'

[36] Al-Ghazālī, *Mi'yār al-'Ilm* (The criterion of knowledge), ed. S. Dunya (Cairo, 1961), p. 58.

(*TT* 320). This description will not do to describe a God for whom there is no alteration (XXXV,41). Talking about God having habits is to ascribe to him far more variability in behaviour than is acceptable to Islam. But al-Ghazālī cannot be referring to the nature of things in his use of the term 'habit' since he clearly sets out to deny they follow a course which can be entirely naturally defined. The habit in question may refer to our own mode of passing judgments upon things. Such a formulation is appropriate if this habit is meant to be the mode of the intellect's procedure in passing judgments upon things, in a manner necessitated by its own nature. But of course al-Ghazālī would not have that. On the other hand, it might mean that most of the time people just make particular judgments, which is a rather unexciting claim if those judgments are not regarded as having some connection with facts which exist independently of those judgments. Averroes adds that: 'If this were so, everything would be the case only by supposition, and there would be no wisdom in the world from which it might be inferred that its agent was wise' (*TT* 320).

Averroes is entirely justified in pointing to the rather confused nature of al-Ghazālī's theory, since when the latter talks about the habitual ordering of nature, he is referring both to the habit of God creating a certain order in events and to the habit of our regarding this order as having some necessary causal nature. Nevertheless, al-Ghazālī is shrewd in his use of argument to suggest that one could adopt the structure of Avicenna's account of causal connection without necessarily accepting at the same time its *impersonal* and non-divine nature. We could then go along with the rules and discoveries of natural science by following the methodological principles of scientific investigation while at the same time acknowledging the direct responsibility of God in establishing the kinds of 'natural' connection in the world which we can come to understand. This is very much part of al-Ghāzalī's strategy in separating the objectionable features of *falsafa* from the useful and valuable aspects of science and logical reasoning which import no principles antagonistic to Islam.

CHAPTER 2

Immortality and the active intellect

It will be recalled that al-Ghazālī did not think that the philosophers set themselves against Islam merely through their adherence to the doctrine of the eternity of the world. They also

were opposed to all Muslims in their affirming that men's bodies will not be assembled on the Last Day, but only disembodied spirits will be rewarded and punished, and the rewards and punishments will be spiritual, not corporal. They were indeed right in affirming the spiritual rewards and punishments, for these also are certain; but they falsely denied the corporal rewards and punishments and blasphemed the revealed Law in their stated views.[1]

He is quite right in claiming that the philosophers did not accept without severe qualification the idea that God will eventually reconstitute bodies and they will live again in the sense that *we* will live again. There are difficulties in the Aristotelian account of the soul for the sort of account which orthodox Islam seems to want to provide and yet be acceptable philosophically. The notion of the soul which the *falāsifa* develop is complex and closely connected with their use of the concept of the active intellect.

The notion of the active intellect in Islamic philosophy stems from what appears to be a casual remark of Aristotle that the intellect is 'part of the soul', which at first had no nature other than its potentiality for thinking, but which later could 'become each thing' (*De An.* 429a 21–2; 429b 6). He adds that here as elsewhere it is possible to distinguish between that which constitutes matter and so is potentially all things, and that which is an agent as a result of its making all things (*De An.* 430a 10–15). A controversy has long existed as to whether the intellect which makes all things is part of us or rather some being with transcendent status, an incorporeal being located in some place in the universe above us. This latter interpretation is certainly suggested by Alexander of Aphrodisias

[1] Al-Ghazālī, *Munqidh*, trans. R. McCarthy, p. 76.

107

and Plotinus. But, as so often in medieval philosophy, the origins of the theory in Aristotle seem far more modest than its later development. Aristotle starts with the proposition that all nature contains both material factors and causal or productive factors. The soul is not an exception, and must contain these factors too, an intellect which can 'become all things' and an intellect which can 'make all things', an intellect disposed to receive thought and an intellect disposed to produce those thoughts. We have already seen the force of the Aristotelian argument that what exists actually is generated from what exists merely potentially. Yet how precisely the active intellect is generated from what exists potentially and brings the human intellect to actuality is unexplained.

This was an omission that the Islamic philosophers sought to make good. Aristotle himself never used the expression 'active intellect', referring explicitly only to the 'passive intellect' and only by contrast to the intellect that makes everything (*De An.* 430a 14ff.). It was Alexander of Aphrodisias who first used the expression 'active intellect' in commenting on this passage. Aristotle actually expressed himself in this sort of way:

Just as in the whole physical world there is, in each class, on the one hand matter (i.e. what is potentially all those things) and on the other something else which is the efficient cause, in that it makes them all (e.g. a craft in relation to its material), so in the sphere of the soul also there must exist this distinction. One intellect is such as to become all things, the other such as to make them all, a kind of positive state, like light: for in a sort of way light makes potential colours actual colours. (*De An.* 430a 10)

The comparison of the agent intellect with light is well chosen, since light is a third factor which must be present besides the capacity (sight) and the seen object, if the act of vision is to take place. This might seem a small point, but it is quite the reverse. In his opposition to Platonic views of the possibility of knowledge as dependent upon self-subsistent forms or abstract entities, Aristotle had to explain how knowledge was possible in the sense of how it is possible for us to receive the abstract concepts which are so important a part of our knowledge. Aristotle's references to something like an agent intellect that 'illuminates' the potential intelligibles concealed in sense objects rather as light reveals the colours of objects which are also 'hidden' in the dark, suggests that in a sense the concepts are already 'there' in the things, and all they need is lighting up. An interesting aspect of the analogy is that light is clearly an entirely different sort of thing than the object of sight or the subjects who see.

Aristotle hints at the independent and substantial existence of the agent intellect as 'separate from the other and pure, being in its own essence actuality' (*De An.* 430a 17–19), and 'once separated from the body this intellect is immortal, indeed, eternal' (*De An.* 430a 22–3). Of course, he is quite hesitant about the exact nature of this intellect, since: 'Our only explanation must be that mind alone enters from without and is alone the divine element. When and how and from where mind comes is a most difficult question, which we must answer carefully and as best we may' (*De generatione animalium* 736b 273). This dilemma was taken up with alacrity by Alexander who understood by the agent intellect an external substance or potency acting upon the individual soul. He identified it with the force of god actualizing the human soul regarded as matter, while the Neoplatonists interpreted it as an emanation of God flowing into and filling the human soul.

Aristotle had used the example of light in order to describe the function of the agent intellect in making possible our application of universals to our sense data. Themistius, like Alexander a celebrated commentator, shrewdly notes the difference between the imagery employed by Plato and Aristotle. While Plato uses the example of the sun, which denotes a unitary being, Aristotle talks about light, which in a sense is one and in another sense is diffused into many things.[2] There are, nonetheless, important analogies between the sorts of qualities which characterize the active intellect and Aristotle's notion of God. Both are immortal and eternal, and both possess uninterrupted activity as a continually operating cause which necessitates their essential and eternal activity. The agent intellect is the cause of our being able to reason about the world, which we experience through the unity of body and soul, which in turn describes our constitution. It 'starts off' the human intellect by presenting it with the basic principles of theoretical reason which later make possible the human intellect's attainment of the perfect state, called by Alexander the 'acquired intellect'.

To understand how these notions of the active and the acquired intellects fit into Islamic philosophy, it is first necessary to consider the cosmological system posited by the philosophers. The universe is generally taken to consist of Aristotle's series of celestial spheres continually revolving around a stationary earth, with each movement being dependent upon incorporeal movers assigned to each sphere. The only causality which exists in Aristotle's system at this level is in terms of motion, but

---

[2] *Themistii . . . De anima paraphrasis*, ed. R. Heinze (Berlin, Reimer, 1899), p. 103.

the use of the Neoplatonic notion of emanation provides a far more 're-ligious' model of the universe. After all, God may be identified with the eternal emanating cause of the existence of the first intelligence, which in turn is the eternal emanating cause of the existence of the second intelli-gence, and so on. Aristotle did not see the need for an incorporeal mover of the lower sublunar world, since he identified causality only with the motion of the universe, not with a sublunar world which does not move as a whole. For al-Fārābī, on the other hand, the ninth intelligence which controls the sphere of the moon emanates a tenth intelligence which he identifies with the active intelligence of Aristotle's *De Anima*. This works as an intermediary between the celestial intelligences and the sublunar world. The active intellect is the intermediary in the sense that it leads the potential human intellect to actuality; it is the heavens and not the active intellect which produce the substance of the sublunar world and accordingly develop the existence of souls in that world. As with Aristotle, the heavens are the cause of the generation and corruption of the lower world, but with the added Neoplatonic feature that specifies the mode of connection as emanation. Al-Fārābī describes the work of the active intellect in such a way that close resemblances emerge with the path that the heavens follow in performing their tasks. After all, the heavens do not act directly to perfect all parts of the sublunar world. Instead, they activate things in the world which then operate on each other until they reach progressively higher levels of existence, through an interaction of the things' own efforts with the continually descending powers of the heavens. Similarly, the active intellect does not complete the perfection of the human intellect by itself. It rather sets off the development of the human intellect and later on provides important knowledge. People dif-fer in their innate ability to receive the first set of very general scientific principles which the active intellect supplies, so that some do not receive any and remain ignorant of virtually everything that is important, while others receive them all. All fairly intelligent people receive enough in the way of such knowledge for them to agree with others on accept-able canons of knowledge and behaviour, while some superior people receive additional and special items of knowledge whereby they are en-abled to understand more deeply the structure of the universe through an understanding of the principles of physics and metaphysics.

Al-Fārābī distinguishes between two types of being, one incorporeal and the other corporeal, the former being actually intelligible while the latter are only potentially intelligible. The development of the human intellect from potentiality to actuality through the active intellect enables us to think about both objects of thought. There seems to be some sort of hierarchy intended here, whereby the human intellect derives abstract concepts of things in the sublunar world by means of the active intellect, deriving concepts of incorporeal beings (such as the active intellect itself) by attaining a higher level of intellectual development initiated by the active intellect. The highest stage is sometimes called that of the 'acquired intellect', which is reached when someone 'perfects his intellect with all intelligible thoughts'.[3] He often characterizes the state of attaining the acquired intellect as one where the active intellect unites with the human soul by producing an emanation which transforms the human being into a philosopher. Once the human intellect reaches the stage of acquired intellect it becomes similar to the incorporeal beings which comprise its subject matter, and so, al-Fārābī argues sometimes, it is immortal in the sense that it is capable of existing without the body. Even before the death of the body it is possible for people to enjoy supreme happiness with souls that continue indefinitely. But only these acquired intellects are immortal, and since they consist in nothing but their thoughts (the very reason for their immortality) they cannot be differentiated from each other, since these thoughts are all the same. They thus possess nothing that might serve as a criterion of distinction between them. This form of immortality is entirely without memory and knowledge of individuals. It is independent of the sense impressions which come to human beings and is unaffected by them, and so we cannot in a future existence retain any impressions for the future from this life.

It is worth noting that in his *Commentary on the 'Nicomachean Ethics'*, sadly not extant, al-Fārābī is reported to have argued that the soul is mortal and that human thought comes to an end. This is because we are unable to grasp abstract forms and so cannot become lasting like them. He also argues controversially that prophecy is a matter of the imaginative faculty alone – a doctrine whose influence on Maimonides we have already mentioned. These arguments of al-Fārābī were rather notorious in medieval philosophy and were in marked contrast with those works of his in which he follows the line that human intellects can grasp intellectual objects by means of insight, the latter being a divine faculty that emanates from the active intellect while at the same time not being identical with it. This divine faculty relates to the objects of the imagination in much the same way as the senses relate to their objects. It grasps, as though illuminated, the intellectual objects, that is the abstract

---

[3] Al-Fārābī, *Al-madīna al-fāḍila* (The virtuous city), ed. F. Dieterici (Leiden, Brill, 1895), pp. 57–8.

concepts applying to celestial principles which are then present in us as objects of the imagination. But these objects undergo a change when they are transferred from the imagination to the intellect in this way. The imagination is closely connected with our ability to receive sense impressions and to play about with aspects of them, but once abstract concepts are regarded as objects of intellect rather than of imagination this connection with the sense faculties is no longer applicable. We would not require bodies to grasp these intellectual objects if they are immortal and unchangeable. If they are immortal and immutable then the soul which cognizes them must share these characteristics. Alexander argued that someone who thought about things which are subject to corruption must himself be subject to corruption, while if the object of thought is not subject to corruption, then neither is the intellect which thinks about it. This is a consequence of the identity of the intellect with the object of knowledge which plays such a large part in the discussion of immortality in Islamic philosophy.

We saw in the previous chapter how the imagination is said to make possible both dreams and prophecy. Some prophets are people who have not perfected their intellect and yet, nonetheless, they receive the active intellect in their imaginations. At the higher level of intellectual development represented by the notion of the acquired intellect, the active intellect automatically comes into play, and the imagination is affected. The imagination occupies what is, in effect, an intermediary position between practical and theoretical reason, and the effect of the active intellect on it is to supply it with knowledge of present and future events as well as abstract ideas and propositions. Since it is characteristic of the imagination to represent its contents in terms of figurative or symbolic language – being a physical faculty capable only of receiving physical forms – it transforms these rational truths into representational language. As for its practical function, the imagination becomes an accurate predictor of future events, as in dreams or visions. What seems to be meant by this is that the normal intellectual processes of working through propositions describing the present to reach conclusions about the future are speeded up by the active intellect, so that both practical and theoretical inferences are run through very quickly. This sort of process makes possible prophecy in people whose imaginations have been perfected. A superior variety of prophecy is available to those who have, in addition, passed through all the appropriate stages of intellectual development that are available to human beings and then have been granted an emanation from the active intellect to bring them to the level of the acquired intellect. The effect of prophecy on the philosopher is to transform his imagination in such a way that he acquires the skill of using persuasive expressions and stories to instruct those less perfect than him in the intellectual truths, and possibly in the practical aspects of life too.

Avicenna extended al-Fārābī's use of the notion of the active intellect in important ways. They both accepted the view, contrary to Aristotle, that the existence of matter in the world must have a cause, but differed over the nature of the cause. As we have seen, al-Fārābī pointed to the celestial spheres, but Avicenna also includes the active intellect as bringing about prime matter, with its potentiality for receiving the forms of all natural objects in the sublunar world as a cause together with the celestial spheres. Avicenna employs the Aristotelian argument for the existence of God from the motion of the universe, adding to it his proof of God stemming from the distinction between necessary and possible existence and the requirement for an absolutely necessary and self-subsistent cause. To Aristotle's demonstration of the existence of the active intellect from the motion of the human intellect from potentiality to actuality, Avicenna adds a proof from the existence of the matter of the sublunar world. Both matter and the forms appearing in matter are emanated from the active intellect, according to Avicenna, and this is not a matter of choice or God's grace but rather a necessary implication of the active intellect's essence. It is within the context of this system that he demonstrates the immortality of the human soul. He argues that human souls are incorporeal substances by using Alexander's principle that only an indivisible incorporeal subject can apprehend intellectual thought. This follows from the principle that what thinks becomes one with the object of thought in the act of thought, and since human souls do receive intellectual thoughts, these souls must be incorporeal. He next argues that the disintegration and destruction of the soul is not necessarily connected with the destruction of the human body, arguing that the soul is produced by the active intellect acting upon some matter already formed in an appropriate manner so that it is disposed to receive it. It follows from this sort of explanation that the soul is not essentially brought about by the body, but rather it is brought about by the active intellect, the body being only the recipient of the soul over a certain period. In that case, the death of the body need not lead to the death of the soul.

It is worth nothing how distant this account of the soul is from that provided by Aristotle. For the latter, the soul is not a thing but rather the organization of a series of life activities. The soul is a substance only in the sense that it is the form of a body which can possibly live. It is the organization of a set of capacities, and nothing more. He disliked the idea that the soul was a separate entity of some sort. Since Avicenna accepts the idea of the soul as a substance he falls into a number of problems. He argues that a substance will only be destroyed if it can be destroyed, and it can be destroyed only if it consists, at least in part, of destructible matter. But incorporeal substances by definition contain no such matter, and so are immortal. How can Avicenna establish the individuality of these immortal souls, and what is to prevent them from transmigrating to other bodies? He claims that the souls are differentiated as a result of their *origin* in different bodies, such that the surviving souls bear some trace of their originally distinct corporeal setting. As for transmigration, Avicenna objects that it is a redundant suggestion since, whenever some material substance is in an appropriate condition to receive a soul, the active intellect provides it with one. In that case there is no possibility that souls will transmigrate into recipient bodies since the latter will already be occupied by souls anyway.

Let us look at the significance of a disagreement between al-Fārābī and Avicenna on the issue of immortality. For al-Fārābī immortality is attained when the human soul reaches the level of the acquired intellect, and the active intellect is a contributory factor in the attainment of this final stage due to its part in starting off the human thinking process. But for Avicenna the human intellect is immortal due to its very essence regardless of a developing perfection. He does consider the nature of the thoughts which the immortal soul can have when disembodied, and sees that this presents a problem. Since the soul when embodied is dependent upon sense perception and thought to prepare it to receive emanation by the active intellect, then one might expect that with the disintegration of the external and internal senses only a very limited notion of thought could survive. Avicenna accepts that if one did not when alive involve oneself in intellectual thought then with the absence of one's faculties when dead there is no possibility of making good this omission later. What he takes to happen is that if the soul establishes a disposition to receive all possible knowledge when alive, then the necessity to maintain contact with the body disappears and moreover the physical link becomes something of a distraction rather than a help in the task of thinking.

There are different varieties of immortal souls, as one might expect given that perfection is not a necessary condition of immortality. Some souls achieve the ultimate in happiness available to human souls due to their complete perfection enabling them to conjoin completely and permanently with the active intellect. Others are less successful at achieving this total conjunction, since they possess less than a perfect disposition for conjunction with the active intellect. These souls just have a basic grasp of the principles of physics and metaphysics. There are souls which do not reach even this level but which nonetheless understand that perfect happiness is only achievable by the development of intellectual thought. There are also souls which are so completely ignorant that they constitute a formless material substratum which does exist, but without any intellectual activity, and so Avicenna sometimes characterizes them as being as good as non-existent. There are other important distinctions to be made, since we have yet to consider the effect of moral behaviour on the character of souls. There are souls which are ignorant and yet have led virtuous lives, and they will lead a peaceful (i.e. painless) existence during immortality entirely uncluttered with intellectual content. Those souls which were steeped in sin in the mortal realm will suffer due to their inability to satisfy their desires. The model which Avicenna has in mind for these disembodied entities is that they both enjoy physical pleasures and suffer physical pains by virtue of the application of their imaginations, so that vivid sensations appear to come to them and affect them.

Some of the problems which Avicenna's account involves are fairly evident. In the first place, he is very unclear on precisely how much knowledge must be acquired in this world for conjunction with the active intellect in the next world to be assured. The claim that some souls seem to be as good as dead given their ignorance appears difficult to reconcile with the original demonstration of the immortality of the soul as such. Again, the survival of the virtuous yet ignorant soul seems to be accepted by Avicenna, yet how can mere virtue replace knowledge among the necessary conditions of immortality if there are to be such conditions? Even more importantly, how can Avicenna provide a description of pains and pleasures in a disembodied immortal existence, since the physical organs which in the human body make possible the application of imagination are no longer there? Not only would it be impossible for the immortal soul to feel sensations, but it would also be unable to imagine them. The imagination is not an immaterial faculty and so it cannot grasp the universal and the immaterial. It can indeed deal with both intellectual and sensible data, transforming them into vivid and persuasive symbols capable of motivating people to action, yet imagination presents its workings in figurative and symbolic language because of its material basis. Once that basis is assumed no longer to exist, there can exist no imagination either. Since the immortality of the soul can only be described in such colourless ways that abstract completely from what ordinary people would regard as desirable features of a future life, why should anyone care about this sort of future life in the first place?

While Avicenna is prepared to accept that the soul is a form, since it is the soul which perfects the various species of living beings, i.e. makes a particular living being a member of a particular species, he regards it as more than just a form. Some things are perfections of other things without being their forms but by being substances separate from them, just as a pilot is the perfection of a ship. So he firmly set himself against the view of the soul defended by Aristotle, perhaps without entirely realizing it. In fact Avicenna's discussion of immortality was also highly controversial in Islam, and much discussed philosophically given its rather unsatisfactory ramifications. A particular aspect of his claim that the soul retains its individuality after separation from the body appears rather dubious, especially when one considers the qualms which Aristotelians have in admitting the existence of an actual infinite number of anything. Given the eternity of the world, and so the eternity of the human and other species along with the processes of generation and corruption, it follows that the present moment has been preceded by an infinite number of people who have died, and so there must also exist an infinite number of souls which are immortal. As we have seen, Aristotelians have no problem in conceiving of an infinity of bodies as such, provided that they only constitute a potential rather than an actual infinity. They succeed one another and do not persist all together simultaneously. But this is far from the case as far as the series of immortal souls goes, they must very much coexist and so constitute an actual infinity. One solution to this difficulty would be to develop some theory of transmigration, so that a finite number of souls 'survived' an infinite number of bodies and was shared around. As we have seen, Avicenna was opposed to theories of transmigration, and especially to the notion that there could be souls waiting in the wings of some prior existence for appropriate bodies to accept them. If there were to be such a variety of souls, how could they be individuated, given their total lack of connection with any body? If there was just one soul, then the resulting individuals would be all the same, which they patently are not, so the transmigration hypothesis must be rejected. The idea that souls can exist prior to their connection with a body is attacked by Aristotelians who argue that the soul can only exist with the body. Avicenna's solution to the problem of the actual infinity of souls is to appeal to the lack of order or position in the numbering of these souls. After all, such souls are immaterial and so without spatial position and they do not causally affect one another, or anything else for that matter. In that case, the sorts of divisions which can be made of actual infinites and which produce problems, such as the distinction between part and whole leading to descriptions of the part applying to the whole, just would not arise. In the course of his discussion in the *Book of deliverance* of the impossibility of things being infinite in number, Avicenna claims that an infinite number is possible in the case of things which, even though existing simultaneously, have no order either in position or by nature, i.e. which are neither corporeal nor interrelated causally.[4] Al-Ghazālī accurately describes this thesis as 'the human souls which are separated from bodies at death can be regarded as infinite in number, and they can exist all at the same time, since . . . that form of existence is without priority and posteriority'.[5] This Avicennan line of argument omits to mention the very real diffculty that God still has to order the infinite collection of immortal souls in order of merit, so that a sort of order is involved in this actual infinity in apparent opposition to Aristotelian principles.

As one might expect, al-Ghazālī, that acute critic of the *falāsifa*, attacked with alacrity Avicenna's account of an infinite number of souls. In fact, he describes that account as being one of the undesirable consequences of the belief in the eternity of the world. He argues against the eternity of the world on the ground that this would imply an infinite number of revolutions of the spheres, which, he argues, is impossible. Of course, Avicenna could reply that an infinite number of things is impossible only of things existing simultaneously but not of things existing successively. Al-Ghazālī responds to this sort of reply thus:

And we say moreover to the philosophers: According to your principles it is not absurd that there should be actual units, qualitatively differentiated, which are infinite in number; I am thinking of human souls, separated through death from their bodies. These are therefore realities that can neither be called even nor uneven. How will you refute the man who affirms that this is necessarily absurd in the same way as you claim the connexion between an eternal will and a temporal creation to be necessarily absurd? This theory about souls is that which Avicenna accepted, and it is perhaps Aristotle's. (*TT* 13)

Averroes agrees that Avicenna's argument is faulty, since matter is the only individuating criterion on the more Aristotelian view that Averroes

4 Ibn Sīnā, *Najāt*, ed. M. S. Kurdi, p. 203.
5 Al-Ghazālī, *Al-maqāṣid al-falāsifa*, ed. S. Dunya (Cairo, Saʿadah Press, 1961), p. 194.

defends, and the immaterial nature of souls means that they cannot be individuated at all. And, even if we could talk of their being individuated, we should not accept that an actually infinite quantity of such individuals is conceivable.

Averroes makes clear that Avicenna's theory is different from that of 'the ancients', so in response he does not defend that theory but just the various philosophical positions on the nature of infinity and the circular movements of the heavens in response to al-Ghazālī. Al-Ghazālī criticizes the philosophical argument which rests on the impossibility of an actually infinite number of essential causes on the grounds that the philosophers (and he means Avicenna) are not consistent in ruling out this possibility. If we think even of only one soul being created each night that the world has existed, we will end up with a temporally ordered series of souls, an order consisting in an infinite number of coexisting individuals. As we have seen, al-Ghazālī quite shrewdly wonders why an actual infinity should be disallowed for space and yet apparently allowed for time, and he also brings in his doubts about the Aristotelian position on infinity and the success with which the *falāsifa* have resolved their account of the eternity of the world even given Aristotelian premises (*TT* 169). Avicenna would perhaps have replied that the difficulty with actual infinity only arises if there *is* such a quantity, or can be thought to be such a quantity, but if there is no such identifiable series (as he argues is the case with immortal souls in time) then there is no problem. Averroes might agree with this but might suggest that this sort of reply rather gives the whole game away. After all, he would argue that there are no great problems here since there is no identifiable order because there are no identifiable individuals. The notion of immortal souls existing at all is, then, rather strange. Of course, Avicenna was quite aware of the fact that there are problems in trying to individuate souls when disembodied. This was in fact his main argument against the possibility of the existence of souls *before* they merged with bodies. He argued that after death the souls which survive are shaped individually and are differentiable by virtue of their prior connection with very different organizations of matter and different behaviour patterns. This is how he explained different achievements with respect to perfection by mortal human beings resulting in different and distinguishable souls which are then immortal. The interesting question remains, though, of whether the sort of connection which exists between such souls and matter is sufficient for us to talk about the separate existence and development of those souls?

This question returns with a vengeance when one considers Averroes' remarks on this issue. Some Qur'ānic doctrines, such as the belief in the provision of reward and punishment in return for individual failings and virtues in this life, are fairly specific about the events of the next life. Yet sometimes when Averroes refers to the consequences of our actions affecting our happiness in the next life he speaks as though those consequences automatically take effect: 'True science is knowledge of God, blessed and exalted, and the other beings as they really are, and especially of noble beings, and knowledge of happiness and misery in the next life . . . right practice consists in performing the acts which bring happiness and avoiding the acts which bring misery: and it is knowledge of these acts which is called "practical science"' (*FM* 63). In his *Commentary on Plato's 'Republic'* Averroes accepts Plato's view that happiness is not a reward and misery not a punishment, but rather both are effects of the corresponding acts (I,XI,5–7). Very much in this vein Avicenna comments: 'it is not to be imagined that after the resurrection there are obligations, commandments and prohibitions for anyone, so that by witnessing reward and punishment they should be scared or refrain from what is proscribed to them and desire what is commanded them'.[6] Avicenna claims that reward and punishment, praise and blame, merely have instrumental value in modifying behaviour.

All these descriptions of the future life fail to mention the significance of the agency of God. This omission can hardly be allowed to pass without comment, since the Qur'ān makes so much of the notion of personal divine judgment and its consequences for the pleasantness or otherwise of the afterlife. The problem for Averroes is quite clear. As an Aristotelian he would regard the possibility of personal immortality as being a difficult notion to comprehend. Matter, the principle of individuation, is precisely the substance which is corruptible and perishes when we die, and so we have to ask two questions. Does Averroes argue that the soul is immortal, and that each individual soul is immortal? In his account of the intellect he compares it with sensibility since both are passive powers which receive their objects from elsewhere. Following Alexander, he calls our intellect the material intellect, and argues that, since it is not physical or a power in something physical, it must be numerically one for all individuals. There could not be more than one given that multiplication within a species is inconceivable without matter. When separated

[6] Ibn Sīnā, 'Essay on the secret of destiny', trans. G. Hourani, *Bulletin of the School of Oriental and African Studies*, XXIX, 1 (1966), pp. 25–48; p. 33.

from matter individual souls are absolutely one. But the species itself is
eternal since the aspects of the human intellect which can be described
as the active and material intellects are immaterial and so not corruptible. So Averroes suggests that all souls become one after death: 'If then
the soul does not die when the body dies, or if it possesses an immortal
element, it must, when it has left the bodies, form a numerical unity'
(*TT* 15).

When talking about how to present this issue to the masses, Averroes
suggests making use of the analogy of sleep with death:

the comparison of death with sleep in this question is an evident proof that the
soul survives, since the activity of the soul ceases in sleep through the inactivity
of its organ, but the existence of the soul does not cease, and therefore it is
necessary that its condition in death should be like its condition in sleep . . . And
this is a proof which all can understand and which is suitable to be believed
by the masses, and will show the learned the way in which the survival of the
soul is ascertained. And this is evident from the divine words: 'God takes to
Himself souls at the time of their death; and those who do not die in their sleep.'
(*TT* 343)

By 'evident proof' here Averroes surely cannot mean what would count
as demonstrative proof for philosophers, but just what seems persuasive
to the masses. This Qur'ānic quotation is taken by him to relate to the
question 'Does scripture contain an indication of the immortality of the
soul or [at least] a hint of it?[7] This is a rather disingenuous question to
produce within an Islamic context.

He goes on to suggest that the analogy between death and sleep can
be used to show that the soul and the body are separable. Indeed, he
ends up by quoting Aristotle: 'Death is a cessation; it must therefore be of
the organ, as is the case in sleep. As the Philosopher says, "If the old man
were to find an eye like the young man's eye, he would see as the young
man sees".'[8] This reference to *De An.* 408b 21 claims that the condition of
the organ makes all the difference to the activity, while the soul remains
unchanged. It is part of a section which rather hesitantly suggests a lack
of resemblance between the mind and the senses. Aristotle follows his
assertion with this amplification: 'Thus senility results from an affection
not of the soul but of the body that contains it, like drunkenness and

---

[7] Averroes, *K. al-kashf 'an manāhij al-adilla* (Exposition of the methods and argument concerning the
doctrines of faith), in G. Hourani, *On the harmony of religion and philosophy* (London, Luzac, 1976),
p. 78.
[8] *Ibid.*

disease. So too thought or contemplation decays through the destruction of some other part within, but is itself unchangeable. Mind is probably something more divine and immutable' (*De An.* 408b 22–9). Yet on the whole Aristotle treats the mind as a unity and with an independence from the body which cannot be absolute, since body and soul form a single complex. His example, and Averroes' application of it, is designed on the contrary to try to separate the mind from the body. The example suggests that poor eyesight on the part of the old man is not due to any weakening of the *power* of sight, but rather to the weakness of the instrument. The implication is that the parts of the instrument or the instrument itself may be injured or destroyed without the powers themselves being destroyed along with the instrument.

Averroes himself is hesitant about saying exactly what his view of the immortality of the soul is:

As for al-Ghazālī's objection, that a man knows of his soul that it is in his body although he cannot specify in which part – this indeed is true, for the ancients had different opinions about its seat, but our knowledge that the soul is in the body does not mean that we know that it receives its existence through being in the body; this is not self-evident, and is a question about which the philosophers ancient as well as modern differ, for if the body serves as an instrument for the soul, the soul does not receive its existence through the body; but if the body is like a substratum for its accident, then the soul can only exist through the body. (*TT* 350)

And indeed towards the end of his *Incoherence of the incoherence* he becomes even more difficult to pin down:

What al-Ghazālī says against them [the heretics and those who believe that the end of human beings only consists in sensual enjoyment] is right, and in refuting them it must be admitted that the soul is immortal, as is proved by rational and religious proofs, and it must be assumed that what arises from the dead are simulacra of those earthly bodies, not those bodies themselves, for that which has perished does not return individually and a thing can only return as an image of that which has perished, not as a being identical with what has perished, as al-Ghazālī declares. Therefore the doctrine of resurrection of those theologians who believe that the soul is an accident and that the bodies which arise are identical with those that perished cannot be true. For what perished and became anew can only be specifically, not numerically, one ... al-Ghazālī accused the philosophers of heresy on three points. One concerns this question [the immortality of the individual soul] and we have already shown what opinion the philosophers hold about this, and that according to them it is a speculative problem. (*TT* 362)

He goes on almost immediately to accuse al-Ghazālī of duplicity and a lack of understanding of Islamic criteria of heresy:

al-Ghazālī asserts in this book that no Muslim believes in a purely spiritual resurrection, and in another book he says that the Sūfīs hold it. According to this latter assertion those who believe in a spiritual but not in a perceptible resurrection are not declared heretics by consensus, and this permits belief in a spiritual resurrection. But again in another book he repeats his accusation of heresy as if it rested on consensus. And all this, as you see, is confusing. And no doubt this man erred in religious questions as he erred in rational problems. (*TT* 362–3)

Averroes is quite clear as to why there is a problem in thinking of one soul surviving each individual body:

Zaid and Amr are numerically different but identical in form. If, for example, the soul of Zaid were numerically different from the soul of Amr in the way Zaid is numerically different from Amr, the soul of Zaid and the soul of Amr would be numerically two, but one in their form, and the soul would possess another soul. The necessary conclusion is therefore that the soul of Zaid and the soul of Amr are identical in their form. An identical form inheres in a numerical, i.e. a divisible multiplicity, only through the multiplicity of matter. If then the soul does not die when the body dies, or if it possesses an immortal element, it must, when it has left the bodies, form a numerical unity. (*TT* 15)

And as he adds at *TT* 308:

The question which still needs to be examined is whether the temporal particulars, which proceed from the heavenly movement are intended for their own sake or only for the preservation of the species . . . it certainly seems that there exists a providence as concerns individuals . . . however, in reality this is a providence which concerns the species.

Insofar as human beings are temporal particulars proceeding from heavenly motion, which in a sense they certainly are for Averroes, then it is only the human species which is immortal, not the particular human beings themselves. Yet later he curiously suggests that there are philosophical supporters for the belief that a principle of individuation exists even in disembodied souls:

in the intellect there is no individuality whatever: the soul, however, although it is free from the matters through which the individuals receive their plurality, is said by the most famous philosophers not to abandon the nature of the individual, although it is an apprehending entity. This is a point which has to be considered. (*TT* 356)

He cannot possibly mean to include Aristotle in his list of these 'most famous philosophers' here. Like Aristotle, Averroes seems quite firm in his view that 'the numerical plurality of individuals arises only through matter' (*TT* 357), and the context makes it clear that Avicenna is at least one of the philosophers he is describing. For Averroes every form in matter is material, and so an immortal soul cannot possibly be in the body, with the implication that there is then no sense in talking about personal immortality.

In an interesting analogy Averroes relates the soul to light:

The soul is closely similar to light: light is divided by the division of illuminated bodies, and is unified when the bodies are annihilated, and this same relation holds between soul and bodies. (*TT* 16)

This analogy is later amplified:

I do not know any philosopher who said that the soul has a beginning in the true sense of the word and is thereafter everlasting except – as al-Ghazālī relates – Avicenna. All other philosophers agree that in their temporal existence they are related to and connected with the bodily possibilities, which receive this connection like the possibilities which subsist in mirrors for their connection with the rays of the sun. (*TT* 63)

As we saw when looking at Aristotle, the use of the sun and light as analogies of the soul is suggestive. Light gives a mirror its very being as a mirror, and could quite easily be regarded as in some ways the form of the mirror. Light brings the mirror to life, we might say. He rejects as a 'shocking supposition' the use of other analogies to indicate that

the soul would come to the body as if it directed it from the outside, as the artisan directs his product, and the soul would not be a form in the body, just as the artisan is not a form in his product. The answer is that it is not impossible that there should be among the entelechies which conduct themselves like forms something that is separate from its substratum as the pilot is from his ship and the artisan from his tool, and if the body is like the instrument of the soul, the soul is a separate form. (*TT* 67–8)

We might add his comment that

The philosophers, however, can answer [the charge that souls will perish with bodies] that it is by no means necessary that, when there exists between two things a relation of attachment and love, for instance the relation between the lover and the beloved and the relation between iron and the magnet, the destruction of one should cause the destruction of the other. (*TT* 357)

Averroes appears to be arguing that form may exist in two distinct ways, one in matter and one entirely separate from matter. It is easy enough to see that this is the case since: 'if the living bodies in our sublunary world are not alive by themselves, but through a life which inheres in them, then necessarily this life through which the non-living acquires life is alive in itself, or there would be an infinite regress' (*TT* 188).

Yet all that these arguments are designed to show is that the soul is immortal. They do nothing to establish the possibility of individual survival in the afterlife that is so important to the religious notion of resurrection in Islam. As we have seen, right at the end of his *Incoherence of the incoherence*, Averroes discusses al-Ghazālī's attack on Avicenna for failing to explain individual immortality, and Averroes stresses the principle that matter is the presupposition of individuation and so it is indeed very difficult to see how personal immortality can be conceived. It is difficult to account for his arguments here, since they so patently seem to fail before al-Ghazālī's blistering critique. Almost as an admission of failure, Averroes is driven to inventing a special sort of matter which might permit the possibility of personal identity when the body has perished:

He who claims the survival and the numerical plurality of souls should say that they are in a subtle matter, namely the animal warmth which emanates from the heavenly bodies, and this is a warmth which is not fire, and in which there is not a principle of fire; in this warmth there are the souls which create the sublunary bodies and those which inhere in these bodies. (*TT* 357)

This move is desperate because it suggests that those who wish to maintain belief in personal survival must then accept the existence of this special substance which grounds it, and since there is no reason to accept the existence of such matter (it is implied) then there is no reason to accept the existence of the individual immortal existents.

Hourani thinks that Averroes may well be offering the existence of this substance of 'heavenly warmth' as a serious argument in favour of personal immortality, albeit in 'bodies' which do not perhaps closely resemble our own.[9] He suggests that this notion would make sense of individuation and is philosophically respectable on Averroes' view given his claim that all the ancient philosophers, even including Galen, held similar sorts of view. He does admit that Averroes is rather hesitant about it, claiming that such topics are confusing and tentative, and that in any case there would be a difficulty in reconciling this view with the Qur'ānic belief in a gap of unconsciousness between our lives and deaths. The soul might be thought in that interval to unite with the heavenly warmth or spiritual matter before it recovers consciousness in its new

---

[9] G. Hourani, 'Averroès musulman', in *Multiple Averroès* (Paris, Les Belles Lettres, 1978), pp. 21–30; pp. 29–30.

material existence, yet this break in continuity could well mean a break in the continuity of the *personality*, something that the theory is supposed to prevent. It is worth recognizing, given Averroes' use of the example of sleep, that such a state of affairs is different from that of sleep where there is material continuity and some mental activity. It is difficult to accept that Averroes means this argument to account for personal immortality in a demonstrative sense, especially when we come to compare it with his extensive defence of the philosophical notion of creation.

The view of the soul as really only one substance which confers form on lots of different bits of matter fits in well with Averroes' discussion of the active intellect as a sort of universal mind which is responsible for both our ability to think and the content of that thinking, and is capable of leading us in stages to even greater levels of abstraction until conjunction with intelligible reality and the active intellect itself becomes a possibility. Averroes was in no doubt that he could combine this account with the Aristotelian view of the soul as the form of the body and hence intrinsically related to the body. The link is made via the material intellect, an instantiation of the passive aspect of Aristotle's notion of intellect, and a substance which has a close connection with the imagination. What Aristotle meant by the material intellect is just the capacity to think and Averroes argued that this disposition requires some substantial form for it to have meaning. The active intellect develops ideas in human minds by actualizing our ability to comprehend the potential intelligible forms in objects. We have seen how in the 'light' metaphors the soul 'brings to life' objects by entering them. In being known the object is, as it were, 'brought to light' by the subject, and the active intellect is seen as both stimulating the knowing subject and illuminating the known object.

In fact, Averroes' accounts of knowledge and intellectual development quite radically do away with individuality as such, so that it is difficult to see why personal immortality should survive. When he talks about the perfection of the intellect and its conjunction with the active intellect he is quite clear in thinking that the individual intellect merges its individuality with the world of infinite and universal form. Even if this stage is never reached, as it is not for most human beings, nonetheless both the actuality and the potentiality of individual intellects are received from the active intellect. The material intellect does indeed acquire individual characteristics due to its involvement with the particular imaginative forms of a specific individual, but it will only retain these aspects of individuality in so far as it fails to develop these imaginative forms into universal and more abstract forms. In other words, we only remain individuals in so far as we fail to progress intellectually. Paradoxically perhaps, it is only when we are dead that everyone loses their unique individuality – once the intellect leaves the body, as it must at death, that is the end of imagination and the participation of the body in thought. Some people might be able to effect this ending of individuality before death, by developing their intellect to such an extent that they merge with the active intellect.

Maimonides seems to reach a similar conclusion, although he appears more sceptical concerning the possibility of knowing the most abstract principles which the philosophers hold up as the summit of intellectual development. In his *Guide of the perplexed* he distinguishes sharply between the sorts of knowledge available to different people, where it is only the prophets, and really only one particular prophet – Moses – who can understand the intellectual objects which go beyond being merely abstractions of corporeal objects. He describes the sort of intellectual knowledge available to us thus:

Know that before a man intellectually cognizes a thing, he is potentially the intellectually cognizing subject. Now if he has intellectually cognized a thing (it is as if you said that if a man has intellectually cognized this piece of wood to which one can point, has stripped its form from its matter, and has represented to himself the pure form – this being the action of the intellect), at that time the man would become one who has intellectual cognition in actu. Intellect realised in actu is the pure abstract form, which is in his mind, of the piece of wood. For intellect is nothing but the thing that is intellectually cognized. (*GP* I,68,163–4)

There is a suggestion that this sort of abstraction is just about all we human beings can manage. After all,

Matter is a strong veil preventing the apprehension of that which is separate from matter as it truly is . . . Hence whenever our intellect aspires to apprehend the Deity or one of the intellects, there subsists this great veil interposed between the two. (*GP* III,9,436–7)

We can apprehend, then, neither God nor the separate intellects because our intellects are so closely related to our bodies.

At a later point Maimonides argues that human beings can acquire no certain theory concerning the principles behind the nature of the celestial bodies or their motions. Only Moses was granted the special favour of being shown such things by God (*GP* III,24). Indeed, given the accepted hierarchy of knowledge, knowledge of the heavenly bodies would have been regarded as some of the knowledge most worth having, yet our knowledge is limited to the features of the sublunar world. Of course, we can think about and even theorize scientifically about the celestial realm, but our knowledge cannot extend to that realm with any degree of certainty. Maimonides emphasizes continually the hesitation which philosophers like Aristotle had about accepting the possibility of a general physics which would comprise the whole of the universe with its laws. This approach owes far more to Alexander of Aphrodisias than to Aristotle himself: 'the opinions held by Aristotle regarding the cause of the motion of the spheres – from which opinions he deduced the existence of separate intellects – are simple assertions for which no demonstration has been made . . . [although they are] of all the opinions put forward on this subject, those that are exposed to the smallest number of doubts' (*GP* II,3,254).

So we have seen that Maimonides is not at all confident about the possibility of human success in cognizing or uniting with the intellectual objects: his claim is that the object of union is too obscure for us to set about sensibly trying to unite with it. He might be thought in that case to be rather hesitant also in his description of the survival of the soul in the afterlife, and indeed he is in the *Guide of the perplexed*. After describing the death by a kiss of Moses, Aaron and Miriam he comments:

The other prophets and excellent men are beneath his degree; but it holds good for all of them that the apprehension of their intellects becomes stronger at separation . . . After having reached this condition of enduring permanence that intellect remains in one and the same state, the impediment that sometimes screened him off having been removed. And he will remain permanently in that state of intense pleasure, which does not belong to the genus of bodily pleasures, as we have explained in our compilations and as others have explained before us. (*GP* III,51,628)

When he considers the familiar difficulty of the existence of an actual infinity of permanently coexisting souls, he remarks:

Now you know that regarding the things separate from matter – I mean those that are neither bodies, nor forces in bodies, but intellects – there can be no thought of multiplicity of any mode whatever, except that some of them are the causes of the existence of the others . . . However, what remains of Zayd is neither the cause nor the effect of what remains of Umar. Consequently all are one in number . . . To sum up: premisses by which other points are to be explained should not be taken over from such hidden matters, which the mind is incapable of representing to itself. (*GP* I,74,220–1)

Indeed, Maimonides suggests that this whole area of discussion is surrounded by obscurity and confusion:

the case of the intellects of the heavens, that of the existence of separate intellects, and that of the representation of the acquired intellect, which is also separate, are matters open to speculation and research. The proofs with regard to them are well hidden, though correct: many doubts arise with regard to them: the critic may well find in them objects for his criticism and the caviller objects for his cavilling. (*GP* I,72,193)

The moral which Maimonides derives from his thesis that there are areas of knowledge which we can only approach cautiously is to build that tentative approach into the definition of the highest degree of scientist and philosopher as someone who goes as far as human knowledge will take him and tries to go no further. In the well-known parable in which God is represented as a ruler in a palace whom various groups of people wish to approach

He, however, who has achieved demonstration, *to the extent that this is possible*, of everything that *may* be demonstrated and who has ascertained in divine matters, *to the extent that this is possible*, everything that *may* be ascertained, and who has come close to certainty in those matters in which *one can only come close to it* – has come to be with the ruler in the inner part of the habitation. (*GP* III.51,619; my emphasis)

Maimonides is, then, of the opinion that when it comes to issues such as immortality and our knowledge of the separate intellects demonstrative argument plays little part. We saw in the previous chapter that he argued that, similarly, we could not come to any definite conclusion about the origin of the world, an opinion he ascribes to Aristotle. Now, we might well be dubious about this attribution of hesitancy concerning the origin of the world to Aristotle, yet Maimonides' strategy of general wariness at the possibility of our knowing highly abstract propositions is one which brings him closer to Aristotle than some other medieval philosophers. For example, Averroes used Alexander's argument for human knowledge of the separate intellect and assumes that Alexander derives this from the work of Aristotle. Averroes argues, as we have seen, that just as light renders an object visible, so the agent or active intellect renders the intelligible that is potentially there actually intelligible. Just as light is the cause of actual visibility and is visible in itself, the agent intellect is the cause of intelligibility and is itself most intelligible, and accordingly a most worthwhile thing for the human intellect to come to know. It is necessary that the material intellect should know this separate intellect since it knows it potentially and such a potentiality must be, in an eternal universe, realized at some time.[10] However, Aristotle had said that, with respect to the most intelligible realities, man is a bat in the light of

---

[10] A reaffirmation of the principle of plenitude.

the sun. He seems to mean that human intelligence is not capable of knowing the most intelligible beings, since our intelligence is dependent upon the imagination and the senses. Averroes reinterprets this analogy and suggests that, while some animals like bats cannot look at the sun, other species can and do look at it. Though some men cannot know the separate intellect, at least one will, since we as a species have the potentiality to receive this intellect.

Yet there can be no doubt that all the philosophers we have discussed held views on the immortality of the soul which are very difficult to reconcile with literal interpretations of religious doctrine concerning immortality and the afterlife. As with the creation of the world, the introduction of Aristotelian arguments – however loosely employed – in the discussion of the soul makes the religious notion of immortality look naïve and ill-founded. Al-Ghazālī was quite right from a religious point of view to point the finger of heresy at the Aristotelian explanations of the soul and its relation to the body.

CHAPTER 3

Can God know particulars?

Al-Ghazālī's third charge of heresy takes this form:

The . . . question is their declaration: 'God Most High knows universals, but not particulars.' This also is out-and-out unbelief. On the contrary, the truth is that 'there does not escape Him the weight of an atom in the heavens or in the earth'.[1]

This interesting charge arises from the way in which philosophers distinguish between our knowledge and God's knowledge. From the point of view of religion, Islam is quite clear in teaching that God knows each and everything that exists in the temporal world; as one might expect, such knowledge is important for his decisions about the fate of human souls after death. In any case, the idea that God would create the world and then ignore it, or at least the corruptible and temporal pieces of it which we inhabit, is not an attractive idea to orthodox Islam. There can be little doubt what view the Qur'ān has of the nature of God's omniscience. Apart from the passage from XXXIV,3 = X,62 above, a much-quoted passage in theological works, there is also the suggestion at L,15 that God even knows thoughts: 'We indeed created man and we know what his soul whispers within him and we are nearer to him than the jugular vein.' He knows exactly which new individuals are produced: 'And no female conceives or brings forth without his knowledge' (XXXV,12) and He knows whatever happens, however apparently insignificant: 'And with Him are the keys of the secret things; none knows them but He. He knows whatever is on the land and in the sea, and no leaf falls without his noticing it. Nor is there a grain in the darkness of the earth, or a green or withered-up thing which is not noted in a distinct book' (VI,59). Also: 'But God is Himself witness of what he has sent down to you. In His knowledge he has sent it down to you. The angels are also its witnesses, but God is a sufficient witness' (IV,164).

[1] Al-Ghazālī, *Munqidh*, trans. R. McCarthy, pp. 76–7.

Yet it is also obvious that there is a radical difference between humans and God, between our way of knowing and that available to God. This has implications for a philosophically respectable view of the content of God's knowledge. We require sensation and the workings of imagination to acquire knowledge, and these are firmly rooted in our physical constitution as creatures with specific organs which are causally affected by the objects around us in the world. These objects are moreover constantly changing, and our judgments concerning them are also variable, not always accurate or decisive, with our grasp of them being only partial. We are necessarily limited to a position in space and time and by a certain upbringing. By contrast, God's knowledge is timeless and eternal. It is universal in the sense that it does not bring about change in God, since God is a unity, without multiplicity, in spite of the multiplicity of the objects of his knowledge. Now, Aristotelians argue that in order to see, hear, feel, taste or otherwise sense it is essential to have a body. Since God does not have a body, he cannot have either senses or any sense-knowledge. Having such perceptions would involve him in feelings – 'where there is sense-perception there is also both pain and pleasure' (*De An.* 414c 4).

Why, then, do we come across anthropomorphic expressions in the Qur'ān relating to God's sense-perceptions? Averroes suggests:

The Holy Law ascribes hearing and seeing to God to remind us that God is not deprived of any kind of knowledge and understanding, and the masses cannot be made to grasp this meaning except by the use of the terms 'hearing' and 'seeing', and for this reason this exegesis is limited to the learned, and therefore cannot be taken as one of the dogmas of the Holy Law common to the masses. (*TT* 274)

Aristotle's first Unmoved Mover is immutable and unaffected by matter. It is pure actuality without any kind of potentiality, it does not think or care about its world of change, even though the harmony and good order of this world depends ultimately upon God as a source for imitation. In the previous chapter, we saw how Alexander of Aphrodisias argued that the object of knowledge is identified with the intellect of the knower, with the implication that knowledge of immutable and eternal things could only be possessed by an immutable and immortal intellect. This principle was extended to make sense of God's knowledge, so that if his knowledge consisted of the ordinary corruptible aspects of our world then the knower must similarly be corruptible and possess sense-faculties just like us. Such a suggestion is clearly difficult for a Muslim to accept, yet if it is not accepted then we seem to be left with the notion of a God who is totally unconcerned with the events of our world and for whom praise and prayers for intercession appear futile. We have seen also how the philosophers defended the notion of immortality, but pointed out that the notion which survives their analysis is not one which provides a view of the afterlife about which we should greatly care. Are the philosophers providing an analysis of God's knowledge which establishes that there is such knowledge, but that it is similarly of no interest to us, because he is not interested in us?

The transcendence of Aristotle's God or Unmoved Mover is such that not only does he wish to spare himself the indignity of idle curiosity ('Are there not some things about which it is incredible that it should think?' – *Met.* 1074b 25), adding later that 'There are even some things which it is better not to see than to see' (*Met.* 1074b 32). The Unmoved Mover does not think about us at all. Al-Ghazālī is clear on the implications of this position:

This then is the principle in which they believe and through it they uproot the Divine Laws absolutely, for this principle implies that God cannot know whether Zaid obeys or disobeys Him, since God cannot know any new occurrences that happen to Zaid, as he does not know the individual Zaid . . . indeed, he cannot know that Zaid becomes a heretic or a true believer, for He can know only the unbelief and the belief of man in general, not as it is specified in individuals. (*TT* 276–7)

Averroes' riposte is a skilful reminder of the difficulties of the religious view of God's knowledge which al-Ghazālī brings against the Aristotelian thesis:

Al-Ghazālī's objection . . . is that it is possible that God's knowledge should be like the knowledge of man, that is that the things known should be the cause of this knowledge and their occurrence the cause of the fact that he knows them, just as the objects of sight are the cause of visual perception and the intelligible the cause of intellectual apprehension. (*TT* 284)

The intellect grasps form as such and the individual is grasped by the sensibility. All that the former can apprehend are universals, it is incapable of distinguishing between individuals since that involves perceiving material differences. Yet this has the implication which al-Ghazālī derives with alacrity that 'God cannot know Muhammad's proclaiming himself a prophet at the time he did' (*TT* 277).

Avicenna tries to get around the apparent difficulty of explaining how the unity of God and his thought can encompass variety by relying on the notion of God's knowledge being essentially self-knowledge. It will be recalled that the model of creation as emanation starts with God knowing himself as the cause of existents other than himself. While it is true that the objects of such knowledge are indeed many and constantly variable, nonetheless the knowledge that there are such objects at the end of the process of emanation and that God is their source can be regarded as just one act of knowledge. The suggestion is that God could, as it were, know everything that exists all at once, where the multiplicity of the *contents* of the knowledge claim does not challenge the status of the claim to be just *one* assertion. Now, Avicenna also makes a distinction between two kinds of multiplicity, one of which consists of the variety of permanent objects of knowledge, such as the genera and species which exist eternally, while the other consists of the everyday events and existents of the contingent sublunary world. He calls the former kind of knowledge 'vertical' and the latter 'horizontal', these descriptions pertaining to the way in which things 'are necessitated in the sequence of order descending from him'.[2] The only way in which one can come to apprehend 'horizontal' knowledge is in a piecemeal and imperfect manner, since it is a matter of a large number of things coming and going into and out of existence, different events taking place at different times, and so on. Were God to apprehend things in this way then this would constitute imperfection in him, yet we are told that his knowledge is quite perfect such that 'nothing escapes his knowledge, not even the weight of an atom in the heavens or the earth'.[3]

How then does God come about his knowledge? Perhaps the best way to answer this question is to see how human beings are said to acquire knowledge and to contrast God's method. Our sensory organs provide the soul with material images which are joined by universal concepts from the active intellect. Objects are in the world, they affect us and we form concepts concerning them in order to be able to describe them in certain ways. But God knows these objects differently, since they are not in existence for him subsequently to discover and to form concepts about, they are there *because* of his causal powers and decisions. By knowing himself as First Cause he is aware of the whole series of effects of his power and the ways in which different types of order, both horizontal and vertical, flow from his essence:

God thinks of his own essence and understands as a result that he is the basis of every existing thing. He thinks of the principle behind existing things which come from him and everything which comes from them. So nothing which exists

[2] Ibn Sīnā, K. *al-ishārāt wal-tanbihāt* (Books of Instructions and remarks), ed. J. Forget (Leiden, Brill, 1892), p. 181.

[3] Ibn Sīnā adheres to this Qur'ānic phrase in *Ilāhiyyāt*, ed. G. Anawati and S. Zayed, p. 359.

is not in some way brought about necessarily by God . . . The First knows the causes and their effects, and what they necessarily produce.[4]

It is important to stress that the model is not one of God having first one thought and then another about some aspect of his creation, as though he were continually running through an inventory. This would be to identify his thought with human ways of thinking and import imperfection into his being. Although God is aware, of course, of the temporal relations between events in the world (since otherwise he would not understand a vital aspect of reality), his understanding of these temporal events is not itself an event which spreads itself over time. Rather, God is said to grasp all at once the nature and construction of reality. As Avicenna puts it:

When our intellect thinks in terms of priority and posteriority, it links them necessarily with time. But this thinking itself does not take place in time but in an instant. When our intellect works with syllogisms and definitions, it operates in time, but the thought of the conclusion and what is defined takes place in an instant.[5]

The idea is that God runs through the appropriate syllogisms which describe the structure of the world in a manner which is both perfect and instantaneous. He can do this because of his grasp of the middle terms of such syllogisms: 'intelligible truths are acquired only when the middle term of a syllogism is obtained. This may be done . . . sometimes through intuition, which is an act of mind by which the mind itself immediately perceives the middle term. This power of intuition is quickness of apprehension',[6] and is identical to Aristotle's notion of quick-wittedness as the ability to guess the middle term in imperceptible time without having to work through a reasoning process to reach it. Avicenna conceives of God's quick wit informing him instantaneously of all the middle terms of the syllogisms which represent the basic structure of the world. This might seem to evade the issue, since the complexity of the world and its contents make the possibility of an overview which is instantaneous difficult to accept. But Avicenna's view is quite acceptable, since it has at its heart the notion of God knowing himself, and thus his creation, all at once. It is appropriate to describe this mental event as intuition since intuition describes the instantaneous grasping of the syllogism's middle term, and God, as it were, timelessly understands the middle terms of

---

[4] *Ibid.*, pp. 359 and 326.

[5] Ibn Sīnā, *Avicenna's De Anima*, ed. F. Rahman (London, Oxford University Press, 1959), p. 237.

[6] Ibn Sīnā, *Avicenna's psychology*, ed. and trans. F. Rahman (Oxford, Oxford University Press, 1952), p. 36.

all the syllogisms and thus the vital nexus of the sort of universe which flows from his essence.

This notion of perspicuity immediately makes one wonder how Avicenna is going to account for God's knowledge of contingent objects. It is one thing to grasp all at once the essential structure of the world by comprehending the basic principles of the world, but quite another to understand every single contingent fact about the contents of the world. Now, Avicenna claims in several places that God apprehends particulars, even contingent and corruptible particulars, in a universal way. What seems to be clear is that he does not know such particulars in all their contingency but just those aspects of them which are general, abstract and universal. It is also clear why Avicenna is prevented from allowing to his notion of God more than this sort of knowledge of the entirely universal attributes of substances. To know individual things which are corruptible, God would require sense organs and would lack perfection in that it would take him time to acquire his information concerning all the different and changing objects in the world. However, it would be a mistake to regard particulars as falling logically into just one class for Avicenna. He distinguishes sharply between particulars which are the only members of their species and particulars which are not. The former set of individuals can be known by God as individuals due to their changelessness; concepts of them are similarly changeless and do not imply change and lack of perfection in the conceiver. It is this aspect of changelessness which means that the material individuals which are the only members of their species, like the sun and the moon, for instance, can be known by God without the application of any sensory apparatus.

It might be thought that we could get around this point by describing a corruptible particular so fully and completely that we could reach its definition. Following the Aristotelian thesis that there is no such thing as definitions of individuals, Avicenna argues that the universal descriptions which are indeed necessarily related to the essence of the individual are, nonetheless, incapable by themselves of picking out the unique individual to which, on this occasion, they belong. At some point or another it is necessary to indicate a particular individual if we are to discover the object of all these descriptions. How could God be expected to know individuals in this way, then, given that he does not possess the ordinary sensory equipment for this sort of experience? God cannot actually *point* to something in the world – he has nothing to point with. By contrast, if the individual involved is the only member of its species, then there is no necessity for God to become experientially aware of it even if it is material, since there is a logical proof which specifies both its characteristics and the fact that those characteristics can only belong to that individual. God will not need to investigate the state of affairs in the universe to discover that such individuals are the only members of their species, he will know by knowing how he has set the universe in motion that they are the unique referents of given collections of quite general predicate terms. As Averroes puts it:

> For the knowledge of individuals is sensation or imagination, and the knowledge of universals is intellect, and the new occurrence of individuals or conditions of individuals causes two things, a change and a plurality in the perception; whereas knowledge of species and genera does not imply a change, since the knowledge of them is invariable and they are unified in the knowledge which comprehends them, and universality and individuality only agree in their forming a plurality. (*T T* 280)

Some arguments which defend the idea of God only knowing 'the universal objects of intellect' are rather more suspect than those provided by Avicenna and Averroes. It is worth considering briefly an argument of al-Fārābī's on this topic. Thus:

> others assent that although the objects of intelligence are present to it, it knows all the partial existences perceived by the senses and represents them to itself and they are impressed upon it, and that it represents to itself and knows what is now not existing but will exist hereafter, what was in past time and has ceased to be, and what is now existing. The consequences for them is that truth and falsehood and contradictory convictions follow each other in succession in regard to all the objects of its intelligence, that the objects of its intelligence are infinite, that the affirmative becomes negative and likewise the negative becomes affirmative at another time ... What it knew in the time of Alexander as existing at the present time, which is nearly 'now' at that time, it knew many ages before it would come into existence, then it knows afterwards at another time that it has been. It knows the thing in the time which was in the time of Alexander, as existing in three times in three conditions of knowledge, viz. it knows before the time of Alexander that it will be, knows in the time of Alexander himself that it is now present, and knows thereafter that it has been and is now over and past ... The holders of this view resort to ugly, hateful deeds, and there arise from it wrong ideas which are the cause of great evils.[7]

Despite the dramatic flourish at the end, this line of attack on the idea that God can know individual events is misplaced. 'Alexander is twenty on Friday' (uttered on Friday) and 'Alexander was twenty on Friday' (uttered on Saturday) are indeed two different propositions, but both

---

[7] Al-Fārābī, *Fuṣūl al-madanī*, ed. and trans. Dunlop, pp. 67–8.

express the same item of knowledge. Now, God's knowledge does not have to be expressed in propositions, and so he can know the same item of knowledge permanently and unchangingly. It is only because we are changing temporal beings that we have to express the one item of knowledge first in one proposition and then in another. When we talk of God's knowledge we must accept the possibility of making a distinction between an item of knowledge and the way in which the knowledge is expressed.

Let us relate this discussion to the previous chapter by looking at how Avicenna would deal with God's knowledge of the human soul. Although the soul is incorporeal and immortal, it changes, nonetheless, and seems an inappropriate object of knowledge for a perfect unchanging knower. Each soul acquires different amounts of abstract knowledge and ethical merit, each soul follows its own path from potentiality to actuality and develops different levels of perfection before death and separation from the body. As we saw before, it is this differing level of perfection which Avicenna wants to use as the criterion of individuality for the souls after their separation from matter. This variability in the soul's development is not the sort of characteristic which is an appropriate object of God's awareness, since these changes affect the very nature of the object itself – they are vital parts of it. Paradoxically, perhaps, it seems that only after death and the end of the soul's flux at a determinate stage of perfection would it become available as an object for God's knowledge. Yet one of the reasons why this discussion is regarded as so important by al-Ghazālī is, of course, precisely that the traditional religious view of these issues is that God is aware of the development of the human soul both before and after death, and the events which affect us when alive are observed by him and form part of his judgments on us when we are dead. It might be said that if God is able to apprehend the level of perfection that each soul had reached by examining the now changeless souls on death, then he would know all he required before passing sentence – after all, that notion of a level of perfection includes moral as well as theoretical development. Al-Ghazālī would surely be correct to claim that this view is far from the orthodox position, even though it might be able to make some sense of divine judgment in this way.

To see what Avicenna meant by talking about certain sorts of change being possible objects of knowledge for God, let us look at his well-used example of an eclipse. He claims that God 'will apprehend every eclipse . . . but in a universal way'.[8] This surely is supposed to mean more

---

[8] Ibn Sīnā, *Ilāhiyyāt*, ed. G. Anawati and S. Zayed, p. 360.

than the assertion that God knows in general how eclipses take place. Yet sensory apprehension of a particular eclipse is denied him, given his non-material characteristics. What he is allowed to know logically is that a particular eclipse with certain characteristics took place at a particular time, or will take place in the future. This sort of knowledge of change does not imply change in the knower since it is merely a matter of adding a time to an event which takes place between definable individuals which are the only members of their species. He sums up his position in this way:

Particulars can be treated as universals if the particulars are brought about necessarily by their causes and are the sole instance of a species. Take the eclipse for example. It can be thought of as a universal when its causes are thought of and when we understand the nature of those causes.[9]

Is Avicenna entitled to this conclusion? I am not sure that he is, especially given his theory of possibility which we mentioned in chapter 1. It will be recalled that the distinction between contingent and necessary entities which Avicenna makes is something of an illusion when the status of God is not at issue. Given the explanation of 'necessary' as 'signifying certainty of existence', we must accept that for Avicenna the objects and events of the world of corruption and generation are just as necessary as the activity of objects which are necessarily existent through something else, like the planets through the activity of God. Of course, if we abstract from the external condition which brings potential objects to actuality, then we can think in terms of such things being mere possibilities, but once we conceive of their condition we have to admit that they are actual and will come about in a certain way at a certain time. On the model of emanation each development is conditioned by its predecessors, and it would be a mistake to think that once we reach the contents of the world of generation and corruption the conditioning comes to an end. To take an example Avicenna uses, it is not just a matter of fact that when fire and inflammable material are conjoined then combustion results – the state of affairs describable as fire and inflammable material in close proximity necessitates the resulting state of affairs. If God is to be denied knowledge of facts like these then his view of the world will indeed be limited. Yet he cannot of course know such facts through observation – he has no body. As Avicenna says, he must know the principles behind such events in a universal manner.

---

[9] Ibn Sīnā, *Ishārāt*, ed. J. Forget, p. 182.

Does it follow that he cannot know the individual event of a particular combustion? God has a perspicuous view of reality since he (and only he) understands how it all fits together and exemplifies certain very general rules and laws. If he did not know that fire was going to break out at such and such a time and place then there must be something wrong with his awareness of the conditions which obtain and necessitate the events of the world. Certainly, when we talk of God knowing that combustion takes place at a certain time and place we do not mean that he experiences it happening as we might experience it happening. As Avicenna states, we cannot expect God to identify contingent individuals in the world without the appropriate physical apparatus, but he can know in a general way what sorts of events will take place in his world since he knows the initial necessitating conditions.

Why should he not be able to map out for himself the entire history and future of each atom of the world and thus grasp the complete train of events and individuals at each and every point of existence? To be sure, *we* cannot do this because we are limited in our point of view. It might be said that this is not a possibility for God because it would lead to a loss in his perfection – after all, he would then be involved in knowledge of a multiplicity of changing events. In a sense this is true, yet the way in which these changes take place is not itself variable and haphazard. On the contrary, the way in which changes take place is determined by the original necessitating conditions. Aristotle often suggests that we know what a thing is when we know its cause.[10] From God's point of view the universals which are predicated of even contingent individuals are inevitably and uniquely predicable of just those individuals if we add spatio-temporal coordinates. As we saw when criticizing al-Fārābī, God is not obliged as we are to describe the world in terms of dated, and so different, propositions describing the same states of affairs which then appear to contradict each other. The distinction between individuals which are the only members of their species and those which are not, like the distinction between existents which are necessary through another and those which are just possible, is more apparent than real. From God's point of view, all individuals are really the only individuals which could have the properties they have, and as such they are all appropriate objects of his knowledge. So in rightly trying to stress the difference between our knowledge and God's way of knowing the philosophers exaggerated the gap by denying God knowledge of much of what we can

---

[10] *An. Post.* 71b 9–12; 94a 20–1; *Phys.* 184a 12–14; 194b 18–19; *Met.* 983a 25–6; 1044b 13.

know. We can use Avicenna's metaphysical principles to argue that God can know what we can know, and a good deal more, but in a distinct and general way.

The argument here, then, is that Avicenna could argue validly given his metaphysical premises to the conclusion that God has knowledge of all particulars, and not only those particulars which are unique in species such as eclipses. It seems that he did not want to derive the full implications of his metaphysical system, quite possibly because he wished to avoid too closely identifying God's mode of knowledge with our own. Were God to know the everyday events of this transitory and mutable world, then would he not be obliged to possess sensory equipment? Avicenna was in total agreement with the rest of the *falāsifa* that this latter possibility is inconceivable of an Islamic deity. Yet it is not necessary actually to have sense-experience for empirical knowledge to be possible. Much of our empirical knowledge is arrived at not through our own investigations, but through the evidence which others pass onto us, and which we accept. We are obliged to wait for such evidence to be presented to us in a piecemeal and imperfect manner since the evidence is on the whole independent of our will. God possesses all the evidence because he has determined that it is to be evidence, that the universe is to be constructed in precisely that way. God's knowledge of the universe is the cause of the universe being one way rather than another. This kind of knowledge is based upon nothing more than his will to create. There is no possibility of anything going wrong. He knows exactly what he wants to make, and no obstacle can stand in the way of his making it. Thus he can know each and every empirical fact of his creation without the necessity to acquire that knowledge through the senses. It is the connection between God's power as a maker and his knowledge of his product which is important here. Interestingly, the significance of this connection is quite clearly expressed in the Qur'ān:

All that is in the heavens and the earth magnifies God; He is the All-mighty, the All-wise. To Him belongs the Kingdom of the heavens and the earth; He gives life, and He makes to die, and He is powerful over everything. He is the First and the Last, the Outward and the Inward; He has knowledge of everything. It is He that created the heavens and the earth in six days then seated Himself upon the Throne. He knows what penetrates into the earth, and what comes forth from it, what comes down from heaven, and what goes up unto it. He is with you wherever you are; and God sees the things you do. To Him belongs the Kingdom of the heavens and the earth; and unto Him all matters are returned.

He makes the night to enter into the day and makes the day to enter into the night. He knows the thoughts within the breasts. (LVII, 1–6)

Al-Ghazālī was quite right to criticize the *falāsifa* for apparently depriving God of the sort of knowledge of particulars which is so necessary if he is to carry out fully his knowing and judging roles. However, the argument in this section has been that it would have been possible for the *falāsifa* to accept that God has knowledge of particulars without contravening any of their philosophical principles. They had only to look at the Qur'ān to see how it might be done.

What is the motive behind al-Ghazālī's attack upon the *falāsifa*? Is it just to dismiss their arguments and replace them with other, more theologically appropriate, arguments? There is no doubt that al-Ghazālī was prepared to argue, and to argue both fiercely and well, in his confrontation with the philosophers. What lies behind this attack is the fervent desire to establish that the existence of God makes a difference to the way the world is and to the human beings in that world. The three key philosophical theses which he declares represents unbelief and must be condemned by Islam are not chosen at random. These three theses are so important because they appear to deny God's influence over his creation. If the world were eternally in existence, if God has no knowledge of particulars such as human actions and natural events, if corporeal resurrection is denied, then there is little point on Ghazali's view in continuing to talk about God. On al-Ghazālī's characterization of the philosophers' position, God had no choice in the issue of creating the world, he cannot know our thoughts and deeds, and he cannot reward or punish in any meaningful way those thoughts and deeds after we die. As we have seen, the interpretation which the *falāsifa* made of Aristotle leads them to conclusions distinctly averse to aspects of Islam. The key doctrine which the *falāsifa* accepted, the principle of plenitude, seems especially objectionable to Islam. The notion that what is possible has happened or will happen at some time, and that whatever is eternally possible is thereby eternally actual, seems to exclude God from any real influence on the world and its affairs. The issues of immortality and knowledge of particulars seem merely to be additional evidence of God's segregation from the world. The idea that the world is characterized by causal relations which are necessary and so independent of the First Cause once they are activated, and the idea that a necessary chain of emanation relates the First Cause to the rest of creation both seem to describe a world in which the significance of the deity is denied. Perhaps the denial is implicit rather than explicit, but it is nonetheless real and thoroughly offensive to the religious enthusiasm of al-Ghazālī.

Al-Ghazālī wanted to emphasize the place of God in Islam and to establish the very real influence which God is supposed to have upon his creatures. One of his most celebrated collections of writings – *The renaissance of the sciences of religion* – is evidence of this, for in its very title the notion of reviving or making more alive is stressed. Al-Ghazālī was unhappy with the dry legalism of much Muslim doctrine and practice, and especially with the abstract intellectualism of both the philosophers and the theologians. The passion and vigour of the faith of the Ṣūfīs impressed him greatly and contrasts markedly with what must have seemed to be the lifeless and debilitating debates of the *mutakallimūn* and the *falāsifa*. He was prepared, nonetheless, to meet their arguments on their own ground, and to try to defeat them by using forms of argument which should (in his view) satisfy them.

We have seen how powerful many of his counter-arguments are, and how difficult Averroes finds it on occasion to defend his philosophical predecessors (especially Avicenna), thus forcing Averroes to try to establish the coherence of basic Aristotelian premises. The arguments which relate to the incompatibility between the philosophers' conclusions and the principles of Islam are especially well directed by al-Ghazālī. Yet the *falāsifa* could, and did, argue that all they are concerned with is demonstrative reasoning, reasoning which cannot establish religious truths. It may well be that their description of the relationship between God and the world is far less detailed than the description offered by the Qur'ān and that their account of God's knowledge of particulars and the nature of survival after death is far thinner than that found in Islam. It is not the task of the philosopher to derive theological and ethical conclusions from his demonstrative reasoning. Religion must follow philosophy and present the latter's conclusions in ways that will be acceptable to the mass of the public.

Al-Ghazālī's attempt to breathe more life into the notion of God than is implicit in the arguments of the *falāsifa* can thus be quite neatly sidestepped. The *falāsifa* could argue that his criticisms of their impoverished notion of God are inappropriate philosophically. Such criticisms should really be applied to arguments which are theological and which relate to religious faith, not to logically valid reasoning which works with certain premises.

In the second part we shall see how al-Ghazālī extended his attack to take account of theories of ethics which seemed to him to make similar errors in the field of practical reasoning to those which the *falāsifa* made in the area of theoretical reasoning. We shall see also how the philosophers developed a model of the relationship between philosophy and religion which attempts to obviate the sorts of criticism which al-Ghazālī makes of the apparently impious conclusions of philosophy.

PART II

Reason v. revelation in practical reasoning

CHAPTER 4

Are the ethics of religion objective or subjective?

It is difficult to overemphasize the significance of legal discussions in the origination of controversies concerning the nature of ethics in Islam. The traditional view of the divine law held that legal judgments must be based upon nothing but the law, and if necessary derived indirectly from that law by some approved technique such as analogy, often interpreted in rather a restricted sense. The more innovatory position of those who adhered to opinion (*ra'y*) argued that in cases where the law provides no obvious guidance one must use one's own rational judgments alone in arriving at conclusions to disputes in law and ethics. This basic conflict was played out in many different contexts, with the 'rationalists' insisting that we can know much of what is right and obligatory by independent reasoning, while the 'traditionalists' acknowledged only revelation as an appropriate source for such knowledge. A great deal of the Muslim establishment – Shāfi'ī, ibn Ḥanbal, al-Ash'arī and a large number of other theologians and jurists – lined up firmly on the side of tradition, believing basically that any other position would deny God's power, for, if we could judge independently of God what is right and wrong, could we not from an independent point of view judge God's actions and assess his moral pronouncements to us? Could we not do away with trying to follow God's instructions since all we need to do is to follow the instructions of our reason?

Quite apart from these theologically dangerous consequences, the 'traditionalists' argued that the results of using independent reason are unsatisfactory since they contradict each other and are incapable of providing the certainty of revelation, or, indeed, even the certainty of reason. The 'traditionalists' did not always differentiate clearly between two distinct 'rationalist' positions, one fairly extreme in that it argued that independent reason is all that is required for the right to be known, the other milder and only claiming that independent reason is required in some cases, scripture in others, and so there is no incompatibility between them. It seems that sometimes they attacked the latter position more fervently than the former since it could be regarded as rather insidiously masking its faith in reason by pretending to believe in the use of both faith and reason as routes to the truth.

This controversy in Islam has been extensively discussed in the works of George Hourani, who fairly consistently takes a critical view of the 'traditionalist' position, and it will be useful to examine his critique first. The 'traditionalists' could be labelled 'ethical voluntarists' because they believed that ethical norms mean *only* what is approved or disapproved, commanded or forbidden by God.[1] The rationale for such an interpretation of ethical terms in the Qur'ān is provided by the stress in many of the suras on God's power. If, the argument might go, God's ordinances comply with already existing objective values then he would be subject to such norms himself, thereby limiting his omnipotence. The analogy between this view and objections to the idea that the universe is eternal should be obvious. As we saw in the first chapter, some Muslims objected to Aristotelian and Platonic conceptions of the universe not being created *ex nihilo* because this would imply that God was subject in his dealings with the universe to following certain previously established principles of natural behaviour. The idea that ethical rules are similarly independent of God is unpalatable to some thinkers.

Perhaps the best starting point for this discussion, as with that of the preceding chapters, is the Qur'ān. Does the Qur'ān discuss ethical terms in such a way that ethical voluntarism is the only feasible interpretation of their meaning? Hourani argues that it does not, and it is by examining his argument (and using his translations) that we shall introduce this discussion and broaden it later to consider the relationship between reason and revelation in Islamic philosophy.

Hourani begins by examining texts which, on the surface, appear difficult to interpret on voluntarist principles. There are texts which refer to ethics and interpersonal human relations. For example, 'The way [of force] is to be taken only against those who do wrong to the people' (XL,42). There are also references to self-inflicted harm as in 'Whoever does that harms himself' (II,231). Hourani argues that the passive use of 'wrong' is even more difficult to analyze on the voluntarist theory, as in 'Except those who believe and do good deeds and mention God often, and overcome after they have been wronged' (XXVI,227). He argues that these sentences could not be interpreted in terms of obedience or

---

[1] G. Hourani, 'Ethical presuppositions of the Qur'ān', *Muslim World*, LXX, 1 (1980), pp. 1–28.

disobedience to divine commands, and concludes that this suggests that the voluntarist thesis is mistaken. For example, in XL,42 we would get 'The way [of force] is to be taken only against those who disobey God in regard to the people', and in XXVI,227 the second conjunction would have to be 'and overcome after they have been affected by an act of disobedience to God'. There are in addition plenty of references in the Qur'ān and classical Arabic to harm and wrong which are unconnected with moral senses of wrongdoing, and the ethical senses of these expressions seem to have arisen from a more descriptive and objective meaning.

A good example of this development of a non-moral into a moral term is provided by *'adl* or justice, the opposite of *zulm* or harm just considered. For example, in the moral use of justice in 'If it [one of two quarrelling parties] yields, set things right between them with justice' (XLIX,9), justice is nothing more than a relation between two persons without any reference to the commands of any third party. Where there is a reference to God's commands, the voluntarist position would result in boringly truistic propositions. The verse 'God commands justice, beneficence, and giving to relatives, and he forbids shameful and blameworthy acts and insolence' (XVI,90) would be analyzed in terms of 'God commands what he commands, and forbids what he forbids'. Hourani points out that the term for justice has emerged in Arabic from the notion of equality and the balanced distribution of weights such as loads on animals. He concludes that the term for justice originally described a tangible and physical notion of even balance and was developed into a moral concept of balance and natural justice. He contrasts his account with that of the eminent jurist al-Shāfi'ī (d. 204/819), 'Justice is that one should act in obedience to God',[2] and suggests that the Shāfi'ite use has no relevance to the Qur'ān. The same sort of approach can be made to the terms for good and evil, *ḥasan* and *sū'*. There are contexts in which *ḥasan* means 'satisfactory' or 'beneficial' and cannot easily be interpreted as 'commanded' or 'permitted'. Hourani wonders how the voluntarists could cope with a verse like,

And it is said to those who fear God 'What has your lord sent down?' They say 'Good. For those who have done good in this world there is a good [reward], and certainly the house of the afterlife will be better and pleasant will be the house of the godfearing.' (XVI,30)

In this context it is difficult to see how 'doing good' when applied to actions can mean 'obeyed the *sharī'a*' (i.e. Islamic law), and there is some

---

[2] Al-Shāfi'ī, *Risāla* (Treatise), ed. M. Shakir (Cairo, 1940), p. 25.

evidence that this particular Arabic term has as its basic meaning an aesthetic rather than ethical sense.

Particular problems arise in applying ethical predicates to God on the voluntarist view. Take for example, 'that he may justly reward those who believe and do good deeds' (X,4), 'God is not a wrongdoer to his servants' (VIII,51) and even the famous 'In the name of God, the merciful, the compassionate' (I,I). There seems to be considerable difficulty in seeing how a voluntarist could make sense of these verses. Hourani identifies the voluntarist position as holding that ethical terms when applied to behaviour and character never have any objective meaning but only refer to divine commands or prohibitions, and compliance or non-compliance with them. All their opponents have to show is that there are *some* uses of ethical terms which purport to be objective and independent of divine fiat. Now, it is possible to argue that Hourani goes too far here in his attack on voluntarism. The voluntarists may accept quite happily all that Hourani and the lexicographers have to say concerning the non-ethical origins of the ethical terms used in the Qur'ān, and yet still insist that when such terms are used morally they maintain an essential link with the notion of divine command. When a moral standard is set by God, then it is reasonable to expect God to adhere to it, so references to God as possessing moral attributes are not especially problematic.

For example, Hourani argues that the voluntarists would have terrible difficulty in making sense of these two verses, which deny that anyone is wronged by God, 'To each one there will be degrees [of recompense] depending on what they have done, so that he may pay them in full for their deeds and they shall not be wronged' (XLVI,19) and 'Whatever you spend on the path of God will be restored to you, and you will not be wronged' (VIII,60). Hourani notes: 'Both grammatically and theologically, fantastic contortions would have to be performed to interpret such sentences in terms of disobedience to God's commands, and the resulting equivalent sentences would be so absurd that they are better left unmentioned.'[3] But why? It would certainly be clumsy to replace the ethical terms with expressions involving God, but most analyses of sentences into another discourse are clumsy and grammatically unappealing. A voluntarist could claim that what is meant by 'wrong' when we use the expression of ourselves or when the Qur'ān uses it is quite simply what God defines as wrong, and accordingly it is behaviour which he forbids, informing us of this fact through the teachings of Islam. Saying

3 Hourani 'Ethical presuppositions', p. 15.

that God does not do wrong is to claim that there is a type of behaviour which God has defined as not to be performed, and he accordingly does not perform it.

Exactly the same move may be made with the other ethical terms we have considered. Arguments which suggest that particular applications of 'good' and 'justice' are used to relate aspects of the conduct of human beings and have nothing to do with God just beg the question. Of course, Hourani is perfectly justified in arguing that many such applications of these terms do not appear to relate to God in any way, but the voluntarist would not want to stay at this superficial level. He would point to the necessity for analysis in order to understand what the ethical terms in the Qur'ān really mean. It is certainly true that there are examples of terms which can be used ethically being used also in non-ethical contexts, perhaps in aesthetic (*ḥasan*) or in physically descriptive (*'adl*) contexts. In such contexts, there is no necessity to look for a reference to God's commands. The voluntarist would insist, though, that when those terms are used as *ethical* terms, they must import some implicit reference to God's commands. There may indeed be strong arguments against such a view, but they are not to be found in the Qur'ān.

The Qur'ān places much emphasis upon the dependence of all human beings on divine guidance, incorporated in religious authorities, for moral knowledge to be possible. The theme of confused and errant individuals being guided by the book runs throughout the Qur'ān. When appropriate guidance appears, the Muslim is obliged to surrender his personal opinions to that guidance, as in 'Say "God's guidance is the true guidance, and we are commanded to surrender to the lord of the worlds"' (VI,71) and 'It is not for any believer, man or woman, when God and his Messenger have decreed a matter, to have the choice in the affair. Whosoever disobeys God and his Messenger has gone astray into manifest error' (XXXIII,36). The connection which is said to exist between a system of beliefs and their clear formulation in a book is an important one, namely, 'What is the matter with the way you make decisions? Do you have a Book in which you study?' (LXVIII,36–7). It would only be fair to punish people after the appropriate revelations and formulation of the revelations in a text. 'We never punish until we have sent a Messenger' (XVII,15) and 'Truly God was gracious to the believers when he raised up among them a Messenger from themselves, to recite to them his signs and to purify them, and to teach them the Book and the wisdom, though before they were in manifest error' (III,164). A frequent alternative to accepting the revelation offered in the Qur'ān and being guided by it is to be misled by one's passions, e.g. 'Then we set you on a path of command, so follow it and do not follow the passions of those who do not know' (XLV,18).

The general tenor of these and many other Qur'ānic verses is that the Book itself is taken to provide the exclusive guide to moral and of course religious knowledge for human beings. Indeed, the only alternative to following this path is to succumb to one's passions, hardly a very tempting moral alternative. But is it as simple as this? Does the Qur'ān rule out explicitly the possibility that we might be able to know how to behave rightly by using nothing to guide us except our reason? It should be emphasized yet again that the Qur'ān is not a philosophical work and should not be expected to make explicit statements on this sort of topic. Yet there are respectful references in the Book to people who are intelligent and thoughtful in the appropriate interpretation of the signs (*āyāt*) of God in the world which permit an inference concerning his caring attitude for human creatures. The Qur'ān itself frequently declares its respect for the human intellect and urges us to use that great gift of God to its fullest capacity. The implication is that some facility in reasoning proves useful to the Muslim when deciding how to interpret scripture to find out how to deal with a moral issue. There are, though, a number of passages which include interesting references to pagans who are described as morally evil even though they could not have known, through the Qur'ān, how to behave morally in the first place. For instance, there is ' "What has pushed you into Saqar?" They say "We were not of those who prayed, and we did not feed the needy" ' (LXXIV,42–4), and also: 'Have we not given him two eyes and a tongue and two lips, and guided him on the two paths? Yet he has not attacked the steep path, and what makes you understand what is the steep path? It is freeing a slave or giving food on a day of hunger to an orphan relative or a needy man in misery' (XC,8–16).

It would seem from these two passages that there are at least *some* duties which anyone, believer or not, is morally obliged to perform. And, if that is the case, then it must be possible to know that there are such duties without scripture. But these passages do not establish that view at all firmly. In LXXIV,42–4 there is a conjunction between feeding the needy and praying, which could well suggest that they go together. Again, in XC,8–16 the sense could be that the various duties mentioned are indeed duties but, without scriptural backing and Islamic motivation, they can only be carried out haphazardly and without any clear direction. They could also be regarded as just prudential rules, or socially desirable norms relevant for *any* community. A large proportion of the Qur'ān consists not just in arguing for the performance of particular kinds of acts but also the cultivation of virtues, or the acquisition of dispositions to carry out such acts. Without scriptural direction, the suggestion appears to be, it might well be possible to carry out particular acts but difficult if not impossible to ensure that the appropriate traits to act in morally righteous ways would be developed in people. So the Qur'ān has yet to admit that there are truths which are both moral and knowable independently of the Book, where 'knowable' means 'knowable as moral truths'.

For the anti-voluntarist, there are more hopeful references to reason in the account of God's reasons for making human beings rather than the angels his deputies (*khalīfa*) on earth (II,28–30). Human beings are capable of knowing the names of things or the essential nature of reality, so that, when God appoints us to govern the earth, he can be confident that we will use our reason to make good use of the gift. There is certainly nothing in Islam which would give support for the decrying of reason; indeed, it is regarded as the means to attain happiness in this world and the next. According to al-Ghazālī, a staunch defender of the voluntarist thesis, even 'Turks, Kurds and the rough Bedouin', whose existence is barely superior to that of animals, know by instinct that they ought to honour the old as a result of their experience and the application of reason.[4] Does it follow, then, that they are capable of discovering their duty without the aid of religion? This is very far from al-Ghazālī's intention. It is always open to him to argue like Juwaynī (d. 478/1085) that those people without the benefit of the Qur'ān who follow some sound ethical principles nonetheless base their practices on moral ignorance rather than knowledge. For example, the Brahmins think it wrong to slaughter animals, which in Muslim law is perfectly acceptable. Some of their other customs are in accord with Islam, yet not all their moral judgments are valid, and indeed perhaps the basis of *all* their moral reasoning is inappropriate. Doing the right thing for the wrong reason may be to strip the action of all its morally commendable features, since it could then be regarded as merely a chance occurrence. Any analysis of someone's ethical system which represents it as a hit-and-miss affair because it is not based firmly on some valid principle or theory is in effect a criticism of that system as a *moral* system.

In fact, al-Ghazālī distinguished between four uses of reason (*'aql*). Firstly, it is the quality that distinguishes us from animals and makes

---

[4] Al-Ghazālī, *Ihyā'*, ed. 'Irāqī, I, p. 83.

possible the development of the theoretical sciences, for which he had great respect. Secondly, it enables us as children to build up a repertoire of necessary truths such as mathematical equivalences. More unusually, reason is also identified with the knowledge which experience produces; and, lastly it is identified with continence and efficiency in carrying out one's practical ends.[5] The connection between reason and morally right conduct is interesting in this context. The traditional distinction is between the *'aqlīyāt*, or kinds of knowledge that are accessible to us through reason alone and demonstration, and the *sam'īyāt* or *al-'ulūm ash-sharī'a wadīnīya*, legal and religious knowledge established through revelation and so not demonstrative in nature. The contrast between these two different types of knowledge will be examined in some depth in both this chapter and chapter 5.

It is evident that al-Ghazālī accepts that at least some ethical rules fall into the realm of rational knowledge, since they could well express rational rules about how people should live together, and so on. There could be a danger in such a position, though, if it slips over into the thesis that even directly religious rules must have some intrinsically rational explanation. For example ibn Miskawayh (d. *c.* 421/1030) relates the Islamic rule that believers should perform the five daily prayers together and not in private to the desirability of stimulating and incorporating the natural human tendency to be companionable. The Friday service which brings together people from different ends of the city, the two main festivals which unite the city with the countryside and the pilgrimage (*haj*) to Mecca which brings together Muslims from all over the world, all are evidences of the purpose of the rules being the uniting of diverse believers. This sort of approach is roundly condemned by al-Ghazālī, who is adamant in upholding the importance of obedience to commands just because they are commands, not because they are rational. He argues that the *haj* to Mecca is quite the reverse from the actualization of a rational decision in ibn Miskawayh's sense, and includes practices which we would not have arrived at by ourselves and which we do not really want to perform. By having the obligation to perform such actions foisted on us, we are better able to acquire the correct attitude of powerlessness and servitude to God. Of course, some rules have rational features, such as the tax for the poor and fasting to help control the emotions. But other rules such as stoning the devils at Mina cannot be justified in this sort of way – these are rituals carried out solely in response to a

5 *Ibid.*, I, pp. 84–5.

command and as part of a policy to subdue our wills to that of the deity.

Al-Ghazālī was concerned to establish the compatibility of mysticism and exact observance of the ritual laws. Although he was sympathetic to aspects of Ṣūfism, he disapproved of that movement's rather cavalier attitude to the observance of the religious commandments. While it is true that virtue is only a necessary condition for the supreme degree of knowledge and love of God that represents true happiness and the end of man, nonetheless the development of moral perfection is essential if we are to be successful in attaining this end. The commandments help, guide and support the struggle to overcome base impulses and to purify our hearts to do God's will. As al-Ghazālī puts it, 'God has wisely made the salvation of mortal beings dependent on their actions and not on their natural feelings, and has put religious law in charge of them.'[6] The exact compliance with the law is upheld by him as vital to the development of morally valid modes of behaviour, and any questioning of the law, whether to defend it in terms of non-religious explanations or to challenge and criticize it, is regarded as objectionable.

Now, it is interesting that, in spite of his scepticism about the value of philosophy and the anti-voluntarist approach which most of the Greek philosophers taught, his comments on the philosophical attitude to ethics should be so mild, especially when compared with his comments on philosophical doctrines with respect to creation, immortality and God's knowledge:

All they have to say about the moral sciences comes down to listing the qualities and habits of the soul, and recording their generic and specific kinds, and the way to cultivate the good ones and combat the bad. This they simply took over from the sayings of the Ṣūfīs ... In the course of their spiritual combat the good habits of the soul and its shortcomings had been disclosed to them and also the defects that vitiate its actions. All this they set forth plainly. Then the philosophers took over these ideas and mixed them with their own doctrines, using the lustre afforded by them to promote the circulation of their own false teaching.[7]

He claims, though, that their remarks on ethics are dangerous, both for those who accept them and for those who reject them. The latter might well be led to reject at the same time the prophetic, Qur'ānic and Ṣūfī aspects of their doctrines, and this would be a great loss. The

[6] *Ibid.*, 1, p. 85.
[7] Al-Ghazālī, *Munqidh*, trans. R. McCarthy, p. 77.

former might accept the philosophical doctrines along with the religious truths, and thus be spiritually damaged. Yet, it is still true to say that al-Ghazālī objects to the philosophical doctrines concerning ethics far less strenuously than those which deal with metaphysical issues.

In some ways this is surprising given the fact that it is for exactly the same reasons, namely, the implication of limitations on God's power, that al-Ghazālī argues against eternal creation and objective ethics. The very notion of God being compelled to behave in a certain way is repugnant to al-Ghazālī. Some theologians argued that, given the sorts of creatures God created, he is morally obliged to provide a revelation that sets out specific instructions and rewards designed to apply to the natures of the creatures on which they are imposed. The imposition of this obligation is not really something that God can do anything about, he is morally obliged to impose it given his nature, the nature of the creatures in the world, and the world itself. Al-Ghazālī objected to the idea of God being confronted with notions of human good and evil which had the status of an extrinsic and independent law. To argue against the notion of the objectivity of ethics, then, al-Ghazālī presents a detailed defence of how specifically religious references can be incorporated into the meanings of ethical terms. He does this by interpreting the key ethical concepts of good and evil (*ḥasan* and *sū'* or *qabīḥ*) teleologically, i.e. in terms of what is appropriate to a certain end and what prevents the attainment of that end. These ends are entirely relative to the agent, in which case an adulterer will think that adultery is good and anything which prevents him from an adulterous lifestyle as bad. Ethical voluntarists would not be happy with this approach since it seems to ignore that dimension of human behaviour which involves people doing things just because they are right, even though they have no advantage to themselves. For example, people sometimes care for others when they have no hope or prospect of reward. Some unbelievers will steadfastly refuse to break their word even though they are threatened with considerable punishment. We might say that they act as they do because those are the right things to do. Some people will risk death in order to avoid committing evil actions even though they have no hope of future recompense in an afterlife. Al-Ghazālī has to put forward a variety of different motives to explain this sort of behaviour. Some people are so desirous of praise for their honesty that the prospect of death is overshadowed by the idea of the praise! Or he suggests that they rigidly adhere to an association of ideas whereby breaking one's word is normally followed by unpleasant consequences.

It may be also that some people feel a natural sympathy for others and help them for that reason. It is possible to doubt the motives of those who act in apparently virtuous ways for no particular end.

Now, these arguments might seem truly extraordinary. What religious person, after all, would defend in this way the idea that an act is good when it promotes our ends and bad when it does the reverse? Yet al-Ghazālī does manage to adapt this seemingly unpromising position into quite a persuasive theory. One of his purposes in setting up such a doctrine is to make it easier to argue that God has no ends. Since God is far too exalted and superior to his creation to have needs, it would be misleading to call any of his actions good in the normal sense. He did indeed create the world with the purpose of revealing his power and will, but he does not benefit from that creation. It is also totally inappropriate to think of God committing any evil actions; he cannot do wrong since doing wrong is a matter of dealing unjustly with the property of others, and since everything in existence is his property anyway, no one has a claim on anything he affects by his actions. Thus he argues that God's actions are not necessary in any way but merely possible – he could have done otherwise. Al-Ghazālī sums up his view in this way:

Our position is that it is possible for God not to demand that his servants take on obligations, and to demand of them unattainable obligations, to cause them pain without compensating them subsequently . . . it is not necessary for him to take any interest in their welfare nor to reward their patience or punish their disobedience . . . he does not have to send prophets, and if he does not then that does not show he is evil.[8]

His first claim is an attempt at challenging the Mu'tazilites' arguments that God is obliged to impose obligations on his servants since he at the same time confers benefits on those servants. Al-Ghazālī objects that God need not have created any creatures at all, and his creation of such creatures was not an attempt at avoiding harm or benefiting himself. He could easily not have created at all. There is no inconsistency in thinking of God as not creating the world, provided that we avoid the philosophical doctrine that God has eternal knowledge and an eternal desire to create, in which case he has no alternative but to create. Al-Ghazālī makes the shrewd point that it is not at all obvious how being put under obligation to God constitutes a benefit to his creatures. Of course, the Mu'tazilites' claim that if we are put under such obligation then we can have the satisfaction of earning our eventual reward, but this seems rather small

---

[8] Al-Ghazālī, *Iqtiṣād*, ed. I. Çubukçu and H. Atay, p. 160.

beer compared with the prospect of God presenting us with entirely
gratuitous benefits without any accompanying burdens (in the form of
obligations) at all. Besides, 'Some . . . have advanced the argument that
there will be compensation in the afterlife for . . . [undeserved] suffering.
These people fail to realise how evil a king's act of slapping a weak person
as a condition for giving him a loaf of bread is, if he could have given
him the loaf without the slapping.'[9] And God, surely, is precisely in the
position of a king who has unlimited power.

Al-Ghazālī reproduces a famous argument in Islamic theology to
'show decisively that God Most High is not bound, in the qualities of
His perfection, to consult the advantage of his creatures'. The argument
goes thus:

> We suppose three children one of whom died as an infant, and one attained
> puberty as a Muslim, and the other reached maturity and embraced unbelief,
> then died. Then God requires each according to his merits, and He will execute
> justice, So He will lodge the one who matured and embraced unbelief in the
> depths of hell, and the one who matured and embraced Islam in the ranks
> of the blessed, and the one who died an infant without embracing Islam and
> sustaining an act of worship after puberty in a rank inferior to that of him
> who reached maturity and embraced Islam. Then the one who died an infant
> will say: 'O Lord! Why have you put me behind my brother the Muslim who
> reached maturity and died? . . . How, then, does that befit justice? And God will
> tell him . . . that [the other] reached maturity and embraced Islam and toiled
> and endured the hardships of the acts of worship – 'So how does justice demand
> putting you and him on an equal footing?'. Then the infant will say: 'O Lord!
> You are the one who caused me to live and caused me to die. And You ought to
> have prolonged my life and caused me to reach the stage of independence and
> guided me to Islam' . . . Then God will say to him . . . 'It was to your advantage
> to cause you to die in childhood: for had you reached maturity, you would have
> embraced unbelief and deserved the Fire.' Whereupon the unbeliever who dies
> after he had reached maturity will cry out from the depths of hell and say:
> 'O Lord, You knew of me that if I reached maturity, I would embrace unbelief.
> Could You not, then, have caused me to die in my childhood? For I would be
> satisfied with the lower rank in which You have lodged the child who yearns for
> the sublime ranks.' At this point it remains for him who claims 'Wisdom' only
> to stop replying and venturing.[10]

Al-Ghazālī intends this argument to show that it is a mistake to ask
whether God's actions are just, and indeed his argument could be taken

9 Al-Ghazālī, *Miʿyār*, ed. Dunya, p. 194. This passage is translated in M. Marmura, 'Al-Ghazālī on
    ethical premisses', *Philosophical Forum*, 1 (1969), pp. 393–403.
10 Al-Ghazālī, *Fadā'ih al-bāṭiniyya* (The infamies of the Batinites), 222–3, in R. McCarthy, *Freedom
    and fulfillment*, pp. 241–2.

by a critic of religion as an admission of the impossibility of reconciling an omnipotent and omniscient deity with a modest conception of justice. The trump card which al-Ghazālī has in his possession, though, is the fact that he thinks there is no point in trying to show that God's decisions are just, since the notion of justice is logically inappropriate as an attribute of divine action. In that case there are no problems involved in the claim that God can impose obligations which are impossible to fulfil. Since the nature of God's transmission of commands to his creatures is similar to an officer addressing an intelligent subordinate, there is no contradiction between ordering the impossible and the order being obligatory on the subordinate. Such an order could not be described as evil, since only acts with personal ends can be called evil, and God has no such ends. He is free to do with his human possessions what he likes. This thesis does at least have the virtue of accounting for the recorded instances of impossible obligation in Islam, like the obligation to become a believer even when God knew that the person would not and could not become one. In addition, although it is obvious from even a casual glance at the world that God does make entirely innocent people suffer without any compensating reward in this life, this does not offend the bounds of justice since he is only playing with his own toys, over which no one else has any claim. There is, then, no objective notion of justice which stands over God and which determines how he is to behave towards his creation.

It is hardly surprising, given al-Ghazālī's strong anti-Muʿtazilite position, that he denied that independent reason is sufficient guide to ethical knowledge. One of the interesting aspects of his hostility to the philosophical and the Muʿtazilite theories of ethics is his attack on their theory of natural connection which lies behind their theories of teleology. The entire mechanism of ends and means, of virtuous acts leading to rewards in this and the next life, is based upon notions of causality which fail to mention God's overwhelming power and influence over all these happenings, and so must be rejected. We saw in chapter 1 how al-Ghazālī attacked the philosophical position on natural causation. Yet it is worth recalling that a problem with identifying his disapproval of philosophical ethics with his attitude to philosophical accounts of causality is that, of course al-Ghazālī did not doubt that science could establish reliable and certain generalizations, nor that we could discover by intelligently examining nature in a scientific manner, constant relations between phenomena. His objections were to accounts of these relations which made mention of God's influence over them nugatory.

Yet, while al-Ghazālī argued that reason is not always a reliable guide to understanding how we should develop appropriate ethical and religious knowledge, it does not follow that reason has no part to play. Reason is important in understanding how the natural world works, where, as we have seen, he accepted the analysis of natural connection offered by Avicenna, albeit radically reinterpreted. His mentor, al-Ashʿarī, stressed the rationality involved in becoming convinced of the truth of Islam. He claimed that the Prophet observed the variety of beliefs and faiths and 'showed them what they did not understand with conclusive proofs of God and his direct explanation, and he proved the validity of his position with demonstrations of God and his signs so that there was no room for any other argument or for any attempt to refute his argument'.[11] But how are we to become persuaded of the validity of the message provided by Islam? It cannot just be a matter of suddenly knowing by some sort of intuition, since all sorts of highly dubious propositions are suddenly 'known to be true' in this way. Al-Ashʿarī suggested that people are led gradually to recognize the authority of the teaching of Islam. There is a rational order of the progress of faith which starts with the acknowledgement of the contingency of the world and its creatures, moves to the impotence of the world with respect to God, the true prophethood of Muhammad and the consequent veracity of his message. In this model the veracity of the Prophet and the validity of his claims and authority are established by signs and miracles which *follow* the conclusive arguments and demonstrations of the first two stages. And, indeed, this seems reasonable, since the whole point of the miracle is to emphasize our contingency and dependence upon an omnipotent God.

We saw, in chapter 1, that miracles are regarded by Islam as very much part of a package of proofs and signs rather than the decisive factor themselves in stimulating belief. Miracles are rational devices provided within the context of prior theoretical rational understanding. So an unbeliever is obliged to become a believer when 'the Prophet has produced a clear proof... and it can be grasped through their natural intellect which was provided as a means of understanding'.[12] The arguments put forward by the Prophet are the best possible arguments which reason can assemble, from which al-Ashʿarī draws the conclusion that people who wish to develop and employ their reason would be well advised to

---

[11] Al-Ashʿarī, *Risāla ila ahl at-tajr bi-Bāb al-abwāb* (Letter to the people of the frontier) (Ankara, Ilahiyat Fakültesi Mecmuasi 8, 1928), pp. 80–108; p. 86.
[12] *Ibid.*, p. 101.

restrict themselves to just those arguments and no other. Interestingly, some Mu'tazilites defend the view that the obligation to know God arises not from knowledge of the contingency of the world but rather from human nature – it is just one of those ideas of which one becomes more aware as one grows older, but it is really there all the time. As the Qur'ān puts it 'Is there any doubt regarding God, creator of the heavens and the earth?' (XIV,10). Muḥammad based his message on this pre-existing knowledge of God. This notion that knowledge of God is innate is sometimes used as a justification for God to punish everybody who refuses to take his revelation seriously. People are obliged to speculate about God's nature and to ask after his rules because we are supposed to know about his existence from the beginning.[13] Before discussing in more detail the nature of the dispute over ethical behaviour between the Ash'arites and the Mu'tazilites it is worth pointing out that there is no justification for thinking that the latter hold reason in greater respect than the former. Indeed, as we have just seen, it might be claimed that precisely the reverse is the case, in that the Ash'arites, as opposed to the Mu'tazilites, more readily admit reason's relevance to the very basis of faith.

In opposition to ethical voluntarism, the Mu'tazilites developed a deontological theory of ethics which identifies the key ethical terms obligatory, good and evil (*wājib, ḥasan* and *qabīḥ*) as 'that for the omission of which the agent deserves blame', 'that for doing which the agent deserves praise/blame'. The consequences of the action do not always enter into the decision as to the moral descriptions appropriate to it; rational people just are in a position to judge accurately on the moral standing of particular actions. What is axiomatic in their system is that human beings can become aware of at least some of their obligations, and the difference between good and evil actions, through the independent use of reason. This has the same force for them as the way in which it is possible for human beings to describe accurately the natural qualities of the objects in the world regardless of their religion or divine guidance.

The claim that there are such general rational rules of ethical conduct is challenged by al-Ghazālī in a number of ways. A rather unsatisfactory argument is to select a putative universal rule and then point to cases where it can quite easily be seen that that rule should not be applied. For example, telling the truth is doubtless held to be universally valid, yet we would all accept counter-examples to it, where perhaps it would

---

[13] E.g. Abū-l-Hudhayl discussed by J. van Ess. 'Early Islamic theologians on the existence of God', in K. Semaan (ed.), *Islam and the medieval West* (Albany, State University of New York Press, 1980), pp. 64–81.

be better not to tell the truth. This sort of objection just ignores the elaborate descriptions by the Mu'tazilites of different kinds of universal ethical truths and the requirement to qualify them in some way in case they are rigidly applied regardless of the consequences. A stronger argument is based on a theme of Avicenna's, where both philosophers distinguish between the undeniability of necessary truths and of the so-called universal moral truths. Al-Ghazālī comments

> that if we want to understand the difference between what we generally accept to be true and what cannot be anything else but true, we should take some basic moral norm such as 'killing a human being is evil and saving him from death is good'. If we imagine ourselves just coming into existence, and being a part of no community and having no prior knowledge of how human beings live, it would be possible to doubt that norm, or even deny it is true. Yet this would not be true of statements like 'two is greater than one' or 'a statement cannot be both true and false'.[14]

This example is not perhaps very appropriate, since it might well be argued that a person in the position described here would not be able to make any judgment at all about such a moral rule, since he would be totally abstracted from any community which provides the appropriate context for ethical life. Such a person would not be in a good position to comment on the moral rule's universality and necessity, since he might not even be able to grasp what a moral rule *meant*. But the general tenor of the argument is valid, namely, that there is an important distinction between necessary truths of logic and mathematics and the sorts of 'truths' which constitute ethics.

Al-Ghazālī points out that if one accepts his interpretation of 'obligatory' as 'necessary to produce benefits', then the Mu'tazilites have a big problem in showing that their list of necessary moral truths is acceptable. For instance, he argues that

> There is no rational requirement that we are grateful to a benefactor, despite what the Mu'tazilites say . . . If gratitude is rational then it must involve some beneficial consequence or otherwise. If it has no beneficial consequences then it could not be rational, since it would be without any point. If it does have a beneficial end, it must either be for the One who is served [i.e. God] or the servant [i.e. us]. It cannot be for [the former] since he is above being benefited and is too holy to have ends. The welfare of the servant applies either to this world or the next. There seems to be no benefit in this world, since he is worn out by study and contemplation, knowledge and gratitude, and these affect his desires and reduce his pleasures. But there is no

---

[14] Al-Ghazālī, *Mi'yār*, ed. S. Dunya, p. 197.

benefit in the next world, any reward there is provided as a favour from God.[15]

As we saw when al-Ghazālī was arguing with the philosophers over the creation of the world, he tends to present his preferred definitions of the key terms and to show how inconsistent they are with opposing views, which is hardly a surprising discovery. Yet at the same time al-Ghazālī is offering examples of his interpretations of such terms to try to persuade others that those interpretations are preferable to the alternatives. In this case, he rejects the idea that from our knowledge of the nature of God we can derive certain principles which would govern his behaviour towards his creatures. Al-Ghazālī's form of theological reductionism does at least have the virtue of clearly specifying how to determine which sorts of moral rules are incumbent upon us, and these are those which 'God has made necessary and ordered with the sanction of punishment if they are omitted, for if there is no revelation, what does "necessary" mean?'[16]

Al-Ghazālī uses his theory to try to skate neatly around what the Muʿtazilites must have thought of as one of their most powerful arguments. This is the argument that there must be at least one duty apprehensible by reason before revelation and this is the duty to verify the genuineness of the Prophet through an understanding of his miracles. Without such an attempt it is not possible to accept the genuineness of the Qur'ān and the moral rules which follow from that acceptance. To argue that one's obligation to accept the Qur'ān and its consequent obligations are all derivable from the Book itself is to indulge in circularity. Al-Ghazālī suggests that if this is indeed a circular argument then it will serve to discredit the argument which has reason as the necessitating motive, for with reference to evidence, 'If one does not examine it rationally, one does not understand the rational need to examine it rationally, and if one does not understand the need to examine it rationally, then one will not examine it rationally.'[17] Given the vast benefits which potentially lie in adhering to the edicts of the Qur'ān, a person would be foolish were he to hear about such benefits and fail to investigate their source in scripture. This investigation would soon come up against the first requirement to see whether the Prophet's miracles are a proof of his divine mission and salvifical purpose. Al-Ghazālī compares someone who requires the discovery of a necessary reason to examine the genuineness of

---

[15] Al-Ghazāli, *al-Mustaṣfā min ʿilm al-uṣūl* (Cairo, 1937), I, p. 39. This book deals with the theory of the sources and methods of knowledge fo rules in jurisprudence.
[16] *Ibid.* = *Ihyāʾ*, I, ed. ʿIrāqī, p. 113.
[17] Al-Ghazālī, *Mustaṣfā*, I, p. 40.

the Prophet with a person who is told of a lion behind him and replies that he will not look around until his informant convinces him of his veracity. His point is that it is hardly prudent to doubt the informant in such a case, where the penalty for being wrong is so great and the cost of the informant being mistaken is so slight. God has sent a prophet to guide us, miracles to establish his authority and our reasoning faculties are sufficient to comprehend the significance of the message and the miracles.

Al-Ghazālī's argument that we can use our reason to perceive the nature and persuasiveness of the miracles and the Prophet seems to come close to the basic Mu'tazilite position. Indeed, they claim that one of the universal moral principles apprehended by all rational people is that one ought to avoid what is harmful to oneself and to seek what is of benefit to oneself. Yet, as the Ash'arites point out, 'it may happen that you will hate a thing which is better for you; and it may happen that you will love a thing which is worse for you; God knows and you know not' (II,212). As al-Ghazālī puts it, directly quoting Avicenna, 'But the true often is other than the praisewothy and the false is other than the repulsive. For many a repulsive thing is true and many a praiseworthy thing is false.'[18]

According to the principles of the Mu'tazilites, we know that in our actions we deserve punishment or reward, and so we are led to wonder whether we shall be punished or rewarded after this life has finished. This is far from being a casual speculation since it concerns not only the matters of this world but in fact the sum of events throughout our existence (in whatever form) which affects us. They argue that we can by reason acquire the knowledge that there exists an omnipotent and omniscient being to whom worship is due and from whom punishment or reward stems. Now, it would have been possible for God to have created us directly in paradise so that we acted all the time in morally correct ways, but in which case we would have missed the opportunity to obtain the greater reward available to us as ordinary human beings who are capable of *deserving* and *earning* rewards. Even in our world, there might be people who only require natural reason in order to carry out all those acts which are morally obligatory and at the same time to avoid those acts which are blameworthy, but on the whole we require something more than just unaided reason to motivate us to behave properly and avoid evil. God has graciously acceded to our frailty here and sent prophets

---

[18] Al-Ghazālī, *Mi'yār*, ed. Dunya, p. 197 and a direct quote from Ibn Sīnā, *Ishārāt*, ed. Forget, p. 401. And yet al-Ghazālī also claims that 'What urges us to follow the path of salvation is nature', *Iqtiṣād*, ed. I. Çubukçu and H. Atay, p. 195.

to tell us what rewards and punishments await us in the next life and at the same time helps us to achieve the former and avoid the latter by detailing various laws and duties which strengthen our disposition to act rightly and so merit the ultimate reward.

There is an interesting distinction here between those obligations which are known and motivated by our reason alone and those obligations which are known and motivated by revelation. There is quite a difference between these two types of obligation, not just by virtue of the different routes to them but in themselves. Norms established by reason are universal while those based on revelation are particular and reveal to us in detail how we are to act if we wish to merit the ultimate reward. We can know by the use of our intelligence the broad direction in which our moral activity ought to go, but the more detailed and specific rules provided by revelation complete the picture to provide us with a practical guide to everyday actions within the framework of the entirely general rational rules. Although revelation provides us with these rules, they are readily seen to conform to the universal principles of reason and the desirability of our attaining our ultimate goal. However, it is problematic whether we could arrive at these rules just by the use of reason. We could determine just about how we should act, at least in general terms, by the use of reason alone, although our attainment of moral perfection and the spread of moral perfection over all classes of society is far less likely than would be the case were we to be provided with revelation.

As we have seen, the arch-opponent of the Mu'tazilites, al-Ash'arī, accepts that there are a number of vitally important truths concerning creation and its designer which can be known by reason alone. For example, one can come to know by reason that the world is contingent, that a certain sort of creator exists and that certain sorts of evidence demand our belief in the veracity of the Prophet's claim to present God's message. Al-Ash'arī stresses those aspects of Islam which point to the *reasonableness* of the assumption that both the Qur'ān and the Prophet's utterances have a divine source. However, we cannot stop with reason if we are to discover how we are to act, for our moral principles can only stem from God's commands and his prohibitions and our reward or punishment is based on whether we act in accordance with or in opposition to God's command. Our knowledge of good and evil and the nature of the obligatory is then only obtainable through our acceptance of revelation in which God details the precise nature of his commands and prohibitions and describes the nature of our ultimate goal and rationale for obedience to God's commands, i.e. the enjoyment of reward in the next life.

The use of reason is extremely important in this respect, and yet can only take us so far. It can take us as far as understanding the source and nature of revelation, and then the obligation to submit to divine authority for the sake of human well-being. The only point that al-Ash'arī can see in *kalām*, or speculative enquiry into the basic principles of religion by a believer, is to reinforce the faith of fellow believers by setting out before them the appropriate methods of attaining the truths, and to refute non-believers or innovators in their erroneous views. In no sense is such reasoning intended to replace the Qur'ān and the Sunna. These both contain in perfect and clear form an account of the source and nature of the revealed law, and they show how the law itself demands affirmation of truths concerning God and his qualities, the contingency of the world and so on, along with practical knowledge of how we are to behave. In spite of this perfection there is a point to *kalām* in that it can deal with questions not obviously settled by the law, and it can reformulate Islamic doctrines in ways perhaps more appropriate for different contexts. Nonetheless, the *mutakallim* must beware of straying from the exact message of revelation in the formulation of his arguments.

The *falāsifa* extended this initial theological point to argue that we are constructed in such a way that our ultimate happiness is the attainment of a kind of perfection that transcends the ordinary circumstances of this life in 'another life' (which need not be interpreted as equivalent to the afterlife). On the whole this state of affairs can only come about in a well-regulated society based on appropriate laws which organize the community in such a way that each person will be enabled to attain this ultimate goal. The law which we obtain through revelation involves both religious regulations concerning our beliefs about God, the future life, death, and so on, and also positive laws regulating the secular and religious behaviour of the religion's adherents. The close connection between these aspects of religion and the recipes for how we are to live led the *falāsifa* such as al-Fārābī to describe a theoretical approach to religion as part of political science. After all, any political theory must embody some account of what it is that constitutes human happiness and how it is to be realized. So the nature of human beings and the world in which they live are important aspects of any account of political science. It would seem, then, that political science involves not just the study of society but also the sum of the speculative sciences, metaphysics, physics, psychology, etc.:

political science is the knowledge of things through which the inhabitants of states in communities reach happiness, each in proportion to his natural capacity. It will be shown . . . that the political group and the collective which is constructed through the combination of citizens in the cities is like the grouping of bodies in the whole of the universe, and we can see that everything which the state and nation contains has something similar to what the universe as a whole contains.[19]

The philosopher acquires knowledge of the world and of God. He sets out to construct an ideal state which resembles the world and which proceeded from God. Then he goes on to imitate God by founding such a state in time and space. Since political science is the study which illuminates the ultimate perfection and goal of all human action, and lists the conditions of the attainment of those all-important ends, it cannot be studied without at the same time (or better, at a previous time) the speculative sciences being studied.

Now, it does not follow that the study of the speculative sciences will in itself provide us with *detailed* constituents of the positive law that ought to be established in virtuous régimes, yet we could thus arrive at very *general* principles which must underpin any such particular law or norm. In fact, these specific parts of the positive law must embody highly abstract and complex metaphysical truths in such a way that they succeed in communicating with the majority of the citizens the nature of these truths without at the same time talking over their heads. The ordinary, everyday law should present these difficult notions in easily digestible form, so that all citizens have the chance to act virtuously and come to know, albeit merely partially, the nature of reality. As al-Fārābī again puts the point, insofar as people become involved in philosophy, we should insist that

the end at which one should aim in studying philosophy is knowledge of the creator . . . that he is one and unmoved, the efficient cause of everything and the director of this world through his generosity, wisdom and justice. The actions which the philosophers should follow are those which imitate the creator in so far as human beings can do this.[20]

We can, according to the *falāsifa*, use our reason by itself to determine the nature of God and his creation, the general principles of ethics and human happiness, and so on. Revelation describes these truths in a manner appropriate to a particular community, i.e. by using the appropriate conventions for that particular time and place. So the application of reason to the nature of the world comes first and revelation is seen to fit that pattern later, by showing how the general principles

---

[19] Al-Fārābī, *Philosophische Abhandlungen*, ed. F. Dieterici, p. 16.
[20] *Ibid.*, p. 49.

of virtuous life established by reason are translated into more specific terms and applied to a particular community. The lawgiver–prophet is required to devise these specific norms, since no amount of abstract thought will arrive at them, yet the framework within which he has to work is that laid down by reason alone.

The implication that this sort of approach has for the nature of the *kalām* should be evident. It is not a speculative science which seeks to establish an entirely theoretical and demonstrative understanding of the nature of God and his creation. It is not concerned with very general rules or truths, but rather with defending the dogmas established by a particular lawgiver–prophet within a certain religious and cultural context. The purpose is to strengthen faith and acceptance of the law by those who are not capable of following the justification on purely philosophical lines, and so must be content to accept a justification in terms of only the 'similitudes' (*miṭālāt*) of the demonstrative truths. Indeed, if *kalām* would only stick to its job here it would never come into conflict with philosophy. *Kalām* proper is limited to discussing rhetorically and dialectically the dogmatic principles of a particular religion, and cannot, without distortion, rise to the task of seeking to establish logically the fundamental truths which are only crudely represented in the religious principles. Unfortunately, *kalām* is sometimes overambitious and theologians argue that the principles and customs represented in positive law are equivalent to the universal truths of the philosophers, and in such cases much confusion and controversy arises. This is solely due to a category mistake, to a misunderstanding of the differing logical natures of philosophy and *kalām*.

At the beginning of his *Book of letters*, al-Fārābī states:

dialectical and sophistical powers, together with philosophy grounded on opinion, or philosophy based on sophistical thinking, should have preceded in time certain, i.e. demonstrative, philosophy. And religion, regarded as a human matter, is later in time than philosophy in general, since it is aimed at teaching the multitude theoretical and practical things which were deduced from philosophy in ways which facilitate the multitude's understanding of them, either through persuasion or representation, or through them both together. The arts of theology and jurisprudence are later in time than religion and are subordinate to it. And if the religion is subordinate to an ancient philosophy, either based on opinion, or on sophistical thinking, then the theology and the jurisprudence which are subordinate to it accord with either of them, but are below either of them.[21]

---

[21] Al-Fārābī, *Book of letters*, trans. L. Berman, 'Maimonides, the disciple of Alfarabi', *Israel Oriental Studies*, 4 (1974). pp. 154–78; pp. 156–8.

Al-Fārābī's model is of a variety of different forms of thinking following each other in time, gradually improving until they reach the level of demonstrative thought. Sophistical thinking which depends upon rules of persuading an audience to accept one's view by poetic exaggeration and literary tricks is superseded by dialectical thinking, which is capable of showing us how to move logically from one premiss to others, but is incapable of establishing the acceptability of that premiss in the first place. This final task can only be completed by demonstrative thought. Religion follows philosophy in time and fulfils the task of instructing the mass of the population in practical and theoretical truths which can be philosophically established by those capable of the activity, so that 'Religion consists of opinions and actions, determined and limited by conditions, which their ruler lays down to the group, seeking to achieve a specific goal which he has, either in them or by means of them, through their active utilization of these opinions and actions.'[22]

Following religion in time comes jurisprudence and theology. The former is required to establish the details of the law, given that the original lawgiver did not go into great depth, and thus accepts the axioms of the religion as true. The theologian defends the principles of religion against opponents and attacks opposing views in general: 'The jurisprudent accepts as given the views and actions of the founder of the religion and treats them as basic principles from which he reasons to necessary conclusions, but the theologian defends the principles which the jurisprudent treats as axioms and so not derived from other things.'[23] Al-Fārābī expresses his view of the interrelationship between these different thought processes and roles thus:

On the whole philosophy comes before religion in the way that the user of an instrument comes before the instrument in time. Dialectical and sophistical thinking comes before philosophy just as the nourishment of the tree comes before the fruit, or as the flower of the tree comes before its fruit. Religion is prior to theology and jurisprudence just like the way someone in charge of a servant comes before the servant and someone who uses an instrument precedes the instrument.[24]

The contrast between the form of presentation of moral rules in philosophy and in religion is important. Although the latter is said only to provide images or representations of the demonstrative truth, nonetheless the link between these forms of expression and the truth is supposed to

---

[22] M. Mahdi (ed.), *Alfarabi's 'Book of religion' and related texts* (Beirut, Dār al-Mashreq, 1968), p. 43.
[23] Al-Fārābī, *Enumeration*, v, pp. 75–6, in Mahdi, *'Book of religion'*.
[24] Al-Fārābī, *Book of letters*, ed. M. Mahdi, p. 132.

be a strong one: 'Every religion exists through inspiration and is blended with reason. And he who holds that it is possible that there should exist a natural religion based on reason alone must admit that this religion must be less perfect than those which spring from reason and imaginative symbolization' (*TT* 361). This is because a religion which involves inspiration or imaginative symbolization will have the capacity to appeal in appropriate language to everyone, not just the wise. In some religions the symbols employed are not up to much: 'The images which symbolize . . . differ in merit. Some are better grounded and adequate in their imagery, others are less so. Some are closer to the truth, others less close . . . If the systems of symbols differ in adequacy, then the one which is best and which has the smallest number of objectionable features, if any, should be chosen . . . and the others rejected.'[25]

Avicenna firmly agrees with al-Fārābī on this issue, arguing that religion cannot be presented without its appropriate symbolization:

> As for religious law, one general principle is important, namely that religions and their laws, produced by a prophet, seek to communicate with the masses as a whole. It is obvious that the deeper truths concerning the real unity, that there is one maker who is exalted above quantity, quality, place, time, position and change, which lead to the belief that God is one without anyone sharing his species, that he contains no parts . . . that he cannot be pointed to as existing in a particular place, it is obvious that these deeper truths cannot be passed on to the multitude. For if this had been communicated in its true form to the bedouin Arabs and the crude Hebrews, they would have immediately refused to believe and would have unanimously declared that the belief which it was proposed they accept was belief in an absolute nonentity.[26]

Averroes occasionally goes further and suggests that inspiration has an even more important function because 'The laws which it [the Qur'ān] includes on doctrine and practice are such as could not be acquired by learning but [only] by inspiration [*wahy*].'[27] As we have seen, the *falāsifa* argued that the law is closely connected with the total conditions of human happiness and the structure of the universe, so that any successful legislation must be based on knowledge of these principles. Yet how can we, with our limited capabilities and finite knowledge come to know which sort of legislation is appropriate? Fortunately 'we find all this determined in the scriptures. And all or most of this only becomes

[25] F. Rahman, *Prophecy in Islam* (London, George Allen and Unwin, 1958), p. 41.
[26] *Ibid.*, p. 42.
[27] Ibn Rushd, *Kitāb al-kashf' an manāhij al-adilla*, in M. Müller (ed.), *Philosophie und Theologie von Averroes* (Munich, 1859), p. 100.

clear through inspiration, or else its explanation through inspiration is superior [to a rational explanation alone].'[28]

In his commentary on this passage. Hourani suggests that Averroes did not really think that inspiration was the best source of knowledge about the universe, nor did he think that it was indispensable to anyone seeking to understand that universe. He hints that Averroes is merely presenting an exoteric view and that he 'could work sincerely as a *qāḍī*, because he believed in the worth of the *sharī'a* as a guide to practice for most people and most cases'.[29] This suspicion of Averroes' real views is misguided, at least in this case. Averroes' claims are quite mild, and he does not suggest unequivocally that *all* topics are best comprehended via inspiration – he qualifies his claim by saying 'all or most'. The idea that he thought that *sharī'a* had only limited worth as a guide to practice for *some* people is entirely unsupported by any evidence. It is not surprising that there are no reports of attacks on his legal judgments.

Hourani goes on to suggest that in his *Commentary on Aristotle's 'Nicomachean Ethics'* Averroes shows how practical reason could be used to 'correct' religious law. He is there considering Aristotle's definition of the equitable as 'a correction of law where it is defective owing to its generality' and relates this to Islamic law concerning holy war or *jihād*. It is generally obligatory on all Muslims to wage war against non-Muslims at all times. Yet it is clear that such a general policy would on occasions be of considerable disutility to the Islamic regions. Following rigidly such a general instruction is said by Averroes to be a result of 'ignorance of the intention of the lawgiver, and for this reason it should be stated that peace is preferable, and war only occasionally relevant'.[30] Hourani comments that 'Such correction of positive law by equity implies the existence of a natural right, to which the Legislator conformed, and by our direct knowledge of which we may interpret his intentions.'[31] This is far from the case, however. All general rules require interpretation, and one often seeks to establish the nature of the intention which those rules embody so that in a difficult case it is possible to compare the original intention with the actual consequences of following the rule. When the comparison reveals some sort of discrepancy we might think about interpreting the rule in a particular way which makes sense of

---

[28] *Ibid.*, p. 101.

[29] G. Hourani, 'Averroes on good and evil', *Studia Islamica*, XVI (1962), pp. 13–40; pp. 38–9.

[30] Ibn Rushd, *Commentary on Aristotle's 'Nicomachean Ethics'*, fo. 248r on Books V, ch. 10; in Latin trans., *Averrois Cordubensis . . . commentarii* (Venice, 1560), III.

[31] G. Hourani, 'Averroes on good and evil', p. 39.

the intention. This is especially clear in the case of the law surrounding *jihād*, since the intention of that law is at least in part to extend the realm of Islam. If the actual practice would in certain circumstances have the contrary effect, it would be reasonable not to declare *jihād* at that time and in that place. There is no necessity to appeal to some knowledge of natural right which regulates the use of positive law.

What sorts of reasons would the philosophers give for the necessity of a prophet and for his embodying his intentions in a law and legal institutions? As we have seen more than once, a prophet is required to teach people how they ought to live, in which ways they ought to control their natural selfishness, and to lead those of them capable of the journey into acquaintance with the basic religious and philosophical truths. It is essential that any prospective prophet be able to reconcile the abilities and interests of the wide variety of human beings in the state, so that; 'the lawgiver is a man who has the power to deduce, through the excellence of his cogitation, the conditions through which these practical intelligibles can be actually realized for the attainment of ultimate happiness'.[32] For the law which the prophet leaves to remain effective once he has gone, it is necessary for his intentions to be constantly at the fore of legal debate, so that legislation does not descend to the condition of merely an empty playing with rules and terms. Again, this shows how important it is that the legislator in the first place be a prophet, since only someone who has such well-developed imaginative powers will be in a position to present the law in such a way that the line of development of those rules which still embody his intentions will remain clear. As Avicenna suggests,

It is necessary for the prophet to institute certain acts which he obliges the people to perform regularly . . . in order to keep alive in their minds [the purpose of the law] . . . These acts should keep in people's hearts the memory of God . . . and the next life, if they are to be useful. These reminders can be either outer words or private intentions. One ought to tell people that such actions bring them closer to God and bring benefits to them . . . They are equivalent to the various kinds of worship people need to follow.[33]

Al-Fārābī goes into detail concerning the distinct types of approach appropriate to different sorts of people:

There are two ways of making people understand, one is to make its essence clear while the alternative is to communicate an image which represents it symboli-cally. Judgment is formed in two ways, through a convincing rational argument

---

[32] Al-Fārābī, *Attainment*, ed. M. Mahdi, p. 45.
[33] Ibn Sīnā, *Najāt*, ed. M. S. Kurdi, pp. 305–6.

or through persuasion. When we understand the nature of existence and work from there via rational argument to conclusions, we practice philosophy. But when imagination receives symbols imitating reality, and judgments are made about these symbols using persuasive reasoning, this is the type of knowledge which was called by the ancients 'religion'.[34]

It would be a mistake to conclude that since the philosophers made this sort of distinction between philosophy and religion, they claimed that some people might be excused the devotional behaviour that religion specifies for its adherents. One might have thought that they would argue that religious practices could be limited to those incapable of a philosophical understanding of the topics which religion deals with in its own imaginative way. But they did not argue in this way. Al-Fārābī for one insists that 'A philosopher must perform the external acts and observe the duties of the law, for if a person disregards a law ordained as incumbent by a prophet and then pursues philosophy, he must be deserted. He should consider unlawful to himself what is unlawful in his community.'[35] One reason for not holding oneself aloof from the masses in religious matters, apart from the obviously prudential motive, is because 'the existence of the learned class is only perfected and its full happiness attained by participation with the class of the masses' (*TT* 360). Yet it is worth for the moment expressing a difficulty in this line of reasoning. If the philosopher understands, as Averroes suggests, 'that the aim of these doctrines lies in their universal character' (*TT* 360), why should he conclude that this universality applies equally to him? Philosophers do not require imaginative symbolization to appreciate important religious points. Why, then, are they required, in the opinions of al-Fārābī and Averroes, to adhere to religious procedural norms in order to behave rightly? If we can be made aware by the use of reason why religious laws and regulations take the form they do, is there any point in also claiming that it is revelation which establishes those laws as *the* laws to be obeyed?

The relevance of this discussion for the issue of the objective or subjective status of ethics in religion is quite evident. If it is possible for some people (e.g. philosophers) to acquire knowledge concerning their duty without relying upon revelation, then it would seem to follow that duty is not grounded in revelation at all, but rather in reason, and revelation is only a *means* of communicating truths to those not capable of using reason as both a method of discovery and a source of ethical norms.

---

[34] Al-Fārābī, *Attainment*, ed. M. Mahdi, p. 44.
[35] Al-Fārābī, *Risāla zainūn al-Kabīr* (Hyderabad, 1930), p. 9. This commentary could well be by Avicenna.

CHAPTER 5

Happiness, philosophy and society

One of the themes which runs through the account of ethics in Islamic philosophy is the conflict between two kinds of ethical system. The moral life of human beings takes place on two different levels, one of which is secular, social, political and physical, while the other is spiritual and religious. When we think of Aristotelian ethics in terms of the doctrine of the mean then we are thinking of fulfilling the commandments and establishing appropriate rules of behaviour for our social life. When we think of moral behaviour in terms of intellectual union with God, in terms of moral and intellectual perfection, then we are concerned with the rules of behaviour appropriate to that spiritual end. As we have seen in chapter 4, there is often taken to be a progression of stages on the way to perfection, with the ultimate aim being knowledge of the supreme being. Once this knowledge is attained it is closely connected with the happiness of the knower – 'when he knew God with a certain knowledge, he admitted that true happiness, which is the knowledge of the deity, is guaranteed to all who know Him' (*GP* III,23,492). Yet this state of knowing God can be interpreted in different senses. Is it a matter of something like personal knowledge? Does it require moral perfection first? Can only someone skilled in philosophy and demonstrative thought really know God?

We are returning here to the issue of the relationship between religion and philosophy which fascinated the *falāsifa*, in particular to the connection between happiness and philosophy. Islamic philosophy tried to resolve a dispute which arose between Plato and Aristotle and which bedevilled *falsafa*. The dispute originates with Plato and his assertion that theoretical reason, *sophia*, is the highest activity of human beings, and our happiness lies in the exercise of reason. Reason for Plato is the sole source of value, and if reason is required for happiness (the latter being a loose translation of the Greek term *eudaimonia*, which might be more properly rendered as 'well-being'), then most people will not be able to achieve this good completely. Only those capable of rational contemplation can succeed in finding this good and its corresponding happiness. This Platonic doctrine created the problem with which the *falāsifa* were confronted, namely, that it seems arguable that one has to be a philosopher to know how to do good, or to achieve happiness. This difficulty in Plato's ethics struck the *falāsifa* particularly clearly since they held that the Qur'ān or the Torah contains the whole of the knowledge of the content of morality in the most perfect form possible. Moreover, this knowledge and its accompanying happiness is available to anyone who takes the appropriate religious steps. Yet as philosophers, and especially as philosophers inspired by the structure of thought exemplified by the Greeks, they were at the same time reluctant to accept that reason is not a vitally important characteristic of good action and happiness.

This conflict between religious faith and philosophical belief in the question of the primacy of reason is well represented, albeit in a different form, in Aristotle's indecision concerning the nature of human beings. According to Aristotle, if something has a function then the good of that thing is dependent upon its function. The function of a thing is generally what it does that makes it what it is. So the function of human beings in terms of which human excellence is measured, its form, is that which makes us human beings rather than something else. Now, Aristotle often argues that that function is reason in a particular employment (it cannot be reason alone since the gods exercise reason too, in which case the possession of reason could not distinguish us from them). Reason permits us to become the only creatures capable of concentrating on what is higher than ourselves. Reason does have a role in the ordering of our practical lives, yet if we limit our applications of reason to practical affairs, then we would regard such affairs as the main object of rational attention. This would be a mistake, since we can use reason to do something unique, namely, to concentrate upon what is higher than ourselves. So 'it is absurd to think that political science or prudence is the loftiest kind of knowledge, inasmuch as man is not the highest thing in the universe' (*NE* 1141a 21–3). Political wisdom should recognize its limits: 'But again it is not supreme over philosophic wisdom, i.e. over the superior part of us, any more than the art of medicine is over health; for it does not use it but provides for its coming into being; it issues rules, then, for its sake but not to it' (*NE* 1145a 6–9). In the *Eudemian Ethics* (1248a 23 and 1249b 20) Aristotle claims that the good for human beings consists in serving and contemplating God, but that position largely disappears in the *Nicomachean Ethics*. In *Magna Moralia* the function of practical wisdom is said to be like that of a steward whose business it is so to arrange things that his master has leisure for his high vocation. The idea is that human beings realize their function most perfectly as human beings when they are on the highest possible point, for them, on the continuum from animal to God. Thus they should make theoretical knowledge their main object, the single end or target at which they aim. Yet acceptance of such a view would surely have awkward consequences for *falsafa*, because it would mean that only a few of God's creatures, philosophers, are capable of fulfilling their function satisfactorily.

The argument that 'Happiness, therefore, must be some form of contemplation' (*NE* 1178b 32) is based upon the notion of a contemplative and philosophical ideal which consists, at least, of the following propositions. Intellectual activity is the highest activity, it is self-rewarding and self-sufficient, and it is the activity of which God either partakes or the one which constitutes his very essence. In the *Metaphysics*, Aristotle tends to identify God with *nous* or contemplation, thus separating the ethical and practical from the theoretical. The highest activity of which we partake is the activity of reason which 'more than anything else in man' is man (*NE* 1178a 8). This activity is described as superior in value, its own end, pleasant in itself, autonomous, leisurely, relaxing and divine (*NE* 1177b 20ff.). Aristotle steers clear from claiming that God himself should be our object. While the object of divine thought is God himself (*Met.* 1074b 34), the objects of human contemplation are 'things noble and divine' (*NE* 1177a 15). The *falāsifa* went further than Aristotle here, and referred to our reason's conjunction with the active intellect, an emanation many times removed from God. We shall see what implications this has for their argument in a moment.

Aristotle had another view of the nature of human beings, and so another view of happiness, and this is the view which the *falāsifa* develop as appropriate to the religious notion of human beings. On this view, happiness essentially includes not just the activity of theoretical reason, but also the full range of human life and action, involving moral virtue and practical wisdom. Aristotle sometimes regards human beings as composite creatures, a mixture of reason, emotion, action and perception all gathered together in one body. In the *De Anima*, for instance, human beings are given a complex soul, which, being a form, defines the creatures whose soul it is. If the form of human beings is complex, combining rational and non-rational capacities, the function of those beings should be correspondingly complex. The function of such a being will be regarded as what it is that counts as the excellent or perfect working or organization of such a function. Aristotle claims that 'man is born for citizenship' (*NE* 1097b 11) and so has interests and projects which require the cooperation of others and his own readiness to fit his projects in with those of other people. If our total organization is to function properly, and if our social and material requirements are to be realized, then we must live in and accept the norms of a well-run state. On the other hand, Aristotle still argues that the life of contemplation is the best sort of life for human beings. It is certainly the case that we must organize our social affairs in the best manner possible: 'But we must not follow those who advise us, being men, to think of human things and, being mortal, of mortal things, but must, so far as we can, make ourselves immortal, and strain every nerve to live in accordance with the best thing in us; for even if it be small in bulk, much more does it in power and worth surpass everything' (*NE* 1177b 31–1178a 2). When comparing 'political' with 'philosophical' concerns and lifestyles, Aristotle comes firmly down on the side of the latter. Contemplation, he argues, cannot fail to provide happiness, and a divine kind of happiness, since it can be exercised at any time and for longer than any other activity (*NE* 1177a 22ff.). Yet one might question whether philosophical and practical reasoning are so distinct that one could talk of them leading to different kinds of happiness. An important thesis which Aristotle employs here is the idea that a difference of objects presupposes a difference of faculty (*NE* 1139a 6–12), so that knowledge of higher objects is equivalent to higher knowledge.

Aristotle does sometimes refer to the view of human essence as composite as 'secondary' (*NE* 1178a 9), which is certainly how it appears from the intellectualist point of view. But it has the advantage (for a religious philosopher) of accepting that a life which consists only of moral and religious virtue as opposed to intellectual perfection is also a happy life. People may be happy in the proper use of their purely human properties as distinct from their godlike reason. Aristotle, typically, did not make up his mind what to say definitively about the function of human beings, and he saw merit in both these views. The intellectualist account acknowledges the truth which Aristotle saw in Plato's identification of the highest activity of human beings and theoretical reason. The composite account accepts that people not capable, nor inclined, to practise theoretical reason are capable nevertheless of leading happy and virtuous lives. As we have seen, according to Aristotle an individual may attain the higher sort of happiness by developing, in so far as he can, the divine in human nature. This leads to a problem for Aristotle, in that the more the individual attains to this end, which he can never fully reach, the less dependent he is upon association with other people. Yet a human being would not be a human being if he did not live in a community with other human beings; otherwise no human life is possible (*NE* 1178b 5–7). So Aristotle argues both that the social virtues are not up to the standard of contemplation and also that those virtues are vitally significant to anything that could count as a happy and human life.

Now, Averroes uses the same sort of technique which Aristotle employed to combine social with intellectual virtues in his account of happiness, but in the case of the *failasūf* happiness is discussed in relation to religious and intellectual virtues. Averroes famously claimed that there is no difference between the aim of philosophy and that of religion. They both seek to secure happiness and the truth. Religion permits anyone to attain these desirable ends, but philosophy is limited to a few people who are attuned to intellectual work, and allows to a few people an investigation in depth by rational methods of the real sense of the divine law. *Sharī'a* and philosophy have the same purpose, but only philosophy can show by demonstrative argument what the nature of this knowledge contained in the law really is. The prophets are said to produce religious laws which are true and impart a knowledge of those actions by which the happiness of everyone is guaranteed. Only philosophers can properly use demonstrative arguments to illuminate the hidden inner meaning of revealed truth. Even al-Ghazālī at times seems to accept this view. Quoting a passage from the Qur'ān (XVI,125–6), he argues: ' "Call thou to the way of thy Lord with wisdom and good admonition, and dispute with them in the better way." God thus taught that some men are called by wisdom [philosophy], and some by admonition [preaching], and some by disputation [dialectic].'[1] For the non-philosophical sections of society, a variety of arguments are available, dialectical for the theologians (*mutakallimūn*) and rhetorical or poetical for the ordinary people (*jumhūr*). All these arguments in the *sharī'a* cohere; there is nothing wrong with non-demonstrative arguments as such, they may be valid but their acceptance is less rational than acceptance based upon demonstrative arguments. The conclusion which Averroes wishes to draw, particularly in his *Decisive treatise on the harmony of religion and philosophy*, is that anyone may know how to act rightly by following the rules of Islam, and so the virtuous life is available to all regardless of their capacity for rational contemplation. What is distinct in these various approaches is just that they will each approach happiness along a different route. The *sharī'a* is

---

[1] Al-Ghazālī, *Al-Qistās al-Mustaqīm* (The correct balance), in R. McCarthy, *Freedom and fulfillment*, pp. 287–332: p. 288.

required by everyone, but philosophy is not. Averroes makes this point by comparing the legislator and the doctor (a frequent Aristotelian analogy too) where the purpose of the doctor is 'to preserve the health and cure the diseases of all the people, by prescribing for them rules which can be commonly accepted . . . He is unable to make them all doctors, because a doctor is one who knows by demonstrative methods the things which preserve health and cure diseases' (*FM* 67).

In fact, Averroes does not only try to show that philosophy and religion are compatible, he also tries to establish the much stronger proposition that religion demands philosophy. He does this by suggesting that Islam instructs its followers to find out things about the world and to use their faculties of reason and enquiry so that: 'If teleological study of the world is philosophy, and if the Law commands such a study, then the Law commands philosophy' (*FM* 44). We should remember, too, that even al-Ghazālī did not disparage philosophy and demonstrative reasoning as such; it was the invalid application of these techniques and their impious conclusions which he criticized. Whether he would have had much sympathy with Averroes' aggressive strategy here is quite another matter, of course. George Hourani claims that Averroes' argument that the law commands philosophy is fallacious on two separate grounds (*FM* 20–1,83). As an argument it is said to commit the fallacy of undistributed middle, since philosophy might not be the kind of teleological study which the *sharīʿa* commands. But, whatever its other demerits may be, Averroes' opening argument does not commit such a fallacy. The philosopher is taking 'teleology' and 'philosophy' to be equivalent, where any teleological study is ipso facto regarded as philosophy. Such an identification might seem far-fetched until it is recalled that Averroes had in mind an Aristotelian conception of science as his paradigm of both philosophy and teleology, a science which would permit the logical derivation of truths concerning both nature and philosophy from indubitable initial premises. Hourani's criticism that philosophy might not be the kind of teleological enquiry required by *sharīʿa* falls down if we accept this Aristotelian view. Philosophy represents an important rational means of understanding the course of nature and the structure of the world, and if *sharīʿa* commands believers to understand the world, then it must command philosophy as the means to that end for those capable of thinking philosophically.

Hourani argues that there is another fallacy in the argument, and this is in the way in which the term 'philosophy' is understood by Averroes. Hourani points out that philosophy in medieval Islam means a lot more

than just the teleological study of the world; it includes for instance, natural science, ethics, psychology, and so on. He is quite clear that such
investigations 'were not simply intended to prove God's power but were
studied for their own interests or with a view to man's happiness' (*FM* 21).
Yet, Averroes seems to have a different conception of philosophy when
he describes it as 'nothing more than study of existing beings (*mawjūdāt*)
and reflection on them as indications of the Artisan' (*FM* 44). Now, it
is difficult to see why Averroes should be thought to be committing a
fallacy here, since it is clear that he meant this description of philosophy
as a teleological enquiry to include all these other aspects of philosophy.
As we saw earlier, Aristotle was confident that describing the *function* of
a thing is the same as defining its essence, what it is to be such a thing.
So, understanding the world, ourselves included, is a matter of understanding how it is organized, which teleological principles are operative.
This is what Averroes means by philosophy and it includes all the areas
which Hourani thinks he has left out. For example, we can be expected
to answer questions in political philosophy only when we know what the
purpose of the state is. Psychological issues can only be resolved once
it is discovered what the purpose and function of the human mind are.
These are all teleological and, for the Aristotelian, philosophical problems. The form of the opening statement which Averroes produces in his
Decisive treatise on the harmony of religion and philosophy could be formulated in
this way: God has commanded us (where we are capable of understanding in this way) to understand his creation, and thereby himself. Such
understanding is philosophy, so God has commanded us to undertake
philosophical enquiry.

   One of Averroes' aims is to show that all these different routes to
happiness which exist in Islam are consistent with one another, and the
task of the philosopher is to demonstrate by argument that this in fact is
the case. *Sharī'a* and philosophy refer to one truth, to one end, since the
former prescribes for religious knowledge and practice while

Its intention as regards this purpose is essentially the same as that of philosophy
in respect of class and purpose. Therefore some people are of the opinion that
these religious laws only follow ancient wisdom. It is obvious that Good and
Evil, beneficial and harmful, beautiful and ugly are in the opinion of all these
men something that exists by nature, not by convention . . . Many people of our
region hold this opinion about our common law. (*Comm.Pl.Rep.* II,vi,4–5)

   In his *Commentary on Plato's 'Republic'*, Averroes argues for the objectivity
of ethics as opposed to the subjectivism which had become orthodox

in Islam. What he sought to show was that the way in which the pagan philosophers of the past discussed important notions in ethics and politics is, at the very least, *compatible* with the teachings of religion. If moral language is to be exclusively definable by reference to the commands of God as revealed to man in the *sharī'a*, then it is difficult to see much of value or interest in Greek moral philosophy, since the latter claims validity for its doctrines on its own terms, regardless of any religious backing. Of course, as we have seen, Averroes was not content to argue that philosophy and religion are consistent. He went on to make the stronger point that the method of reasoning involved in philosophy explains in paradigmatically rational form why *sharī'a* has the characteristics it does, and this rational explanation is permitted, indeed *demanded* by Islam.

The end of human beings in the moral philosophy of Averroes as in that of Aristotle is happiness, represented as an action of the rational soul in accordance with virtue. Again, they both see happiness as not simply one thing, but rather as mixed as human perfection. There are many human perfections, although wisdom or contemplation definitely holds the highest rank: 'The human perfections are, in general, of four kinds: speculative, intellectual and ethical virtues, and practical conduct, and . . . all these perfections exist only for the sake of the speculative ones and as a preparation for them, just as the preparation which precedes the ultimate end exists for its sake' (*Comm.Pl.Rep.* i,i,9–15). Human perfection and happiness consists in the union with the active intellect. As Averroes states at the end of his *Incoherence of the incoherence*, 'those who are entitled to it [the truth] are, as Galen says, one in a thousand' (*TT* 363).

The example of such a person which he gives is of Aristotle: 'For I believe that that man was a rule in nature and a paradigm which na-ture uses to demonstrate the ultimate human perfection in the material order.'[2] After all, Aristotle established and completed the speculative sci-ences, determined the possibilities of human knowledge and has through his efforts made more likely our attainment of perfection. The end of human beings, union with the active intellect, can only be accomplished after the perfection of the speculative intellect in the individual. This implies that only the philosopher can be united with the divine life. This is rather nice for philosophers, perhaps, but not very appropriate to a religious philosophy designed to apply to all human beings, or at least to all believers. Averroes does not seem worried that all people do not (indeed, cannot) attain the ultimate human perfection. He limits himself

---

[2] Ibn Rushd, *Commentarium magnum . . . de Anima*, Latin trans. ed. S. Crawford (Cambridge, MA, Harvard University Press, 1953), p. 288.

to arguing that some individuals attain this perfection, and necessarily so given the thesis which we have already examined in some detail that something which is always possible must become actual at least once. He accepts that since some (i.e. most) people will never reach this end, then in fact they never had the possibility of achieving the ultimate end. But Averroes is not really concerned with human individuals. It is the human species which interests him and to which he relates his moral and political philosophy. Since human perfection is multiple, it is attained through participation in a society or group rather than by individuals. The philosopher achieves his end through knowledge while other people approximate the ultimate end through virtue. There are thus two radically distinct ends for human beings, that of union with the active intellect and that of ethical perfection – neither of which permits personal immortality. As we have seen, for Averroes only the species is eternal.

Does this theoretical perfection which philosophers can realize provide everything needed for the attainment of ultimate happiness? If it does, then what is the value of religion and *sharīʿa*, other than in urging us to acquire this theoretical perfection? If theoretical perfection only provides us with knowledge of ultimate happiness, and what leads to it, there still remains a need for something else which brings into actual existence what is known theoretically. Religion and *sharīʿa* are frequently given the task of filling this gap between theory and practice by the *falāsifa*. Averroes' account of the four human perfections is heavily influenced by al-Fārābī's remarks on this topic, the latter explaining in detail why knowledge of the theoretical sciences or virtues is not enough for the attainment of happiness. Someone must possess the will and decide to bring the four human perfections required for the attainment of happiness into actual existence in the community. The four human qualities (theoretical, deliberative and moral virtues, and practical arts) must be present in a political community for happiness to be present. For such happiness to be brought about, four corresponding kinds of science have to be employed. These include: (i) theoretical sciences which make intelligible those things which are certain and demonstrable; (ii) rhetorical sciences which present the demonstrable conclusions in a persuasive manner; (iii) dialectical sciences which explain how different positions may be defended; and (iv) a mixture of all three in an appropriate way for each individual nation. According to al-Fārābī, Plato specifies in the *Republic* that, in order to avoid becoming a false philosopher, anyone seriously involved in theoretical science 'should have correct views on the opinions of their religion, adhere to the ethical standards of their religion and not abandon all or most of them'.[3] Nonetheless, all these sciences are to be used to fulfil the purpose of theoretical science which is, after all, ultimate happiness for human beings.

One might interpret Aristotle's apparent hesitation at accepting wholeheartedly either the composite or the intellectualist view of happiness as a matter of his not being able to make up his mind about what human beings really are, and so being uncertain concerning the nature of human happiness. Averroes has fewer problems in knowing what we are, or what our function is, for this is to a degree specified by Islam, and indeed every faith. But he uses the different accounts which Aristotle provides to describe the different ways in which people can approach happiness. This distinction is necessary because people are themselves different in their capacities and interests. Indeed, one of the excellences of the *sharīʿa* is held to lie in the fact that it makes possible for *everyone* the attainment of happiness in a specifically appropriate form for that person. So no one is excluded from happiness by reason of innate ability – it would indeed be a problem in a religion to have a creator who formed his creatures differently with the result that some but not others were capable of being happy. Averroes takes Plato to task on this point, claiming that Plato's account of society deals only with two of the three classes of the state, the guardians and the philosophers. The laws of the state provide for happiness based upon theoretical knowledge for only the élite, whereas the *sharīʿa* guarantees the whole of humanity happiness – provided they are all Muslims. On this interpretation, Plato's model is limited to a section of society and so is unsatisfactory as a general account of the political entity. The *falāsifa* could take up this criticism and regard Islam as satisfactorily adapting Plato to cover the whole of society, since the revealed truths of Islam are equally available to all, along with its corresponding happiness.

It is worth pointing out that such a criticism of Plato would not really be justified. He certainly does not go in for much discussion of the artisan and agricultural sectors, yet they are not ignored in his theory. In the *Republic* he asserts that 'we have laid down, as a universal principle, that everyone ought to perform the one function in the community for which his nature best suited him . . . that principle is justice' (432B). Earlier, at 420A, he claims that 'our aim in founding the commonwealth was not to make any one class specially happy, but to secure the greatest possible happiness for the community as a whole . . . For the moment, we are

---

[3] Al-Fārābī, *Attainment*, ed. M. Mahdi, p. 48.

constructing, as we believe, the state which will be happy as a whole, not
trying to secure the well-being of a select few.' Plato certainly thought
that his theory should cover all aspects of society, and the happiness
of all classes. The function of every citizen is to do just one thing, and
the state and its inhabitants will be best organized, with the greatest
consequent happiness, if every citizen engages in just one craft, that for
which he is naturally fitted (a point which Averroes also stresses in his
Comm.Pl.Rep. i,xviii,6). In fact, one of the most notable features of Plato's
political philosophy in the *Republic* is its comprehensiveness. The activities
of every part of the state and of every member of the state is regarded
by Plato as relevant to the character of the state and the happiness of
its citizens. In Plato's state the important distinction is not between the
quantity of happiness enjoyed by its citizens, but between the *quality* of
happiness. This brings out the problem with translating *eudaimonia* as
'happiness'. The élite live better in the sense of having more significant
lives than the rest. It might be said that they live at a higher level because
they really understand what virtue is, as opposed to the masses, who just
accept what they are told and act accordingly.

   It might, however, be claimed that what Averroes is really objecting
to is the way in which Plato seems to regard the masses as necessarily
incapable of grasping the truth. It is perhaps surprising that Averroes of
all people would make such an objection, since he also frequently doubts
the capacities of the mass of people to grasp the truth in its unvarnished
reality. In the Allegory of the Cave, Plato develops the idea that the masses
cannot see the truth directly, but must be satisfied with an imitation of
reality. This is a claim which Averroes cannot entirely accept given his
belief in the existence of a divinely revealed law available to all believers
plus the necessity of agreeing that there are parts of *sharī'a* which are
to be accepted without question. This reflects the important distinction
between a *nāmūs* and a *shar'*, between man-made law and prophetically
established law. The man-made sort of law may have all kinds of virtues
but it will not be as general in character as the divinely inspired religious
law. In any case, the man-made law might have as its rationale some story
or allegory which is designed to persuade citizens to act in accordance
with it, while at the same time not really providing an argument for
accepting and following the law. In the epilogue of his *Commentary on
Plato's 'Republic'*, Averroes claims that he is really only interested in those
arguments of Plato which are capable of proof by demonstrative means.
The Myth of Er, which suggests that there is punishment and reward
in the afterlife as a result of our behaviour in this life, is patently not

such an argument and so Averroes declines to comment on Book X of the *Republic*. He points out that in any case it is perfectly possible to be virtuous without believing in such tales and stories, through adhering to the religious law.

It is important, nonetheless, to pay some attention to those parts of Averroes' *Commentary* which involve stories that he does discuss. For one thing, he talks about the Allegory of the Cave, although with significant omissions. Why does he do this since this is obviously not an argument capable of demonstrative assessment? It is not an argument of any sort, but just a story which suggests in highly graphic detail how different sorts of people have different perspectives on the nature of reality. He also uses Plato's discussion of the story of the metals which are in the souls of citizens, a story which Plato commends to the rulers of the state as a useful ruse to persuade its citizens that there is a preordained and naturalistic explanation for their inequality. Such a story provides more backing for the view that everyone is fitted to one, and no more than one, skill. This, too, is far from being a demonstrative argument, and one wonders why Averroes considers it at all. We shall discuss the nature of Averroes' treatment of these stories in chapter 6, but for the moment we can say that he is interested in them because they suggest that people may be led to the truth in all sorts of different ways. The happiness of all believers is assured by the truth of Islam, but there is scope, within the context of that religion, to approach aspects of the truth indirectly, where this is in the interests of the masses. Some of Plato's stories show how this may be done. But, in the end, there is no difference for Averroes between what the masses and what the philosophers know. The only difference lies in the way that philosophy can show how the revealed truth of Islam may be established as demonstratively valid. Since the truth of Islam lies in revelation through prophecy, all believers believe for the same reason. But the philosopher can justify the belief in another way as well as through acceptance of revelation. Similarly, Averroes argues that both the philosopher and the ordinary believer can be happy, but they will be happy in different ways. The ordinary believer's happiness will lie in his observance of the *sharī'a* and social norms, while the happiness of the philosopher will lie in addition to such observance in his personal development of intellectual virtues. According to Averroes, Islam can account for the happiness of both types of person.

It is interesting to see how he uses the different approaches to the question of human happiness and essence which Aristotle employs and fits them into a theological context quite neatly, using the composite view to explain the happiness of everyone and the intellectualist view to explain the happiness of the philosopher. The Islamic background provides him with a suitable theoretical framework in which to reconcile both views as applicable to different kinds of individual. The *sharīʿa* was provided for the use of the masses in order to show them how to attain knowledge and happiness appropriate to them as non-intellectual beings, while the philosophers have been provided with their rational abilities in order to comprehend the deeper meaning of the law and to achieve a different kind of happiness. This explains why the Qur'ān is written in figurative and anthropomorphic language.[4] It is designed to enable anyone to understand and believe as much as he needs to understand and believe in order to be happy and lead a good life: 'In short, the religions are, according to the philosophers, obligatory, since they lead towards wisdom in a way universal to all human beings, since philosophy only leads a certain number of intelligent people to knowledge of happiness and they therefore have to learn wisdom, while religions seek the education of the masses as a whole' (*TT* 360). This form of presentation of the *sharīʿa* is, in fact, evidence of the kindness of God, in making his revelation available to all regardless of their capacity to reason (although it might be added that since God presumably also established their lack of capacity to reason beyond a certain level in the first place, presenting the revelation in this form is only *fair*).

Within the context of Neoplatonic thought the philosopher is regarded as a seeker of contact (*ittiṣāl*) with the spiritual forms or Platonic ideas, since achieving this contact with what is real as opposed to what is merely appearance is a prerequisite to union (*ittiḥād*) with God, or immersion in the deity, which is the ultimate end of the rational being. The philosopher seeks to rise above the masses and their dependence upon the world of appearance, to rise to the level of reality which is attainable only through the use of reason. Reason is regarded as a divine faculty, the use of which makes people similar to spiritual beings whose entire *modus essendi* is rational and not material or animal. As we have seen, the *falāsifa* tried to bring the happiness of the philosopher and the ordinary person closer together by insisting that they can only realize their ends within the framework of an adequately organized state. In such a state, the ordinary people are given the opportunity to act in accordance with the sorts of social and religious virtues which

---

[4] There was a good deal of discussion in Islamic philosophy and theology about the sort of language used in the Qur'ān.

are appropriate to them, while the philosophers, in addition to carrying out these general norms of observance, are provided with a sufficiently stable environment in which they can pursue their goal of intellectual perfection. Now, the *falāsifa* did not just intend to show that the aim of intellectual perfection is compatible with the other aims that people have in the community, in the same way that Averroes did not intend to show that philosophy is merely compatible with religion. They went onto the offensive with an argument, derived from Plato, to demonstrate that the best sort of state for anyone at all is one which is organized by philosophers.

The argument goes that, if the state is organized by those capable of intellectual perfection, it will make the diverse natures of the rest of the citizens cohere in such a way that *all* will benefit, albeit in different ways. Referring to the goal which rational beings have of perceiving reality insofar as this is possible, ibn Bājja (d. 533/1139) comments: 'It is clear that this goal is intended for us in our nature. But this is possible only in political association . . . men were fashioned opposite to each other in their stations so that through them the state should be perfected in order that this purpose be achieved.'[5] Why is government taken to be a part of the philosopher's function according to Plato? For a theoretical and a practical reason. The philosopher is trained to comprehend reality, to perceive the essence or common factor which pervades all existing things, and so only he is able fully to understand the nature of justice or government. Only the philosopher really understands what 'government' is and what it is that different uses of this expression have in common. With such knowledge the philosopher is taken to be in a position to bring about conditions in the state in accordance with his complete understanding of justice and government, so that all sections of society will be able to achieve their best possible way of living compatible with the best possible way of living of everyone else. The practical reason is that the best ruler is the person in society who least wishes to rule, and the philosopher really only wants to contemplate reality in coming into contact with the spiritual forms.

What sort of role does the philosopher have in a society which does not look to him as its ruler? According to ibn Bājja, in the imperfect state the philosopher cannot govern others, even though this is his function, and so is left with no alternative but to govern himself. He should try

---

5 Ibn Bājja, *Risālat al-wadāʾ* (Letter of farewell), ed. A. Palacios, *Al Andalus*, VIII (1943), pp. 1–87; p. 37.

to develop in himself those virtues and characteristics which he would,
if given the chance, instil in the state. The imperfect state is characterized by ignorance, lack of self-control, absence of respect for truth
and desire to satisfy the animal instincts. The philosopher who turns
away to govern himself will then seek to achieve temperance, knowledge and a control over his animal passions by his intellect. Does the
solitary philosopher, the *mutawaḥḥid* described by ibn Bājja, then reject his Platonic obligations to society and turn his back upon it in
order to govern himself? Plato does warn after all that the philosophers in the imperfect state may well develop an evil character since
their capacity to exercise reason will not be directed towards the attainment of knowledge of reality but rather in benefiting themselves
and satisfying their animal instincts, characteristic motives in imperfect societies (*Republic* 487B–497A). The *mutawaḥḥid* is not necessarily
guilty of such a vice, since he insists that he has no way of exercising
his duty to society given the way in which society regards his function. Since rights and duties are correlative, his duty to participate in
society is relative to having a right to direct and control society, and
if this right is not recognized, then the corresponding duty does not
arise. Indeed, the *mutawaḥḥid* could make an even stronger point that
in societies where philosophers are not respected in the appropriate
way they are often in actual danger of death or persecution as a result
of their practice of philosophy. This is the point of calling these soli-
taries *nawābit*, i.e. plants or weeds, a term taken over from al-Fārābī but
originally from Plato, which emphasizes the way in which philosophers
in such societies are regarded as useless, harmful and fit to be rooted
out. In such societies, 'they have sprung up, like a self-sown plant, in
spite of their country's institutions; no one has fostered their growth,
and they cannot be expected to show gratitude for a care they never
received' (*Republic* 520B). After this heartfelt passage Plato directly contrasts this state of affairs with the position of the philosopher in the
ideal state, who has been educated and trained to rule and whose accepted position in society is that of its director. The *mutawaḥḥid* does
not ignore his duty when he leaves society to its own devices, he rather
recognizes that in the present state of affairs there is no possibility of
this duty being carried out. Living within such imperfect conditions
is of very real disadvantage to the *mutawaḥḥid*, since Plato, al-Fārābī,
Averroes and ibn Bājja all agree that without society the philosopher
will not be able to achieve the highest perfection. Ibn Bājja characterizes the imperfect state: 'But the three classes which either exist or can

exist are the weeds [the philosophers], the judges and the physicians. The happy ones insofar as they can exist at all in these states, enjoy an isolated happiness. For the just government is only the government of the isolated, be he one or be they more, while neither nation nor city state is in agreement with their opinion.'[6] Ibn Bājja then draws the conclusion that the philosopher should by his self-government separate himself from society and approach as closely as possible by himself to the state of perfection.

This sort of position is surely very reasonable. It would be surprising, to put it mildly, if it were argued that philosophers must take part in the state's affairs if there is general opposition to their participation. As al-Fārābī puts the point, 'If . . . he finds no role, the fact that he has nothing to do is not his fault, but the fault of those who either do not listen or who think that they do not need to listen to him.'[7] Clearly, the responsibility does not lie with the philosopher if society rejects his contribution and renders him socially impotent. In such a state of affairs the philosopher 'will certainly suffer one of two fates, either death or deprivation of perfection'.[8] It certainly is al-Fārābī's view that a human being cannot achieve perfection in isolation, but it does not follow that the *mutawaḥḥid* has no option but to become involved in his present society. It may be that the philosopher in such an imperfect state would do best to preserve himself and his skills until such time as the state of society is more receptive to his influence, or so that he can pass on his learning to others in the hope of a future improvement in the social atmosphere. Averroes expands this point:

When by chance a true philosopher grows up in these [imperfect] states he is in the position of a man who has come among wild beasts. He is indeed not obliged to do harm along with them, yet he can also not be sure in his own mind that these wild beasts will not oppose him. Therefore he will have recourse to isolation and live a solitary life. He will [thus] be lacking the highest perfection which he can attain only in this [ideal] state. (*Comm.Pl.Rep.* ii,iv,7–14)

Plato clearly recommends isolation and withdrawal when to do otherwise would be useless (*Republic* 496CDE). The highest perfection would then not be available, but other meritorious activities remain. Ibn Bājja illustrated Plato's point about the importance of pursuing limited goods with medical examples. At one point he claims: 'If a limb is cut from

---

[6] Ibn Bājja, *Tadbīr al-mutawaḥḥid* (Rule of the solitary), ed. A. Palacios (Madrid, 1946), p. ii.
[7] Al-Fārābī, *Attainment*, ed. M. Mahdi, p. 49.
[8] Al-Fārābī, *The philosophy of Plato*, in M. Madhi, *Alfarabi's philosophy*, p. 64.

the body, it is essentially harmful, though incidentally it may be advantageous to one whom an adder has stung, and his body is relieved by cutting it off.'[9] The suggestion is that there are cases where one cannot achieve a type of perfection (bodily perfection, for example) and at the same time live. In such cases it is necessary to separate the diseased from the healthy parts, otherwise everything will perish. The philosopher must then separate himself from those sections of society which are diseased, so that he may maintain his integrity at the same time as being available to cure the disease at the appropriate time. Saying that man is a political animal does not mean that he must always play a part in the state. Man is also naturally a creature with a certain number of limbs, but there are occasions when the removal of some of them is necessary to preserve life. This principle, that the philosopher's obligation to participate in society is relative to the nature of the society is profoundly realistic, and must have struck a deep chord among the *falāsifa* when considering their strategies in often unsympathetic social environments.

[9] Ibn Bājja, *Tadbīr*, trans. in D. Dunlop, 'Ibn Bajjah's "Tadbīru l-Mutawaḥḥid" ', *Journal of the Royal Asiatic Society*, April (1945), pp. 61–81, p. 76.

CHAPTER 6

How to read Islamic philosophy

MYSTICISM

It is difficult to overemphasize the significance of what might be called mysticism within the Islamic philosophical world. Virtually all the major thinkers wrote on *taṣawwūf* (mysticism) or at least expressed some interest in it. Even al-Fārābī, one of the driest writers of philosophical prose, was reputed to be a mystic, although there is no evidence of this from his extant works. (On the other hand, the music which he is taken to have composed and which has survived does suggest some commitment to mysticism.) This interest in mysticism has lead some commentators to describe Islamic philosophy as incorporating the idea that it is impossible to pursue wisdom without at the same time pursuing God. That is, Islamic philosophy is taken to be much more holistic than, say, Western philosophy, which sees itself often as the technical investigation of particular concepts which we employ in our thinking about the world. This is even true of non-analytic philosophy, which often manages to get by without any explicit mention of God or even any general unifying principles of a transcendent nature. Some would defend the idea of philosophy as essentially holistic, an idea which the West has rather lost due perhaps to the Enlightenment and the growth of materialist theories. This possibly rests on a rather romantic conception of the East as the repository of a more holistic notion of life, while the West represents a more piecemeal conception. It is worth pointing out that such a conception is held by many and very diverse thinkers, and like all generalizations it is flawed. There were many Indian thinkers, for example, who were as thoroughgoing materialists as anything seen in the West, and there were of course many Western thinkers committed to holistic ideas and the centrality of God to understanding the nature of our key principles.

On the other hand, it is true that even the type of Islamic philosophy which we have been discussing here makes far more reference to religion than does the Peripatetic philosophy from which it takes its name. For one thing, the major thinkers did not just write on one or two aspects of philosophy, but on the whole of philosophy, and not just on philosophy. They tended also to be lawyers, physicians, political leaders, scientists, and so on, and it is hardly surprising that they felt the need to discuss the general principles which might hold all these different concepts together. One of the problems with the Peripatetic (*mashshā'ī*) theories is that they do not provide much of a role for God, in that he seems to play little direct part in the nature of the world and our place in it. Al-Ghazālī is quite right to be critical of this, and not only on the theological point that a theory which provides no powerful role for God must be flawed from an Islamic perspective. His argument was stronger, and it took the form of suggesting that if a thinker uses the concept of a person but gives that person no significant role in actually doing anything, then the personhood characterized by that concept is highly suspect. Al-Ghazālī points out that the philosophers constantly talk about God but give him nothing to do, and so they are really talking about nothing.

One of the useful features of mysticism is that it provides at one level a role for God in a world which has no role for him at another level. This comes about by making a sharp distinction between the intellectual understanding of the world and our emotional reaction to it, between reason (*'aql*) and its ability to structure the nature of reality, and our actual experience (*dhawq*) of reality. From an entirely rational point of view one can explain the structure of the world and our role in it without making any direct reference to the will of God and his specific actions. This is because the world has always been there and he had no choice about how to create, since he had to create in the best and most rational way possible. Yet we also expect to have a personal relationship with God, to the degree that this is possible, and we experience our religion as more than just a set of rituals which has grown around a series of logical principles. There can be a 'science' of this experience in just the same way that there is a natural science and a system of logic, and such a science would have as its task the explication, description and organization of our religious experience.

This sounds very different from the normal way of understanding mysticism, which often takes the form of an antinomian contrast with rational approaches to faith. That is, the mystic does not have respect for the laws of religion since he has another and more direct route to the truth, that of experience of God. Also, the techniques of the mystic are often far from clear, and highly subjective. There is no reason to think that he has hit the mark, as it were, apart from his self-observation, and this is far from scientific in the sense where science is aligned with objectivity. There were mystics in the Islamic world who could be characterized in this way, but the system of mysticism is just as systematic as any other form of intellectual enquiry, and there was a great deal of suspicion even within Ṣūfism of the various ecstatic and emotional states into which some of their peers threw themselves. This led to the creation of a basic divide in Ṣūfism between Ṣūfīs who emphasized the significance of direct experience of God in their beliefs and practices, and those who did not, a fact which is not always acknowledged. Even those Ṣūfīs who argued for the possibility of experience of God did not suggest that this could be acquired in just any way at all, but insisted that it is only possible through a long and arduous training, inevitably under the leadership of a shaykh who would supervise every stage of the journey to the truth. On the whole, also, they insisted on a serious attitude to the norms of social and religious behaviour, rather than their replacement by other and more dramatic forms of spiritual expression.

Some writers on mysticism overemphasize the distinctness of this form of thinking as compared with alternatives. It is sometimes said, for example, that for the mystic the ideal model of reasoning is circular as compared with the linear reasoning of logic, since circular reasoning replicates the nature of reality by the process returning to its starting point, in just the same way that in reality everything is in a sense just one. Linear reasoning, which starts with premises and then arrives at a totally distinct conclusion, something new which has been developed out of those premises, misrepresents reality in that it suggests that something new and entirely different can emerge out of what is unlike it. Secondly, the mystic sees the meaning of the world as lying outside the world, as being higher than the world, while the non-mystic sees the world as basically containing its own meaning. This is often a contrast which it is easier to express aesthetically, of course. One may enjoy a song, appreciate the words and be moved by the music, and that is the end of it. On the other hand, one may see in the song something deeper and more generally appropriate to understanding our role in the world, and on this view the ordinary understanding of the song is merely superficial. The mystic feels the need to go further, the non-mystic does not. One of the interesting features of this contrast is that it is to a degree about how one should assess different kinds of experience. The mystic regards ordinary experience as insufficient without supplementation by something extra, something more significant which frames, as it were, ordinary experience and raises it to a new level.

Let us take as an example here the thought of probably the outstanding mystical philosopher in the Islamic world, ibn al-'Arabī, a thinker whose ideas have been a topic of constant interest ever since he died in 638/1240, and not only in the Islamic world. One of his themes is the importance of understanding the oneness of being, what it means for God to be one. This is of course a central principle of Islam, but it is not a principle which ibn al-'Arabī thinks is really taken to heart by most Muslims. What does it mean to say that God is one, that nothing is associated (*shirk*) with him? For many theologians this means that the Qur'ān should not be seen as something which God created, since that would make it secondary to him and interpret it as one of his characteristics, and so it would be associated with him, thus interrupting his unity. The precise way in which God 'has' his qualities turned out to be a controversial issue in Islamic theology, since it was and remains important to describe this relationship in such a way as not to suggest that God is more than just one thing. We, by contrast, are precisely more than one thing, I am now typing the words you are reading, but there was a time when I could not type and there will be a time in the future when I shall not be typing, so although to a degree I am just one person, I am not entirely undifferentiated and a unity. It is important to describe God's qualities in such a way as to make it clear that he is one and undifferentiated, so that he has his qualities in an entirely different way in which we have ours.

But there is an implication of this which ibn al-'Arabī argues we do not tend to draw, and that is that the world cannot just be the product of God, because that would interfere with his unity. If the world is a thing, and God is a thing, then the world is a thing which is separate from God and, its dependency on the divine notwithstanding, it seems to get in the way of divine unity. After all, our world, appropriately labelled by the *falāsifa* the world of corruption and generation, changes all the time, as we do, and this seems to be incompatible with the idea of a creator who is perfectly one. This idea produced problems for the *falāsifa*, who had to explain how an unchanging God could know of the frequent changes in the world without changing at the same time, and as we have seen it was one of the planks of al-Ghazālī's assault on philosophy itself. As al-Ghazālī argued, unless we can understand that God knows what happens in this world in much the same way that we know, we cannot understand how he could judge us, or what it means for him to send messengers and see what effect they have. But ibn al-'Arabī takes the issue one step further, and wonders how we can differentiate our world at all from the divine without falling into the sin of associating him with others. Now, as with al-Ghazālī this is not merely a theological point, but is taken to be a significant intellectual criticism, since if God is one (as is taken to be the rational conclusion) then any view of the world which makes him out to be more than one is clearly fallacious, regardless of the particular religious context within which the argument is expressed.

Now, if the world is not to be an obstacle to divine unity, it must be an aspect of that unity, not something separate from it. It follows that the world, our everyday world, in some sense is not separate from God, but is rather part of him, but not part of him like being associated with him. Rather it is an aspect of his essence, and the apparently distinct forms of the world are merely our misleading ways of seeing it. We think of ourselves as individuals and the changing events of our world as being separate from each other, and from God, but in reality these are all aspects of perfect unity. What we need to do if we are to improve our knowledge is to realize the unity of everything, and abstract from the discrete to form a concept of the one. This is hardly a simple process, and it is one for which divine assistance is necessary (hence the significance of good works), yet what we will eventually appreciate is the unity of everything, if we are successful in perfecting our thought. It is at this stage that some of the enemies of this form of Ṣūfism would suggest that this is really pantheism and to identify the world with God as an aspect of his unity is definitely unacceptable, the most blatant form of *shirk*. The idea of *wahdat al-wujūd*, of the unity of being, does not after all have to mean that absolutely everything is one, it need only mean that the basic principle behind the creation and existence of everything is just one, so the diversity of the everyday world can continue to enjoy an independent existence, to a degree, as nothing more than the contingent consequence of the unity of being, but not part of that unity. This is how Ṣūfīs like al-Ghazālī would put it (although al-Ghazālī was a rather untypical Ṣūfī in many ways, in particular in his lack of reference to instruction by a shaykh) since for them the events of this world are merely what is brought about by God, and he could have brought about anything he wished. The suggestion that the world is an aspect of divine unity rather gets in the way of this notion of divine freedom of choice, since presumably if everything is a part of divine unity, God has to create in a particular way, in whatever way fits in with that conception of unity. Like a neoclassical architect, he would have to select between a few ways of embodying particular principles in practice, since if he did not follow those principles the consequent structure would not display the unity of that design. Al-Ghazālī insists on God's complete freedom to do whatever he wishes to do, unrestrained by any principles or preconceptions. This hardly fits in with the idea that whatever is produced by God is a feature of absolute unity.

Although as we have seen there were many thinkers who argued against Ṣūfism, or at least against particular forms of it, it would be wrong to represent Ṣūfism as essentially opposed to philosophy in the sense of *falsafa*. It would be difficult to argue that it was essentially opposed since it was pursued by so many of the *falāsifa*! There are certainly reasons we could produce as to why the *falāsifa* might have not been enthusiastic about mysticism, yet they did not on the whole take up and develop those reasons. Was this because of a desire to pursue a more holistic way of doing philosophy, a way which involves incorporating God and the meaning of the world in the analysis of the world itself? Not necessarily. It was not a case of philosophy versus mysticism but of philosophy and mysticism dealing with different areas of human thought and experience. Philosophy deals with those forms of human expression which are capable of being at least partially encapsulated within the structure of the syllogism. We have to take seriously here the idea of the organon, something of great significance within Islamic philosophy during this period. This is the thesis that every form of human expression, however loose and evocative, is capable of being represented in terms of the syllogism, i.e. as a kind of reasoning process.

This enterprise does not get any purchase on religious experience itself, since it is experience and needs to be felt and not analyzed. There is nothing wrong with analyzing such experience, of course, and this does take place within the framework of Islamic philosophy, in particular when it looks at the nature of statements such as those dealing with prophecy and responding to the *sharīʿa*. What mysticism does, though, is to develop different concepts of the complexity of religious experience and devise a route to improve one's grasp of that experience and take it on to ever-higher levels of self-awareness and eventually on to experience of the divine, in some sense. To take an example, if someone asks me what carrots taste like, I need to help them capture that experience themselves, and if I have to rely on purely descriptive techniques then it will be difficult although not impossible to give them some idea of the taste. The Ṣūfī shaykh is in the position of someone who knows the taste and is trying to help others experience it, but who cannot just give them carrots to try, he must lead them gradually and carefully along a route at the end of which they too will have the opportunity to taste what he has tasted. Of course, he can to a degree describe that taste to them, and unless he could it would be difficult to motivate them to set off on the long path to reach the taste, but there is far more to the taste than merely the description of the taste. What is difficult to capture is not so much the experience, although that is difficult, but the fact that there is little more to the taste of carrots than the experience. In just the same way the experience of God is so overwhelming that it often seems to defy description, or at the very least the description which can be given of it is so inadequate that it pales into insignificance compared to the experience itself.

But this argument seems to prove too much, if it proves anything at all. It shows that dealing with experience is a very different activity as compared with dealing with other aspects of human life, and it would seem to follow that there is no possibility of a science of experience in the same way that there is, say, a science of dialectic or poetry. There are sciences of the latter in the sense that there is organized knowledge about how they work, what they are and so on. There is also a science of mysticism, an *'ilm al-taṣawwūf* or sometimes it is represented as *'ilm al-'irfān*, where *'irfān* is the special kind of knowing which occurs in mystical forms of understanding. The argument for such a science is that coming to acquire an experience can be just as systematic and rigorous a matter as can working through logical syllogisms which describe the rational structure of a way of speaking. In some ways it is even more difficult since its eventual successful outcome is by no means guaranteed, because the experience may never be grasped (in the language of ibn al-'Arabī, it is for us to approach the door, and for God to open it). It is actually a familiar difficulty which we have of getting someone to understand what a particular experience is like when she or he has not experienced it yet, and although we have been talking about experiences which are religious, we can appreciate how difficult they are when we think about the difficulties of explaining the nature of experiences which are apparently much simpler, like the taste of examples of food and drink, or the fragrance of a spring day in the Appalachians. Hence the need for a science of coming to such experiences, and the possibility of such a science based on the gradual build-up of linked experiences, the personal development of the individual to acquire even more sophisticated ways of experiencing, culminating hopefully in the experience which is being sought.

Pursuing this aim is not to go against anything in analytical philosophy, and so there is no contradiction in being a *failasūf* and also a mystic.

Some *falāsifa* such as ibn Rushd seem to have been thoroughly opposed to mysticism, and in his case this is perhaps because he held that the meaning of the world really is not higher than the world, since from examining the world and using our reason we can work out everything we need to know about that world. He is unusual in his apparent lack of interest in mysticism, and he obviously regarded it as what Kant came to call *Schwärmerei*, or wild ravings. The important point to make is that his conclusion was not inevitable, he could have joined the vast majority of the Peripatetic school and investigated both *falsafa* and *taṣawwūf*, both the structure of different kinds of language and also different kinds of experience. So the description of Islamic philosophy as holistic unlike much modern Western philosophy is not really accurate. It is true that the *falāsifa* did discuss a much wider range of thought and experience than their modern peers, but they did not really bring all these ideas into a whole, nor did they think of this as an important task. After all, the distinction between language and experience is wide enough to allow for different treatments.

If there can be said to be a theme in Islamic philosophy, and it is always difficult to argue for any philosophy having a central theme, it is that there are a variety of routes to the same destination. If we are aiming to establish the truth, there are a number of different ways of doing this, some are theoretical and philosophical, while others are practical and religious. It is tempting to suggest that philosophy and mysticism are two different routes to the same truth, but we should be careful about such a conclusion. The problem with identifying both systems of thought is that they are very different. From the point of view of the *falāsifa*, philosophy is an entirely demonstrative process, starting with certain premises and using them to move on to valid conclusions, which themselves could go on to serve as certain premises in further syllogisms. This is not the case with mysticism, which is not based on a certain premiss but rather on a belief or an experience, and proceeds by investigating that belief or experience. Once that belief or experience is accepted the process of reasoning can get under way, but this is a form of language which the *falāsifa*, and especially ibn Rushd, classified as dialectical, since it starts from a premiss which is accepted 'for the sake of the argument' but for which there is no demonstrative proof. That would be a problem for Islamic philosophy if it really was Islamic, that is, if it really based itself on Islam and the principles of religion. Then it would accept as true a whole range of principles which could not be established in any other way, the principles of Islam, and the conclusions of Islamic philosophy would be irretrievably contaminated by those initial premises, however wonderful they might be in themselves as expressions of the truth directly transmitted to humanity by God through his angel. So the science of mysticism is not as demonstrative an exercise as philosophy itself. Insofar as mysticism concentrates on experience, it is also very different from philosophy, which concerns itself entirely with connections between concepts and regards experience as the subject matter of the subjective rather than the objective. Not only are philosophy and mysticism distinct enterprises, it is not even clear that they are after the same truth. Philosophy looks to a conclusion, while mysticism looks to an experience, and while the experience may well be linked to the conclusion, the result of mysticism is not something known but something felt.

ILLUMINATIONISM

If *falsafa* and *taṣawwūf* are the extremes representing very different approaches to how to do philosophy, then illuminationism or *ishrāqī* thought comes somewhere in the middle. This approach was pioneered by al-Suhrawardī, often described as al-Maqtūl (the slain) because of his unfortunately early death through execution in 587/1191, and was really taken up with immense enthusiasm by a long line of Persian thinkers, and it remains influential to this day in the Persian cultural world.

A sign of *ishrāqī* philosophy's intermediate status can be observed in the very different interpetations which exist of it. Some commentators like Hossein Ziai stress its analytical side, and this is certainly important. For example, the *ishrāqiyyūn* criticize in great detail aspects of Aristotelian logic. Al-Suhrawardī leads the way by attacking the Aristotelian notion of definition, with the intention of attacking the Peripatetic theory of knowledge. The *mashshā'ī* philosophers valued above everything starting with definitions, which they argued embody demonstrative knowledge and represent the very best way of starting the reasoning process. Yet is it possible to select the qualities of a thing which it has to have essentially to be the thing it is? That is, are definitions possible? If not, then dictionaries seem to lose their point, but it might be argued that dictionaries merely represent some of the central qualities of a term, not those without which the term would have an entirely different meaning. We can only really define a term if we know which of its properties are essential and which merely superficial, but if we know this then we know the definition before we know it, as it were. Defining a term is equivalent to claiming to know it before it is known, which cannot be right. Even if the Aristotelian gets over this hurdle, he would need to know what the definitions of the essential properties are in order to understand those properties, and the notion which they subsequently make up, but to know those definitions would involve knowing the definitions of even smaller semantic constituents of those terms, and so on. Definition as the bedrock of reasoning only works if we can ground it in something else, in this case other definitions, and this process of support will go on and on, clearly with the result that we never reach bedrock.

Al-Suhrawardī does not conclude that we can do without such premisses, and establishes an *ishrāqī* concept of definition based on the pure intuition or consciousness of the thing in question as a result of its contact with the purity of the knowing subject itself. Definition is attainable through an analysis of the reflection of the thing which is to be defined in the consciousness of the subject concentrating on that thing (note the light imagery here). This concentration manages to extract the essence of what is pereceived in much the same way that light brings out the nature of what it illuminates, and where without the light the character of reality would remain 'in the dark'. As with *mashshā'ī* thought, the *ishrāqiyyūn* pursue the idea of a hierarchy of knowledge and its progressive purification through achieving ever greater degrees of self-awareness. The main distinction is that for most of the Peripatetics knowledge is described as a matter of the cognizing subject connecting with the Active Intellect, while the *ishrāqī* replaces this with a connection that the knowing subject has with itself. The knowing subject comes to terms with the known object through the realization that they are both just aspects of the same essence, and the distinction between them is a matter of different forms of illumination. The very best form of knowledge is intuition, the immediate and incorrigible grasping of something's essence, as in a flash of illumination. To take an example, people sometimes come to know quite suddenly that they are not in love with someone, or it might be better put that they are no longer in love. This intuition changes everything and makes us see the world entirely differently, and it results from seeing the world in a particular way, different parts of the world being illuminated and other parts suddenly put in the dark. There is no questioning this experience, it is not as though one could argue that one should be in love with someone, and demand acceptance of such an argument in someone's experiential life. This sort of example makes *ishrāqī* thought seem quite like *taṣawwuf*, mysticism, in that it emphasizes the significance of experience, and indeed the imagination which is such an important part of illumination. Like mysticism, illuminationism also argues for a science of such experience, and tries in that way to modify its subjective aspects. On the other hand, unlike mysticism *ishrāqī* thought places much more reliance on analysis and examination of concepts, as an explanation of the progressive deepening of our experience.

The name of this form of thought comes from *ishrāq* which means 'rising (of the sun)' and which is also linked to the Arabic for 'east'. The use that *ishrāqī* thought makes of the notion of immediate and intuitive knowledge leads it quite often to be identified with ibn Sīnā's Oriental or Eastern philosophy, if any such form of philosophy really existed, and which is taken to be his deeper teaching as opposed to his work within the Peripatetic tradition of philosophy. The problem with *mashshā'ī* thought from the *ishrāqī* perspective is that the former is too limited in its understanding of both what counts as knowledge and also what counts as reasoning. Al-Suhrawardī sets out to replace Peripatetic philosophy with an entirely new form of logic and ontology. As we have seen, he rejects the Aristotelian account which takes definition as equivalent to genus and differentia since he argues that this is a process of explaining something in terms of something else which is less well known than itself. The project of starting the whole process of scientific investigation with a definition and moving from there to develop more and more conclusions is essentially flawed, according to al-Suhrawardī, since the starting point is no more certain than the conclusion. If we really could know the definition of a proposition then we should not need to carry out the reasoning process, which in fact reveals some of the aspects of the definition. This would be because we would know what the definition was, and so what followed from that proposition, before we bothered to use the definition as a premiss in the reasoning process. Starting reasoning with a definition assumes that we understand the notion of definition, whereas in fact we do not have this sort of information. So using definitions is to explore the obscure with the equally obscure, a profitless occupation.

Al-Suhrawardī also criticizes the particular categories defended by the Peripatetics as the basic concepts of form, claiming that they can be reduced to five and still encompass the same conceptual range. The main epistemological notion he develops is that of knowledge by presence (*al-'ilm al-ḥuḍurī*), which is used to describe a kind of knowledge which has such an immediate relationship to the truth that it supersedes propositional knowledge, and is far more perfect than it. It is knowledge about which one cannot be mistaken, and the light of our self brings to our awareness important aspects of the truth. This idea of light comes to replace the traditional philosophical vocabulary of Islamic philosophy. Light flows through the universe and makes us aware of different levels of being, which then exist for us when they are illuminated, and the differences between distinct things is based on their relative degrees of luminosity, not in their essences. It is hardly surprising that some thinkers identified God with the Light of Lights, the basic light out of which all subsequent light emerges and which does not itself receive light, which is completely one and independent of any other light in the universe.

It is important to distinguish between *ishrāqī* thought and Ṣūfism, and yet there are important issues on which they come together. One such is the concept of the imaginal realm, and it is interesting to see how this concept may be interpreted as mystical or as quite the reverse, as descriptive of a basic aspect of human thought. The notion of the imaginal world was produced largely by ibn al-ʿArabī and al-Suhrawardī. The imaginal world connects the lower world, our familiar world of generation and corruption, with more abstract levels of reality, where the perfect and pure ideas exist. Why do we need an ontological realm between the ordinary ideas of our world and the purer ideas of the world of ideas? For example, when I am learning the properties of triangles I may start by looking at the properties of a particular triangle and not realize that what I have learnt is generalizable to all triangles. Once I acquire this further knowledge, though, I seem to have moved from the relatively crude concepts of our ordinary world to the more universal concepts of theoretical mathematics.

The imaginal realm is important because it represents the way in which we may use ideas which are not entirely structured by our experience and which are also not entirely abstract. We have personal experiences, and these often work their way into our more abstract speculations, so that, for example, if I think about God's love for humanity I may think first about the people whom I love and extend that idea to God. I may come to understand that the notion of love has much more variety than I have myself experienced, and I would find it impossible to love certain people. Also, a lot of the actions which are taken to be evidence of divine love seem to be nothing like that at all, and I can only classify these actions as love if I take a very different attitude to love than I find in my experience. This is where imagination or the imaginal realm becomes important, it enables us to work from where we start considering experience to broaden that experience and the concepts which initially rest on it. Al-Suhrawardī describes the imaginal world as linking our microcosmic reality (what is important for us) and the macrocosmic nature (what is important for everything) of objective reality. The forms of the imaginal world are material insofar as they use physical imagery, but abstract insofar as they point to what is higher than it. It is more real than our world, since it is not limited by experience, but not as real as the higher world of pure ideas. In the imaginal world we have imaginal bodies (*al-jism al-khayalī*) as in dreams which differ from our physical bodies in that these imaginal bodies can wander freely around a range of ideas and experiences which would not be possible for our ordinary day-by-day bodies. When we use our imagination we are not limited by our personal experiences or the range of our bodies, but may extend our thinking in different and novel directions, using ideas with which we are familiar and developing them.

We should take note of the view of creation as emanation, a result of ibn Sīnā's defining influence over Islamic philosophy. The major contrast between ibn Sīnā and Aristotle lies in the responsibility for matter which for the latter is not God. Aristotle's God is the cause of the world, but not of its matter. There is then something in existence apart from God and what he produces, namely, matter. A controversy arose as to whether this ultimate source of existence can be described in terms of substance and accident, in terms, that is, of the categories, which for ibn Sīnā is impossible. It is impossible because whatever brings about the form and matter of the universe cannot be defined in the same terms as the things within that universe, since that ultimate cause must transcend that which it creates and even the processes by which creation takes place. After all, when I make toast in the morning for my breakfast I am presumably operating at a higher level than the bread itself, which merely waits to be transformed into something else. The source of being is a limiting concept, and we should not expect to be able to use the same ideas when describing such a concept as we can when describing what that concept makes possible. The only way we can grasp the nature of the source of being is through contemplation of what it is for a perfect thing to bring about another thing. We should think of this as the way in which a thinking thing brings about its thoughts, but it has to be in a pure and autonomous way, not as a result of the ordinary ways of thinking to which we are subjected by our life as members of the world of generation and corruption. Those thoughts have to flow from our self as aspects of our contemplation of ourself, a contemplation which succeeds in picking out the most important aspects of our being. They should not be seen as reflecting external realities, for then they would be dependent on those realities for their content and be essentially passive rather than active.

The light has to flow from the subject and in the ultimate sense it brings out aspects of the being of the source of light, and at lower stages of being it actually establishes the existence of external objects. What moves these objects from the realm of possibility to actuality is the light which makes them part of the ordinary world.

According to ibn Sīnā, we cannot talk about the world and God, as though these were two different entities. This was the point which particularly aroused al-Ghazālī and many other opponents of *falsafa*, and ibn Taymīyya is a good example here of someone who was even more opposed to *falsafa* than al-Ghazālī. Ibn Taymīyya points out that linking God and the world in this close way is to restrain the quantity and quality of divine creation. Without God there is no world, and the world is merely a result of God's self-contemplation, so that in a sense there is no God without the world either. Everything is one in the sense that it all originates with God, and the rational structure of reality could not be otherwise, according to ibn Sīnā. After all, how could God not create the most rational arrangement of things in the world? This is a point which is emphasized by Mullā Sadrā, according to whom God is equivalent to existence itself. What this means is that the answer to the problem of why anything exists lies in the existence of God and his role as the ultimate source of the existence of everything in the world. Ordinary language is always going to find it difficult to explain how this is to be explained, since ordinary language rests on a form of existence which it itself cannot explain. It might be argued that the move from the notion of the *wajib al-wujūd*, the Necessary Existent, to the doctrine of *waḥdat al-wujūd*, the unity of being, is really quite smooth. Yet there is a need for the existence of various intermediaries which bring together the different levels of our thinking in order to represent the nature of reality, and it is precisely this which is made possible by the ideas in the imaginal realm. It might also be argued that light is itself the perfect mediating notion, since it brings what already exists to our attention by moving it from darkness to light. We might suggest that it is only when we notice something or when it affects us that it really comes into our world, and yet we are aware that a great many things exist without our being able to experience them. I am sitting on a chair right now fairly confident that there is not a monster behind me about to devour me, but I can imagine the existence of such a creature. There would be no difficulty in such a monster being created, and some people look under their beds at night to make sure there is no such being hiding there. Between the idea of a thing and the instantiation of a thing there is a gap, and this is the imaginal realm, the gap between how things might be and how they actually are. The notion that what bridges the gap is light, or a principle like light, was very attractive to many Islamic philosophers, and formed the basis of the *ishrāqī* school.

ISSUES OF INTERPRETATION

It might seem strange to have a discussion of how Islamic philosophy is to be interpreted which is over and above how the arguments which make up that philosophy are to be assessed. Is it not just a matter of looking at the arguments, picking out interesting points and judging the strength or otherwise of the reasoning process which they contain? Students of philosophy are accustomed to discussing philosophical passages almost as though they had just been produced and were without any tiresome interpretational difficulties. One might be asked to assess a particular argument in Plato, Kant or Aquinas without a great deal of knowledge of their circumstances and surroundings being thought relevant. And, although it might be difficult to work out what their argument was, since the language might be rather opaque to us now and the problems no longer especially interesting, we should not on the whole wonder whether their argument expressed their real views or whether they were trying to conceal those views by writing in a special way. Many interpreters of Islamic philosophy suggest that the approach which we should adopt to this form of writing is precisely that of seeking out what is hidden in the text by the author, and they put forward a dazzling variety of hermeneutic techniques which are supposed to help us in this. If they are right, then the approach which has been followed so far in this book might be regarded as naïve, since the arguments themselves have been taken rather at their face-value without any much more profound interpretative devices employed. It is important, therefore, to say something about how we should read Islamic philosophy before reaching a conclusion.

Perhaps the best place to start is with Plato. In his *Republic*, Plato advocated the use of a variety of devious methods to persuade ordinary people that they ought to behave in particular ways. He was not opposed to the use of occasional lies to deceive the enemy or the insane: they are 'useful . . . in the way of medicine . . . to be handled by no one but a physician' and the physician in the *polis* or state is the ruler (*Republic* 388), an analogy often used by Averroes too. Averroes claims in his *Commentary on Plato's 'Republic'* that 'the lie employed by the ruler towards the masses is right and proper for them; it is like medicine for illness' (1,xii,5). In fact, Averroes discusses these passages of Plato with apparent approval (*Comm.Pl.Rep.* I,xvii,5–6; I,xix,1). In his introduction to his translation of the *Commentary*, Ralph Lerner claims that Averroes 'does not preclude the use of invented stories in the *sharī'a*'.[1] It would be remarkable were he to be right and Averroes was indeed an advocate of the idea that God set out to deceive his followers in his revelation. This is precisely the charge which the *falāsifa* were obliged to answer, especially after the attacks of al-Ghazālī, which very much concerned Averroes. Yet do not such attacks have a point, given that the *falāsifa* did seem to support different approaches to different people, with some getting more in the way of truth than others? The distinction which they frequently made between what is hidden (*bāṭin*), and so available only to those capable of demonstrative reasoning, and what is open (*ẓāhir*), or on the surface, does indeed give rise to the idea that God's law embodies lies, and that the apparently orthodox pronouncements of the *falāsifa* themselves contain lies to conceal their real and highly irreligious views.

The root of the confusion is that commentators and the orthodox *fuqahā'* (jurists) tend to lump together all statements which are not designed to communicate the truth under the description of lies. Plato and Averroes were far more subtle in their approach. To a degree the confusion is understandable since the Greek term *pseudos* can mean 'fiction', 'lie' and 'error' in different contexts. Plato even refers to one of his myths at *Republic* 414c as a *pseudos* or tale. On what grounds might Averroes distinguish between these different senses of *pseudos*?

In the first place, he seems to accept that lies may be used for the benefit of the state by rulers who are aware that they are lies. Sometimes it is better to mislead someone or some group than to tell the truth. This type of lie should be distinguished from a story which expresses in an easily digestible form what could have been said without it. The Allegory of the Cave is a good example of such a story, as is the tale of the different metals in the souls of different classes in society. Averroes does not appear to object to these stories, except insofar as his comment that we could do without them goes, where 'we' refers to 'we philosophers'. Such stories should not appear in a philosophical work, argues Averroes, since they are more properly employed in presenting pictures to the masses who are unable to appreciate the force of rational argument. On the principle that philosophers should stick to demonstrative arguments, such stories should be abandoned, since they are used precisely because no argument

---

[1] Ibn Rushd, *Averroes on Plato's 'Republic'*, trans. R. Lerner (Ithaca, NY, Cornell University Press, 1974), p. xxvii.

can be given, in order to bring out a point which Plato feels he cannot establish more surely in another, more rational, way.

Why Averroes should accept these allegories as fit to be discussed, but at the same time reject the first book, the opening of the second book, and the last book of the *Republic* for consisting 'only of dialectical arguments' (*Comm.Pl.Rep.* III,xxi,5) is indeed a puzzle. It may be that he objects to the dialogue form which Plato uses (and al-Fārābī would be a precedent here, as we shall see), and the examples which Plato uses to suggest rather than demonstrate his conclusion – all methods suspect to an Aristotelian. But this general observation would not explain what Averroes finds so objectionable in the Myth of Er that not only does he refuse to discuss it but also says precisely what it is that he does not think worth discussing (*Comm.Pl.Rep.* III,xxi,3). A suggestion is that what is distinct about the Myth is that it offers a rival eschatology to Islam which includes enough similarity in doctrine about being rewarded or punished for what we do on earth in the afterlife to be confused as more than just a myth. The stories about the cave and the metals are both obviously not supposed to describe anything which actually is the case, but the Myth of Er comes close enough to religious doctrine to be regarded as antipathetic to Islam. The Myth makes a claim which it represents as a myth, and which is similar to a claim made by Islam as an aspect of prophetically revealed truth, a claim about punishment and reward in the next life. So Averroes feels obliged to be scathing about the Myth in the *Republic* but not about all the stories which Plato uses. The Myth would actually be dangerous to Islam, whereas the other stories are merely superfluous to a rational explanation sought by the philosopher.

Why is Averroes so eager to condemn stories in general if he was prepared to accept so many provided by Plato? No doubt al-Ghazālī is an important factor here. Al-Ghazālī had accused the *falāsifa* of attributing to the Prophet the will to seduce and confuse the masses by revealing what is not true and concealing what is true. This is his interpretation of the claim which the *falāsifa* sometimes made that the Prophet used the rhetorical method to speak to the masses in a way which they would understand, while he kept the truth for the *falāsifa*. The argument presented by the *falāsifa* claimed that this was done in the general interest, because the masses would not have understood any but rhetorical arguments and stories. In that case, the Prophet could not reveal the truth to them in any other form. Al-Ghazālī interprets this as meaning that the masses are lied to and that this is represented as acceptable because it is in the general interest. Although the *falāsifa* pretend to defend prophecy, he claimed that they in fact contradict its claims and degrade it to a medium of falsehood. He interprets every story, allegory and metaphor as a lie. Within the context of this sort of attack it becomes comprehensible why Averroes stresses his opposition to the use of stories if they mislead people concerning the nature of the truth. He tries to make clear throughout his work that his position is not that philosophers by demonstrative argument can understand the truth, whereas the masses through rhetorical argument are misled in this regard. According to him, the philosophers and the masses both know the same things to be true; it is just that they know them in different ways.

Averroes' position would have been clearer had he pointed out directly that not every allegory or story is a lie. A lie is a statement which is designed to mislead people concerning the truth, but a story in the philosophical sense is merely a statement which is untrue, and patently so. A similar distinction is relevant to accounts of prophecy which stem from al-Fārābī and which connect prophecy with imagination and creativity. When a *failasūf* claims that accounts of prophecy are to be interpreted as accounts of creative imagination he is not claiming that those accounts are not true, in the sense that they are lies. It may well be that those accounts are not true but that they are constructed in such a way as to communicate the truth generally to the public. The orthodox opposition to philosophers such as Maimonides often criticized him for implying in his description of prophecy that the events described were not historically true, which runs totally counter to their presentation in scripture. This is to interpret every story which is not itself true as a lie, and so to represent Maimonides as claiming that reports of prophecy in scripture are lies! Yet, as we have seen, it is possible for a biblical or Qur'ānic account to be a story and yet not a lie, and this sort of possibility is important for Averroes. Yet Averroes does sometimes speak with regret of the way in which Plato uses such stories – he suggests that they are often unnecessary to make Plato's point. It is worth noting how different Averroes' view here is from that of the philosopher who so heavily influenced all the *falāsifa*, al-Fārābī.

In his *Agreement of the opinions of the philosophers Plato and Aristotle*, al-Fārābī talks about Plato's style of writing, his use of myths, allegories and symobls to make his point instead of a clearer and more direct approach to such issues as would surely be possible. Al-Fārābī thinks that what is behind this technique is Plato's intention to reserve philosophy for those who are capable of doing it and who have the requisite merit to receive it. He refers to a letter from Plato to Aristotle in which the latter is blamed for writing in a clear and demonstrative form which could be understood more widely than the dialogue approach of Plato. The implication is that there is no value in popularizing philosophy. Aristotle replies that although his work is indeed less obscure than that of Plato, it is still presented in such a form as would prevent its being taken up by the masses who are incapable of really grasping it and who would otherwise misrepresent it. The desirability of obscurity in philosophy is something of a theme in Islamic philosophy, with the intended result that philosophy is reserved for the elect few and protected from the power of orthodox theologians and the rulers of states unsympathetic to philosophy. Surely in his reply Aristotle is correct, namely, that it is very unlikely that the arguments which he uses will have much attraction for the masses. The same may not be said of some of the stories of Plato which are often designed to appeal to the masses as justifications of a policy which is in their objective interests but which they cannot understand as being such by demonstrative argument alone. Averroes does not really accept al-Fārābī's account of why Plato wrote in such a form – the former thinks that that form of presentation is not appropriate to philosophy per se, although it is only actually to be condemned when it is put in a form which may seriously mislead by partially resembling the truth, like the Myth of Er.

This fascination, which is so common among the *falāsifa*, with different philosophical styles and techniques, and especially for what those different approaches may be regarded as concealing, is interesting. The *falāsifa* themselves speak of the importance of concealing dangerous doctrines and presenting their ideas in such a way that they will not disturb the faith of the masses or the suspicions of the theologians. Were we to ignore this aspect of their thought then we might well miss a great deal of significance. This fact has been taken very much to heart by many commentators on Islamic philosophy, and it has resulted in what I shall call the esoteric interpretation.

According to the esoteric interpretation, much more is required of the interpreter than just the ability to read the text and the capacity to deal with the philosophical points made in it. What is required is a key to understanding the peculiar way in which the text has been composed, and that key is to be found by paying attention to the way in which the text incorporates the conflict between religion and disbelief within a specific cultural and historical context. Now, the great merit of the esoteric interpretation is that it tries to place the text within the context from which it arose, since otherwise it is impossible to grasp what the purpose of the text is. The argument throughout this study is not opposed to the esoteric interpretation as such, but is rather opposed to an assumption which is crucial to it, namely, that the conflict between religion and philosophy is of *overriding* importance to the construction of Islamic philosophy and all the arguments within that philosophy.

The esoteric interpretation emphasizes two common features of Islamic philosophy. Firstly, it is well understood that the *falāsifa* were often operating in unsympathetic conditions and were obliged, out of prudential considerations, to represent their views as perfectly in order with the established beliefs of Islam. Secondly, these philosophers presented their views in such a way as to disguise their real opinions and intentions, so that any reader who wants to understand the text must pierce the outer skin of orthodoxy to arrive at the kernel of philosophical argument. Since the text is riddled with all kinds of devices that are designed to mislead and pacify the ignorant but at the same time to encourage the wise to persist with the argument, any understanding of the text's real purpose involves understanding these devices and reading the text in accordance with an appreciation of their role. So the conclusion of the esoteric interpretation is that we must examine such texts with suspicion and ask ourselves what the author was really getting at; only then can we grasp what the author is about in his work. The esoteric interpretation thus provides a methodological paradigm in terms of which samples of philosophy are to be studied and analyzed.

There is a good deal to be said for such a paradigm, since an important distinction has to be made between exoteric (*ẓāhir*) and esoteric (*bāṭin*) works. There are also works which fall between such clear cases, works that are exoterically orthodox and yet have features pointing to aspects of the argument that only those fit and proper to understand such philosophy would appreciate. In that case, the faith of the masses is not challenged while the wise élite is provided with an account, albeit disguised, that discusses the philosophical aspects of a certain problem. This strategy is apparently followed by God in his gift of the Qur'ān, which is itself a representation of two doctrines, one exoteric and to be accepted by all believers, and one esoteric and available only to those capable of recognizing it.

Averroes rather neatly categorized the different kinds of texts involved in terms of different sorts of reasoning, each type being appropriate to a different group in society. So demonstrative reasoning is appropriate to a different group – philosophers – than dialectical reasoning, which is right for theologians. Rhetorical, sophistical and poetic formulations of an argument are designed for the masses. It is one of the excellences of Islam, according to Averroes in his *Decisive treatise on the harmony of religion and philosophy*, that it provides the possibility of assent to its doctrines for anyone, regardless of intelligence or social position. He severely criticized the mixing up of these different types of reasoning, arguing that it can result only in mystification and disbelief. Certain representations of one's views are appropriate for certain purposes; like tools they should be directed to an end rather than employed haphazardly. The trouble with writing a book is that it may end up in the hands of those for whom it is not intended and actually do them damage, in the sense of endangering their faith. It may, on the other hand, do the philosopher damage, in that its publication may lead to the popular, albeit erroneous, belief that he is advocating disbelief, or at the very least, heresy.

This caution towards writing does not provide grounds for caution towards philosophy itself, though, since the philosopher can in conversation distinguish between those to whom it is worthwhile or safe to talk and those who should not be addressed on such issues. That is the problem with writing, it is indiscriminate and so unsatisfactory – a fact that explains the tendency of *falāsifa* like Maimonides to address their more controversial work to a specific individual who has reached a certain level of intellectual and ethical maturity. As Plato puts it: 'once a thing is put in writing, the composition, whatever it may be, drifts all over the place, getting into the hands not only of those who understand it, but equally of those who have no business with it; it doesn't know how to address the right people and not address the wrong' (*Phaedrus* 275e, trans. R. Hackforth).

A point that the esoteric interpretation makes is that the *falāsifa* try in their written work to duplicate the sorts of controls and safeguards they could apply to their oral teaching. The *falāsifa* tried to write in such a way that whoever read them would find only what it was in his capacity to understand. An ordinary person would not find his faith threatened by reading even a specifically philosophical work, since the way in which it is written would put him off from continuing with it, while a philosopher would put up with the contradictions, repetitions and dryness of the text. This, it will be recalled, is how Aristotle is taken to have justified the clear presentation of his thought in his works – 'If I have written down these sciences and the wisdom contained in them, I have arranged them in such an order that only those qualified for them can attain them' (al-Fārābī, *Agreement between Plato and Aristotle*, p. 85). But this strategy concerning the presentation of philosophical views to the public suggests a question:

what really are the beliefs of the practitioners of this form of writing? Did the *falāsifa* set out to deceive people with their apparent orthodoxy and hidden heterodoxy?

The *falāsifa* themselves were very aware of this issue. At the beginning of his *Ḥayy ibn Yaqẓān*, ibn Ṭufayl (d. 580/1185) catalogued briefly the inconsistencies between the opinions expressed by the same author in different works in the case of Avicenna, al-Fārābī and even al-Ghazālī. He does this in such a way as to suggest that such comparisons were commonly made at the time. For example, he makes this observation about al-Fārābī:

> In the *Ideal Religion* he affirms that the souls of the wicked live on forever in infinite torments after death. But in his *Civil Politics* he says plainly that they dissolve into nothing and that only the perfected souls of the good achieve immortality. Finally in his commentary on Aristotle's *Ethics*, discussing human happiness, he says that it exists only in this life, and on the heels of that has words to the effect that all other claims are senseless ravings and old wives' tales. This makes mankind at large despair of God's mercy. (p. 100)

Ibn Ṭufayl makes a good point here. There certainly does appear to be a marked distinction between the claims the *falāsifa* make in their popular works and the claims they make in works unlikely to have been of much interest to the general public. For example, al-Fārābī's accounts of Plato and Aristotle in his more popular writings (like his *Agreement* and *The virtuous city*) present a different view of these thinkers, and one more in line with Islam, than those in the more specialized works on the Greeks like his *Philosophy of Plato, Philosophy of Aristotle* and *Attainment of happiness*.

One of the most distinguished of the supporters of the esoteric interpretation, Leo Strauss, has also remarked upon the fact that al-Fārābī's *Summary* of Plato's *Laws* is markedly different from its supposed source, Plato, and imports all kinds of religious expressions and concerns which are entirely absent not just from Plato (as al-Fārābī knew him) but from al-Fārābī's own book *Philosophy of Plato* itself. Strauss has also emphasized the significance of the distinction between Maimonides' *Mishneh Torah* and his *Guide of the perplexed*, the former being a standard work of jurisprudence (*fiqh*) and the latter a discussion (according to Strauss, forbidden by the law) of how to explain difficult passages in the law to those confused by what they find in it. He spends a great deal of time in pointing to Maimonides' judicious and self-conscious use of contradiction to put off those not capable of appreciating his teaching. What all the contrasts are designed to show (and many more are available from the works of the *falāsifa*) is that we must approach this type of thought in a very special way, not just because it is concerned with problems that may be specifically medieval, but because the way in which it is written is intended to ensure (insofar as this is possible in a writing) that it will be read by only a certain type of reader. Unless we understand this basic fact about such writing, we shall not be able to enter into it but will be condemned to have only a superficial grasp of exactly what is happening when we confront such a text.

The esoteric interpretation is in fact a reaction against an older type of interpretation, according to which the *falāsifa* managed or thought they had managed, by and large, to reconcile Islam and philosophy, and their writings showed how this feat could be accomplished. This type of interpretation was itself a reaction to the earlier view (largely based on the nature of Averroism in medieval Christian Europe) that the *falāsifa* were rationalists who rejected the values and beliefs of the community of Islam in favour of what they had learnt from Aristotle and Greek logic. The esoteric interpretation rejects the position that the reconciliation was successfully carried out as a view that 'was, in fact, propagated by the Muslim philosophers themselves in their effort to convince their fellow Muslims that the teachings of philosophy did not contradict the revealed teaching, and that philosophic activity, far from undermining religion, was undertaken in defence of the faith'.[2]

It is significant that both the esoteric interpretation and previous types of interpretation all share a certain assumption – that the conflict between religion and philosophy, an aspect of the clash between belief and disbelief, is a constant theme and interest of the *falāsifa*. They are merely taken to differ in their answers to the question of how the *falāsifa* deal with this constant theme, whether by dissimulating their genuine anti-religious philosophical beliefs or by bringing their religious and philosophical beliefs into a genuine harmony. Often when there is a dispute in philosophy between two alternatives, both of which seem capable of reasoned support and argument, it is impossible to settle the dispute because it presupposes a common assumption which is false itself. The common assumption here is the idea that the conflict between belief and disbelief is a crucial theme of Islamic philosophy (*all* Islamic philosophy), and this common and often tacit presupposition deserves some critical attention.

---

[2] Al-Fārābī, *Al-Fārābī's philosophy*, trans. M. Mahdi, p. 3.

It will be suggested here that there are aspects of *falsafa* which are not touched by this presupposition. We should re-examine the influence that Greek philosophy had on the Islamic philosophers. What the *falāsifa* learnt from the Greeks was not limited to a number of interesting doctrines which appear to be inconsistent with Islamic revelation, such as the eternity of the world or difficulties about corporeal immortality, and so on, although the opposition to *falsafa* often centres upon such issues. What was learnt from the Greeks was an entirely new way of thinking, a system of constructive logical thought which provided its users with great conceptual power. This capacity for logical thought was largely, but certainly not entirely, represented by Aristotle, which is why he fascinated the *falāsifa*, not because he supported theories of the eternity of the world or the impossibility of corporeal immortality. What made such awkward theories interesting was that Aristotle seemed to arrive at them using the principles of valid demonstrative reasoning, and so they presented a problem in so far as they were examples of respectable logical thinking that result in conclusions which are possibly opposed to aspects of Islamic teaching. The conflict between religion and philosophy in the medieval world is often represented as being a conflict between orthodoxy in religion and such issues as the age of the world and the nature of immortality, and that indeed is how it is represented in many of the discussions which touch directly on these issues. But Aristotle's thinking in these areas was felt to be so problematical by the *falāsifa* because it was based upon arguments which they could accept as formally valid, and appeared to oppose what they accepted on the basis of revelation. What *specifically* interested the *falāsifa* was the form of the argument, not the conclusion or its premises. In their works which are directed at other philosophers and not the general public they did not go in much for discussing Islam, *not* because they were not really devout Muslims, but because they were writing philosophy, and Islam is a religion and not a philosophy.

Of course, the obvious rejoinder in defence of previous interpretations of *falsafa* will point out that the *falāsifa* spent much time in apparently reconciling philosophy and religion. This does not show, though, that this conflict was of great importance to them *as philosophers*. To be sure, it was a problem which they discussed, and the editing and translating of *falsafa* has often concentrated upon such works, but it would be a mistake to conclude from this fact that such a theme was the major problem or interest for such thinkers. Works dealing with the reconciliation of philosophy and religion are frequently overshadowed in both size and importance by the expository commentaries and analyzes of the Greek philosophers and logicians. The conflict between religion and philosophy did not arise for the Greeks in the form of an opposition between a revelation and a philosophy as it did for the *falāsifa*, and so there is very little discussion of this topic in their discussion of the works of the Greeks. In any case, did the *falāsifa* have anything to hide? The argument that religion and philosophy are radically different forms of knowledge is not to downgrade the former in favour of the latter. For example, al-Fārābī claims that 'religion . . . is aimed at teaching everyone theoretical and practical knowledge which are derived philosophically, but in ways which enable everyone's understanding of them, either through persuasion or representation, or through a combination of them'.[3] Al-Fārābī's point is that 'religion cannot go against the demonstrative knowledge available through philosophy since religion is a reflection and more digestible formulation of that knowledge. Religion establishes its truth in a unique and non-philosophical way. Its truth is based upon revelation, whereas the truth of philosophy is based on demonstrative reasoning. In both cases the means of defence can be dialectical, but the means of gaining knowledge of more than just that one's opponent is mistaken are different. Yet it is a theme of *falsafa* that this difference does not imply that the answers must be reflections of the same truth, which is itself established in different ways.

In their enthusiasm to defend the esoteric interpretation of Islamic philosophy, some writers have even argued that it is important to relate what the *falāsifa* have to say in their technical works to the conflict between religion and philosophy. They argue that the apparently logical comments which the *falāsifa* make have an extra-logical reference and aim, so that in uncovering this reference we may discover what the work is 'really' about. We can examine a relatively uncomplicated example of the esoteric interpretation being applied to the relationship between demonstrative and dialectical reasoning in the work of Averroes.

In his *Short commentary on Aristotle's 'Topics'*, Averroes correctly represents Aristotle's thesis on the distinction between two types of valid reasoning, one type which is called demonstrative and which is based upon true premises, and the other type which is called dialectical and which is based upon merely probable premises. Now, on the esoteric interpretation this discussion of Aristotle must be taken to conceal something because it fails to mention religion. In spite of this failure, Averroes

---

[3] Al-Fārābī, *Book of letters*, ed. M. Mahdi, p. 131.

is taken to refer to religion 'indirectly'. As Butterworth says in his account of the text, 'the whole presentation appears very arid, and one cannot help but wonder why Averroes would have been content to insist upon all these technical considerations, in order to make such a minor point. The answer is relatively simple: the tedious technical discussion is a screen for a more important substantive argument.'[4] It may well be thought, though, that since Averroes was commenting on Aristotle, a writer not noted for his exciting style, it is hardly surprising that his discussion is rather dry. Of course, someone uninterested in logic might find such an argument 'very arid', 'minor' and 'tedious', all descriptions which are used by Butterworth. However, Averroes, like Aristotle, thought that the distinctions which can be made between demonstrative and dialectical reasoning are very important if we are to understand why and how different arguments work or are invalid. Like any other logical distinction, it is of great interest to the logician, and that in itself justifies the process of establishing logically the distinction.

Butterworth follows the esoteric interpretation in thinking that Averroes could not be really interested in this 'minor' point except for its usefulness in attacking the dialectical theologians by showing that they do not really know how to use dialectic. In his *Short commentary on Aristotle's 'Topics'*, Averroes does not mention the theologians (*mutakallimūn*), which might be thought to present a problem for this interpretation. But no, this omission is 'masterfully subtle: rather than attack them openly here, he pretended to ignore them as though this were not the place to speak of them'.[5] This is presumably the employment of 'Another device [which] consists in silence, i.e. the omission of something which only the learned, or the learned who are able to understand of themselves, would miss.'[6] Additionally, providing 'an attentive reading of the treatise ... in order to uncover Averroes' teaching it is as important to ask about what is implied as to ask what is said'.[7]

Butterworth may well be right in thinking that Averroes' argument implies that the arguments of the so-called 'dialectical' theologians are invalid – that would be a reasonable application of a point made in a treatise on logic. Yet to present Averroes as interested in the logical point only to refute particular theological arguments is going too far. The theologians whom Averroes considers present arguments which in

---

[4] C. Butterworth, *Averroes' three short commentaries on Aristotle's 'Topics', 'Rhetoric' and 'Poetics'* (Albany, State University of New York Press, 1977), p. 25.

[5] *Ibid.*, p. 26.

[6] L. Strauss, *Persecution and the art of writing* (Glencoe, Ill., Free Press, 1952), p. 75.

[7] Butterworth, *Short commentaries*, p. 28.

his view are invalid, but he does not conclude that there is anything invalid about dialectic itself just because it is sometimes incorrectly used. Butterworth claims that 'Averroes enabled the reader to call the whole activity of the dialectical theologian into question. If the art of dialectic cannot be used for most kinds of theoretical investigation, then it cannot support the complicated theological disputes characteristic of dialectic theology.'[8] Yet what Averroes does in fact seek to show is that dialectic as an argument form may be invalidly used and that even if valid the conclusions are only as sound as the premisses, and the premisses may be untrue. There is nothing *wrong* with using dialectic. It may be successfully used in refuting the arguments of an opponent, as Averroes famously does in his attack on al-Ghazālī's *The incoherence of the philosophers*, and we should then logically know that such an opponent's argument is invalid. But we will not know whether the premisses and conclusions of an argument are true. Such propositions cannot be proved dialectically. Averroes' point here may be illustrated, as so often, by al-Ghazālī's stress upon the limitations inherent in the use of dialectic. According to al-Ghazālī:

Dialectical reasoning is the weakest form of guidance. The real searcher after truth will not be convinced by an argument based on the presuppositions of his opponent, since those presuppositions need not be true in the first place. For the ordinary person they are in any case beyond his grasp, while the dialectical adversary, even when he is silenced, normally does not change his opinion. He criticizes his own defence of his position, thinking that if only the founder of his school were still alive and available he would know how to overcome the theologians' arguments. Yet most of what the theologians say in their arguments with other sects is nothing more than dialectic.[9]

The point which Averroes is interested in making is that dialectic is limited in its possible application; it may refute the arguments of opponents, but cannot support one's own position in any stronger way than by refuting alternatives. As al-Ghazālī points out, this does not provide a great deal of backing for one's own position, since both it and its negations may be based upon a false premiss.

Now, it is important here to get the order of priority right when discussing the relationship between Averroes' logical arguments and

---

[8] *Ibid.*, p. 27.

[9] Al-Ghazālī, *Mīzān al ʿAmal* (Criterion of action) (Cairo, 1912), p. 160. For a detailed account of how the term *jadal* or dialectic was understood in Islamic philosophy, see J. Van Ess, 'The logical character of Islamic theology', in G. Grunebaum (ed.), *Logic in classical Islamic culture* (Wiesbaden, Harrassowitz, 1970), pp. 21–50.

their theological application. The attack upon the *mutakallimūn* can be mounted because they often logically err in their applications of dialectic, and often try to use dialectic to establish as true the premises of their arguments, something which dialectic is just not capable of doing. There is no necessity to approach Averroes' commentaries with suspicion and ask what is the significance of what is missing, or of what is implied as opposed to what is said. There is nothing to be uncovered, no mysterious forms of representation require interpretation. Averroes is merely presenting a commentary on Aristotle's logic, which is by no means a slavish adaptation of the Greek text, but which is entirely unenigmatic. It is written in a manner perfectly consistent with the standard form of philosophical logic of that period. The references to the *mutakallimūn* (not, it is worth noting, in the commentary on the *Topics*, but in the commentary on the *Rhetoric*) are merely contemporary illustrations of logical points which Aristotle made. But the esoteric interpretation assumes that the conflict between religion and philosophy must have been something uppermost in Averroes' mind even when 'apparently' commenting upon Aristotle's logic; even a commentary on logic must, it is felt, be a reflection of an obsession with such a conflict. Such a thesis is without foundation, and seeks to find what is not there and never was intended to be there.

It might be admitted in defence of the esoteric interpretation that it is not an appropriate method for dealing with logical works of *falsafa*. After all, there is little cause for dissimulation concerning logic, since it is hardly likely to be read or understood by non-philosophers, nor could it easily be thought to be antagonistic to Islam, or any other religious doctrine. Butterworth's application of the esoteric interpretation to logic could then be seen as over-enthusiastic. Logic merely deals with rules of reasoning and has nothing to do with religious doctrines. But the *falāsifa* did not restrict their interest in Greek philosophy to logic; they were interested in more sensitive areas in so far as religion is concerned, such as ethics, politics and metaphysics. Perhaps the esoteric interpretation is more successful in these areas in explaining what it is that the *falāsifa* are about and how they express themselves to their intended audience. This is, of course, to be expected; they were often careful not to appear to challenge the accepted norms of Islam in their writings, and their works are often presented in such a way as to put off or placate the ignorant and orthodox non-philosophers while at the same time stimulating the interest of the philosophically minded.

A good example of how this is supposed to work can be found in Strauss' account of al-Fārābī which is paradigmatic of the esoteric interpretation. According to al-Fārābī, Plato presents his teaching 'by means of allusive, ambiguous, misleading and obscure speech'[10] and was a master of dissimulation. He is famously supposed to have criticized Aristotle for the relative simplicity and clarity of his style which makes it open to anyone, as we have seen. The esoteric interpretation thinks that this discussion of dissimulation should alert interpreters of al-Fārābī's writings to wonder what he is really getting at.

What strikes a reader of al-Fārābī's *Summary* of Plato's *Laws* is how different that summary is from what it is supposed to summarize. It almost seems to be of a different book. It is even quite different from al-Fārābī's own account of Plato and his philosophy, which discusses Plato without any special regard for religion in general or Islam in particular. But the *Summary* talks about God, *sharī'a*, the afterlife and divine laws, managing not to mention the term 'philosophy' once. Strauss suggests that al-Fārābī disguised his real opinions about Plato in the *Summary* by the use of non-committal expressions which signify neither agreement nor disagreement. Strauss catalogues some of the different ways in which al-Fārābī refers to Plato's doctrines and claims that the different expresions used can be seen sometimes to express different shades of agreement or opinion concerning their importance. A tentative conclusion is made by Strauss:

Al-Fārābī may have rewritten the *Laws*, as it were, with a view to the situation that was created by the rise of Islam . . . He may have tried to preserve Plato's purpose by adapting the expression of that purpose to the new medium . . . he may have desired to ascribe his revised version of Plato's teaching to the dead Plato in order to protect that version, or the sciences generally speaking, especially by leaving open the question as to whether he agreed with everything his Plato taught and by failing to draw a precise line between his mere report and his independent exposition.[11]

According to Strauss and the esoteric interpretation, then al-Fārābī must be up to something in his *Summary*; after all, 'al-Fārābī agreed with Plato certainly to the extent that he, too, presented what he regarded as the truth by means of ambiguous, allusive, misleading, and obscure speech'.[12] Strauss himself makes many allusive and suggestive comments about what that truth is from al-Fārābī's point of view. The description which Strauss provides of the *Summary* succeeds in clouding it in the

---

[10] L. Strauss, 'How al-Fārābī read Plato's *Laws*', *Mélanges Louis Massignon* (Paris, Institut Français de Damas, 1957), p. 322.

[11] *Ibid.*, pp. 330–1.

[12] *Ibid.*, p. 333.

same sort of mystery and ambivalence which Strauss claims is integral
to the work. But there is insufficient justification for such an approach
to al-Fārābī. The *falāsifa* were, it is true, often interested in dissimulating
their genuine views, but the sort of strategy which Strauss' al-Fārābī
demands to be understood surely defies credibility. According to Strauss,
to understand al-Fārābī we are not only to have the *Summary* with us but
also the original *Laws*; yet the former is meant only 'to be a help to him
who desires to know [the Laws] and to be sufficient to him who cannot
bear the toil of study and meditation'.[13] The procedure which Strauss
demands of the discriminating reader involves a good deal of ingenuity.
The reader must compare and contrast chapter with chapter, noting what
is added to the original and what is omitted from the original. Then he
must pay close attention to the ways in which al-Fārābī introduces his
discussions of Plato – e.g. does he say that Plato mentioned a subject
of exceeding usefulness,[14] or does he say that Plato mentioned a useful
subject?[15] Strauss mentions all sorts of apparently irrelevant points, such
as that at the beginning of the eighth chapter 'mentioning' is referred
to five times and is contrasted with Plato's 'intimating' another aspect of
the same subject in the beginning of the book.[16] Strauss also points out
that al-Fārābī does not discuss some Platonic themes, that the *Summary*
uses the personal pronoun unlike the *Philosophy of Plato*, and that the
distribution of 'thens' in the *Summary* is uneven. The brilliance of Strauss'
analysis is evident through the fact that he manages to take up all these
points, and many more, and argue that al-Fārābī was doing something
very complicated and devious when he wrote the *Summary*. He does not
feel able to come to any definite conclusion about what the *Summary* is
about, and only asserts that although 'we would be foolish to claim that
we are in a position to explain these difficulties... On the other hand,
it cannot be denied that in reflecting for some time on writing like the
Summary, one acquires a certain understanding of the manner in which
such writings wish to be read.'[17] Strauss is arguing that to understand
the text completely we should have to be in the position of an original
reader, and because our understanding of that point of view is necessarily
limited, our comprehension of the text must be limited, too.

[13] Al-Fārābī, *Compendium legum Platonis*, ed. and trans. F. Gabrieli (London, Warburg Institute, 1952),
   4, 20–1.
[14] *Ibid.*, 42, 20–1.
[15] *Ibid.*, 11, 5:21 5; 27, 18; 32, 3.
[16] Strauss, 'How Farabī', p. 326.
[17] *Ibid.*, p. 338.

But, if the points which Strauss makes about the difficulties in reading the text are separately examined, they can be seen to be not difficulties at all, but rather normal ways of going about writing philosophy. The esoteric interpretation concentrates upon the distinction between the real opinion of the author and what is offered merely as a sop to public opinion and its prejudices. Yet it might be suggested that the *falāsifa* present theories which they argue are true, or, at least, are interesting and relevant, and that the question of the precise authorship of such theories is not really important. Strauss is convinced that this is a question which does and must arise, and which demands an answer, and since the *failasūf* is reluctant to provide the answer, his teaching must be obscured and hidden by means of the techniques we have already mentioned (and a good many more). This approach presupposes that it is normal for Islamic philosophers to differentiate exactly their views from the views of others with whom they are not clearly in dispute, and that when they discuss the works of others they must make clear which argument is original, which merely commentary, which application of the text is not to be found in the original, and so on. It will be urged here, though, that this presupposition fails and so there is no need to try to discover some subtle explanation for possible confusion between the *failasūf*'s views and the Greek source.

If we think of *falsafa* as more like ordinary philosophy and less like esoteric literature, we can explain the 'techniques' which Strauss thinks the *falāsifa* employ in more conventional and less exciting ways. For example, the different ways in which al-Fārābī refers to points which Plato makes may just be stylistic variations which indicate his opinions of the varying relevance, importance and truth of Plato's thought at different stages, rather than due to a 'hidden' meaning, or an obstacle in the way of unsympathetic comprehension of the real point. It is not important for al-Fārābī as a philosopher to distinguish precisely where he diverges from Plato or what his opinion of Plato's various points are. The fact that the *Summary* and Plato's *Laws* (not to mention al-Fārābī's *Philosophy of Plato*) are different from one another in important details has a simple explanation which Strauss himself provides – the *Summary* is not a representation of Plato's views, but rather an account of his art of *kalām*,[18] his technique of defending the laws and religion. Al-Fārābī is showing how Plato would defend law within an Islamic context – hence the introduction of Islamic and religious topics foreign to the original *Laws* and

---

[18] *Ibid.*, p. 325.

Philosophy of Plato. No dissimulation is required here as an explanatory hypothesis. Al-Fārābī himself suggests that the *Summary* is more than just a commentary on Plato by his use of the personal pronoun and his use of specifically Islamic expressions like *sharīᶜa*; it is clear that he did not wish to represent Plato as a Muslim. The question is not whether al-Fārābī used dissimulation (*taqīya*) in his writing. The answer is, of course, that he did. The question is whether it was used as frequently and in the ways that the esoteric interpretation considers to be the case. The best way to tackle this question is by looking at alternative accounts of works subjected to the esoteric interpretation to see if they are convincing. The evidences which Strauss selects in favour of the esoteric interpretation are not compelling and are perfectly capable of an alternative and less forced interpretation as aspects of a normal philosophical discussion.

But, it would no doubt be argued by an adherent of the esoteric interpretation that the account of the *Summary* as an ordinary philosophical work ignores the beginning of the book. Here al-Fārābī speaks at some length of a story about a city in which a holy ascetic is sought by the ruler with the intention of killing him. The holy man disguises himself as a drunken musician and safely passes through the gates of the city after telling the guards, perfectly truthfully, that he is the holy man for whom they are to keep a look out. Strauss takes the moral of this story to be that al-Fārābī is prepared to tell the truth (i.e present his opinions about the *Laws*) but only if he is able to disguise it in such a way that he will not suffer for it. The *falāsifa* were eager to avoid the fate of Socrates, who was put to death, according to them, for his failure to disguise his teaching adequately.[19] But this story does not provide incontestable support for the esoteric interpretation. It may be interpreted in other ways. For example, it may be that al-Fārābī wishes his readers to think that he has disguised his views, so that only those who are capable of understanding and appreciating his teaching will recognize that he has not disguised his views at all. Such an interpretation is not as fanciful as it sounds. After all, in the story the holy man misleads the guards by telling the truth and getting them to think that he is not telling the truth at all. Perhaps al-Fārābī uses the story to get people to think that he is not telling the truth, while he *is* expressing his real opinions after all. In that case, Strauss would be in the position of the guards, in that he naïvely assumes that when he is thus presented with the truth, he is in fact presented with a disguise. Such an interpretation may seem over-subtle,

---

[19] Al-Fārābī, *Al-Fārābī's philosophy*, trans. M. Mahdi, p. 66.

but it is surely not more so than the lengths to which Strauss' use of the esoteric interpretation leads him.

A more plausible interpretation of the story is: al-Fārābī is arguing that the philosophical complexity and difficulty of his book is such that it will prevent those who might dislike its opinions from understanding them. It is worth recalling that al-Fārābī thought that Aristotle's style of philosophy was a form of dissimulation, in that it excludes those incapable of philosophy from grasping his teaching. Al-Fārābī did not suggest that this teaching needed to be hidden because it has features which make it unwelcome to, say, a religion. His point is that those who are not able really to understand Aristotle might *think* that his philosophy is religiously suspect, and so persecute those who expound it. A deeper understanding of philosophy reveals that it is by no means antagonistic to religion. It may be that al-Fārābī used his story of the holy ascetic to suggest that the appropriate way to write philosophy, if one is incapable of Platonic style, is the *grave et meditatum* approach favoured by Aristotle and himself. In that case, interpreting that sort of philosophy will call for no special skills at puzzle-solving that are not already required in the interpretation of any philosophical thought written in the Aristotelian manner.

The aim of this section is very limited. The argument has been that the esoteric interpretation should not be generally applied to all texts of *falsafa*. Are there not, though, some texts which do indeed call for this interpretative approach? Maimonides' *Guide of the perplexed* seems an ideal candidate. It is replete with contradictions, omissions and repetitions, and a whole gamut of confusing and obscuring techniques which Strauss catalogues in his introduction to the work.[20] But the *Guide of the perplexed* should not be regarded as a paradigm of *falsafa*. Strauss himself points out that 'the very existence of the *Guide* implies a conscious transgression of an unambiguous prohibition',[21] i.e. not to explain the secrets of the Torah in a writing. To get around such an explicit law it is necessary to employ all sorts of complicated and powerful devices to ensure that only those fit to study the secrets can sift through the book and receive them. In Islam there is no such 'unambiguous prohibition', although many Muslims argued that both the use of analogy and interpretation with respect to the law should be carefully restricted. The

---

[20] L. Strauss, 'Literary character of the *Guide of the perplexed*', in his *Persecution and the art of writing*; and 'How to begin to study the *Guide of the perplexed*' in Maimonides, *Guide of the perplexed*, trans. Pines.

[21] Strauss, 'Literary character', p. 48. But there are good grounds for thinking that on the contrary the question of permitting or prohibiting the study of philosophy arose only in the wake of the anti-Maimonides controversy.

Guide of the perplexed is, in many ways, a unique work. Strauss' approach to Maimonides leads him to discover dissimulation even where it is not present, or not present to the extent he expects. The *Guide of the perplexed* is a work whose whole rationale is the conflict between religion and philosophy, and it is unrealistic to expect it to serve as a reliable model of *falsafa* in general. It is always tempting to use the esoteric interpretation because it is so enjoyable to try to unravel the tricks and puzzles which the author allegedly sets the reader, and to display one's interpretative virtuosity to the full. It is worth fighting this temptation and directing effort rather to understanding the philosophical arguments themselves.

When we consider the *Guide of the perplexed* we should be careful before we accept that the contradictions in it are a useful means of interpretation. Contradictions can sometimes be interpreted merely as the combination of different views to inform the reader of the variety which exists. In the previous discussion of prophecy and the creation of the world, which Maimonides related to each other in the *Guide of the perplexed*, it was suggested that he might merely be setting out the different positions which could be taken up on both those topics. This interpretation would be regarded as terribly naïve by the esoteric interpretation. The latter would see the *Guide of the perplexed*, and much else, as replete with irony, in the sense in which an ironic claim is intended to get across not the proposition the writer makes but the very contradictory of this proposition. It is very difficult after all to detect irony when it is directed against one's own beliefs. One of the main signs of irony is contradiction; contradiction between various things that appear to be said in the dubious-looking passage and contradictions between this passage and what the writer repeatedly and characteristically says elsewhere. Socratic irony was specifically the pretence of ignorance, of the form saying that p ('I am ignorant') while meaning not p ('I am not ignorant at all'). Aristotle obviously thought that speaking ironically was no bad thing, since his notion of the *megalopsychos* – the 'great-souled' person and best of human beings – does so in speaking with the many (*NE* 1124b 30). No doubt there are contexts in which irony as an interpretative hypothesis works well, but it has been suggested here that the esoteric interpretation consistently overdoes it. Islamic philosophy may be regarded as perfectly ordinary philosophy in that irony is not generally revealing or important in working out what the actual argument being presented is. In any case, philosophers will be more interested in the validity of the arguments concerned rather than in the 'real' intentions of the disputants, this being an issue rather for historians who might well be more interested in the question of 'hidden meanings' than in the argument form itself. By all means let us look carefully at the style of Islamic philosophy, yet without forgetting that it is philosophy and that its interest lies in its arguments and not in its style.

AVERROES AND ARISTOTLE

There has been quite a lot of discussion about the precise relationship between Aristotle and ibn Rushd.[22] It is not possible to be precise about this relationship, given the limited state of our access to the works of ibn Rushd, and the limited nature of his access to the works of Aristotle. He did not have the entire corpus of Aristotle available to him (nor do we), and he did not have them in their original language. He also inherited a tradition which attributed to Aristotle a number of texts which we now know are not by him, something which ibn Rushd was also apparently capable of discerning. We should not overdo the problems here, though, since he did have a great many genuine Aristotelian works, well translated, where several translators had each tried to improve on earlier work. He also had access to a tradition of commentary which is certainly different from that current today, but which was both closer to Aristotle in time and part of a continuing tradition of the development of Greek philosophy. We should not so readily accept that the ways in which we see Aristotle today are the only feasible applications of his thought.

There is a tendency for many to downplay the contribution which ibn Rushd plays in the understanding of Aristotle. For one thing, the cultural context within which he was working was very different from that of the Greek world itself. Borges has represented well in his story 'Averroes' search' the impossibility of ibn Rushd's making sense of the basic examples in Aristotle's *Poetics*, since tragedy and comedy as dramatic forms were unknown in the world of al-Andalus. The point is often made, for example, that much of the *Poetics* was literally meaningless in Arabic since it dealt with forms of cultural expression entirely unknown within the Islamic world.[23] It is also suggested that ibn Rushd was concerned for religious and political reasons to reconcile Aristotle with Islam, and so he may have had interests and concerns which are entirely foreign to the Aristotelian enterprise itself. In his defence, it might be said that the tempestuous nature of ibn Rushd's career does not suggest that he was very

---

[22] There is an extensive literature on this issue. See further reading list below.

[23] See D. Black, *Logic and Aristotle's 'Rhetoric' and 'Poetics' in Medieval Arabic philosophy* (Leiden, Brill, 1990) and S. Kemal, *The poetics of Al-fārābī and Avicenna* (Leiden, Brill, 1991). The story 'Averroes' search' is in *Labyrinths* (New York, New Directions, 1964).

successful in placing philosophy within an acceptable political context, but this does not prove that he did not set out to reach this end. Then there is the well-known fact, frequently referred to by ibn Rushd himself, that on occasions he draws conclusions from what Aristotle says which are not explicitly drawn by Aristotle himself. There is obviously great scope here for the transformation of Aristotle into an entirely different sort of thinker, one whose thought can be regarded as more 'orthodox' from a religious point of view. Finally, there is the organization of his commentaries into three forms, the small, middle and large, which enable him to present Aristotle in a wide variety of different ways, perhaps for different audiences. The small and middle commentaries are often far more than just slimmed-down versions of the large commentaries, and there is scope for arguing that ibn Rushd was often using Aristotle rather than being genuinely Aristotelian. Of course, one could try to get around this apparent difficulty by arguing that it is only the large commentary which represents ibn Rushd's 'real' view on Aristotle, but this seems to me to be wrong. I shall argue that the smaller commentaries are taken by him to be just as Aristotelian as the larger, albeit structured differently.

I have argued in this book and throughout the rest of my work that the project of asking what ibn Rushd was trying to hide in his writings is unlikely to be very productive.[24] There is little to be learnt from considering how his treatment of Aristotle might have been consciously modified by him to take account of Islam. Of course, we tend to transform any thinker whom we admire into someone who fits in more neatly with our broader views, if we can, but we do not need to do this at the level where we are considering the detailed views and arguments of such thinkers. Ibn Rushd had a theory which is well known, that religion and philosophy are merely routes to the same end, different routes, it is true, but nonetheless alternatives. These routes are taken to be appropriate to different travellers. So it would not matter if a thesis produced by Aristotle was apparently not in line with religion; we can be assured that it is merely a way of getting to the same conclusion as religion, albeit by a different route. Although this doctrine has sometimes been dramatically called the 'double truth' thesis, this is not the case. It is the fact that there is only one truth which makes religion and philosophy reconcilable. There is only one truth, and if there are two methods each of which is valid, then

[24] See my 'Ibn Rushd,' in *Encyclopedia of philosophy*, ed. W. Craig, pp. 638–47 and *Averroes and his philosophy* (Richmond, Curzon, 1997). See also M. Campanini, *L'Intelligenza della fede: Filosofia e religione in Averroe e nell'Averroismo* (Bergamo, Pierluigi Lubrina, 1989) and 'Introduzione', in *Averroe: Il Trattato Decisivo* (Milan, Rizzoli, 1994), pp. 7–32.

they must both arrive at that same truth. If there were more than one truth then there would be no need to argue that religion and philosophy are different routes to the same end. They might just as easily, indeed, far more easily, be different routes to different ends, which they do in fact seem to be anyway according to many who look at the apparent contrast between them.

We can perhaps form some idea of how ibn Rushd's philosophical views changed over his lifetime, as of course is also the case with Aristotle. Ibn Rushd started off being thoroughly immersed in the Neoplatonic philosophical curriculum of the time, and especially the works of al-Fārābī, ibn Bājja and ibn Sīnā. Then he took a critical view of this sort of philosophy and rejected much of it as inauthentic with respect to the Aristotelian text itself. His access to that text was accomplished very much with the help of Alexander and Themistius, whose views he later went on to shrug off also as unrepresentative of the meaning of Aristotle himself. So there is no doubt that ibn Rushd saw himself as firmly within the Aristotelian tradition, so firmly within it that he could on occasion reject the views of some of the most important commentators on Aristotle, and even aspects of the translations themselves.

The divergences between ibn Rushd and Aristotle

Despite the spirit in ibn Rushd's works of 'getting back to Aristotle', there are many divergences between the view of Aristotle, as we now understand it, and the explanations of that view by ibn Rushd. To decide how Aristotelian ibn Rushd is we could look at all those divergences, compare them with the agreements in view, and then come to some sort of answer.[25] Perhaps it would be useful to proceed in a slightly different manner, by asking not how close the account of Aristotle provided by ibn Rushd is to Aristotle himself, but by asking how close the account of Aristotle provided by ibn Rushd is to *Aristotelianism*. This has the advantage of abstracting from the precise number of texts which were available to ibn Rushd to the general conclusions which he drew from the texts he had. It also has the advantage of taking account of the conclusions which ibn Rushd drew and which he thought were Aristotelian yet which he acknowledged were not Aristotle's. There are many such conclusions, and it is hardly surprising that this should be case, given the style of Aristotle's main works. If we are to compare the style of the commentaries

---

[25] See J. Jolivet, 'Divergences entre les Métaphysiques d'ibn Rushd et d'Aristote', *Arabica*, 29 (1982), pp. 225–45.

with the style of that on which they are commenting, we immediately notice that they are different. Aristotle is often quite hesitant in what he suggests, and 'suggests' is the right term here. The style is cautious and speculative where Aristotle feels unsure of the truth of the matter, and we know that he often argued that there is no point in applying a general standard of precision to an area of discourse when a different standard is appropriate. Ibn Rushd does not in any way copy this style, and it might be suggested that this is because he is concerned to evade the objections of those enemies of *falsafa* like al-Ghāzalī who accuse Aristotle and his followers of often failing to use proper demonstrative argument. Such an explanation would be entirely fanciful. A commentary on a text cannot replicate the style of the text itself, since it is a commentary. It is an analysis of the text, not a repetition. We should not then be surprised that ibn Rushd does not in his commentaries copy the style of the original. The question is whether he copies the style of the argument itself, not the text. A commentary which replicates the style of the original text is a pastiche, not an interpretation, and we should not be surprised that ibn Rushd does not indulge in this. There was a tendency in much medieval commentary on Aristotle to treat the words of the first master as canonical. To give an example, in the *Guide of the perplexed* Maimonides discusses whether the world is eternal or created. The *falsafa* tradition tended to accept the view that the world is eternal, while the naïve religious approach (both Islamic and Jewish) sees the world as created by God. Maimonides suggests that given our distance from the time of creation the only thing we can say is that the world could be either eternal or created, a position of doubt which he sometimes credits to Aristotle, and if Aristotle could not be sure about the answer, then how could we? We may regard this attribution of hesitancy to Aristotle here as disingenuous, but on the other hand it does make a useful point, which is that Aristotle offered more of a methodology than a system of doctrines. It was to the former rather than the latter that ibn Rushd applied himself.

Ibn Rushd on the intellect

There are a large number of topics which we could examine; but the most studied thus far has been without doubt the nature of the intellect, since this was the most controversial in the transmission of ibn Rushd's thought to medieval Jewish and Christian Europe. In his account of how we think, Aristotle wonders what leads to thought itself, and the brief comments which he made led to a vast commentatorial tradition. Thinking requires a cause, like everything else, and the name for this cause was provided by Alexander as the *poietikos nous* or agent intellect which is equivalent to 'that which is as it is through making all things' (*De anima* 430a 15–17).[26] Now, the link between the agent intellect and the material intellect, the latter being the physical basis of thought, should be quite simple, in that the former should be the form of the latter, in much the same way as the soul is the form of the body. On the other hand, sometimes he refers to the agent intellect as like light, which is very different from a form but more of an efficient cause. But if it is a kind of cause it would still be rather a special cause if it is going to fit in nicely with the description of the agent intellect as 'separable, impassible, unmixed' (*De anima* 430a 17–18).

Not only was there disagreement about the precise nature of the agent intellect, but there was just as heated disagreement about the nature of the material intellect, the physical basis of thought. The material intellect is just a part of our physical constitution, it is the basis of individual human thinking, but how can it actually be used in the acquisition of knowledge? Knowledge, after all, is only acquired through the grasping of universals, and how can something which is essentially part of the world of generation and corruption, and individual, acquire such knowledge? On the other hand, if the material intellect is not itself physical, how can it play a part in ordinary sense perception, and does everyone have one such material intellect or is it shared by everyone?

This was much debated in the Greek world. Ibn Rushd argues that there is only one material intellect, but also that it can only operate with sensory input, which limits it to individuals.[27] The argument that the material intellect must be eternal and incorporeal fails to make sense of our experience of thinking, which operates through images and ideas of individuals, material which cannot in itself be either eternal or incorporeal. Yet this does not present a good argument for the corporeal nature of the material intellect, since we are told that this can receive all material

---

[26] The relevant Greek commentaries are Alexander of Aphrodisias, 'De anima and De intellectu', in *Scripta minora*, ed. I. Bruns (Berlin, Reimer 1887); Themistius, 'Paraphrase of De anima', in *Commentaria in Aristotelem graeca* (Berlin, Reimer 1889), and *The Arabic translation of Themistius' De anima*, ed. M. Lyons (London, Cassirer, 1973).

[27] For excellent accounts of this topic see H. Davidson, 'Averroes on the material intellect', *Viator*, 17 (1986), pp. 91–137, 'Averroes on the active intellect as a cause of existence', *Viator*, 18 (1987), pp. 191–25, *Al-Fārābī, Avicenna and Averroes on intellect* (Oxford and New York, Oxford University Press, 1992); A. Hyman, 'Averroes as commentator on Aristotle's theory of the intellect', in *Studies in Aristotle*, ed. D. O'Meara (Washington, DC, Catholic University of America Press, 1981); and M. Mesbahi, *Ishkaliyyah al-'aql 'ind ibn Rushd* (Beirut, al-Markaz al-thaqafiyya al-'arabi', 1988).

forms. If it had a particular matter, how could it receive any sort of form?
The argument is that the existence of a certain kind of matter in the material intellect would limit what could inform that matter, yet according
to Aristotle nothing can limit what can be received. Aristotle suggests that
the material intellect is incorporeal when he classifies it as separable.[28]

Alexander makes much of this point, and interprets the material intellect as the ability of something material to receive a particular kind of
input. Ibn Bājja took up this point and identified the material intellect
with imagination, a point on which ibn Rushd was later to criticize him
soundly. The images on this account would be produced by the material
intellect, whereas Aristotle has them acting on that intellect. Ibn Rushd
also argues that the intelligibles, the more abstract version of images,
cannot be received by the imagination since it is the imagination which
produces the intelligibles, and so would be receiving itself. Lastly, if the
material intellect is the imagination, then the form of the former is the
images, and it could not receive other forms, which we are told it does
receive, i.e. the intelligibles. The main problem with identifying the material intellect with the imagination, according to Averroes, is that this
does not do justice to the Aristotelian thesis that the material intellect
is eternal. Imagination clearly is not eternal, it is based on our sensory
organs and thus on us, and we are not eternal.

The position which ibn Rushd arrives at is similar to the proposal made
by ibn Bājja. Both material and agent intellects are eternal because they
are not things, but the capacity to do things, in this case the capacity
to find out. For it to be possible for us to make judgments about how
things are in the world we need to look for both a material cause and
an efficient cause. The former is the material intellect and the latter the
agent intellect. Both are eternal in the sense that they characterize what
it is to be a human being, what sort of activity human understanding
is. Human thought can be directed towards abstract and pure concepts,
which aligns it with the eternal, or with more prosaic ideas which require

---

[28] Ibn Rushd wrote short, middle and long commentaries on the *De anima*. See the Long Commentary (*tafsīr*) *Commentarium magnum in Aristotelis De Animalibros*, ed. S. Crawford (Cambridge, MA,
Medieval Academy of America, 1997, trans. into Arabic, B. Gharbi, Tunis, Académie tunisienne
Beit al-hikma des sciences et des arts 1997); the Epitome or Short commentary *Talkhīs kitāb al-
nafs*, ed. A. El Ahwani (Cairo, Maktabat al-Nahdat al-Misriyyah, 1950) (despite the title which
al-Ahwani gives this text, it is more of a short than a middle commentary); *Epitome de anima*,
ed. S. Goméz Nogales (Madrid, Consejo superior de investigaciones científicas, 1985, trans. *La
Psicología de Averroes: Comentario al libro sobre el alma de Aristoteles*, Madrid, Universidad nacional
de Educación a Distancia, 1987); and the Middle Commentary or Paraphrase *Averroes' Middle
Commentary on Aristotle's De Anima*, ed. A. Ivry (Cairo, Egyptian Academy of the Arabic Language
and Supreme Council of Culture, 1994).

images. Sometimes we can do both at the same time, as when an image stands both for what it represents and for something far more abstract, like an example in geometry. It is through not fully appreciating Aristotle's theory of imagination that ibn Rushd gets into the problems he finds with ibn Bājja. The imagination is not only a way of dealing with physical images, it is also a way of transforming those images into far broader and abstract ideas.[29] This means that the material intellect can be both physical and eternal. It is physical in the sense that it is the site of the image-making function we have, and we could not produce images unless we had senses and ideas stemming from the application of those senses. It is eternal because those ideas can be generalized and purified to become entirely abstract, no longer containing any feature of their origins in the individual and imperfect sensations out of which they arose.

How can something be both eternal and physical, though? This seemed to ibn Rushd to be a terrible problem, and one in which ibn Bājja's analysis sinks. But what we should be aware of here is that according to Aristotle the material and agent intellects are not really *things*. There are things which lead to knowledge, but the fact that knowledge requires a passive and an active principle is precisely that, a principle. It is a characteristic of what it is to be this sort of creature, a human creature, with a particular way of finding things out. The fact that we require two sorts of causes for thought to be possible is a fact about us, and it is not a variable or temporary fact, but something eternally characterizing and limiting us. It is presupposed by all our attempts at finding out, and in that way is common to everyone. This does not imply, as the critics of ibn Rushd suggested in Christian Europe, that if one person knows something then everyone knows it. What it does mean is that if anyone knows anything, or has experience of anything, then the principles which make this possible are common to everyone else who is entitled to make that claim.

There is a tendency in much of the literature about ibn Rushd as a commentator to assume that as he got older he got better, i.e. closer to Aristotle himself. I do not think that this is the case. As his views developed he became more and more tied up in the faculty approach to interpreting Aristotle, the approach which was after all part of the curriculum established by Themistius and Alexander. This technique treats the notions of material and agent intellect as though they are things, things whose properties then require defining, but they are not things at

[29] The significance of imagination in Islamic philosophy is discussed in some detail in my *Brief introduction to Islamic philosophy* (Oxford, Polity, 1999).

all. They are ways of doing things, in this case finding out about the world, and about what is higher than the world. It is not surprising that Aristotle should be taken to have been talking about things when he talks about the different intellects. After all, in modern times Kant was interpreted in precisely the same way, as having outlined a series of faculties which are parts of our rationality, and which we actually possess as parts of our mind. The existence of these faculties have been either defended or attacked, but that whole enterprise is misguided, since he did not argue that we have to have particular faculties for knowledge to be possible. Rather, he argues that if knowledge is possible, then certain concepts and ideas have to be used. The notion of transcendental psychology does not therefore get a grip in the critical philosophy. Kant is not arguing for the existence of certain faculties, he is arguing for the existence of certain ways of thinking and suggests that those ways of thinking characterize us as creatures. What justifies us in using those ways of thinking are the concepts which comprise the definition of objectivity, and not anything about our psychological constitution. Of course, we do have a particular psychology which makes it empirically possible for us to have objective knowledge, but the existence of such a psychology is not something which Kant tries to prove. But a hermeneutical tradition arose in which the notion of a transcendental psychology figured prominently. In precisely the same way the interpretation of Aristotle went very much in the direction of converting what he had to say about different kinds of causes into different kinds of things, and by the time of ibn Rushd we find not only a material and agent intellect, but also a speculative intellect, an acquired and a passive intellect.

And why not? After all, if something causes something else to happen, or is the material context within which that event takes place, then it is natural to think of these causes as things. This can be confusing, though. Ibn Rushd objects to ibn Bājja's identification of the material intellect with imagination by arguing that this would mean that the images are both produced by the material intellect and yet also act on it. Yet what is wrong with this? We use images in our thinking, and we produce these as a result of our sensory contact with the world of generation and corruption. Once we have the images we can go on to use them to develop further images. The imagination is not just a repertoire of images which are produced and consumed, as it were, but the ability to create images is stimulated and increased by the images which were produced in the past. So the images can both create the material intellect and be acted on by it, in the sense that imagination is affected by images and also creates images. Another objection by ibn Rushd to the identification of the material intellect with the imagination is that the former would then have the image as its form, and a substance can only have one form. How, then, could it receive the intelligibles, which have a different form? We might challenge the assertion that a substance can only receive one form, but even leaving this aside, and also leaving aside that the material intellect is not a substance, why cannot it have both images and intelligibles as its form? The latter are merely a more abstract version of the former and have the same form. For example, to take an Aristotelian illustration, a particular triangle is a limited instance of a triangle, with particular dimensions, yet it is also an intelligible in the sense that it is a theoretical ratio of proportions in space, explaining in a particular way a general point (*De Mem* I, 449b30–450a7). This is actually how geometry is taught, the teacher draws a figure on the board, and uses that individual figure to explain a general point. If the student is unable to generalize from that figure to what it means for all such figures then he has not grasped the point, which was not really to talk about the particular but about the general.

We need to take seriously the Aristotelian argument, often neglected by commentators, that there is no such thing as knowledge of individuals. There is a tendency to concentrate on his role as a naïve realist, and assume that he had no problem with our having knowledge of the ordinary things and events in the world. He certainly did think that our ordinary sense perceptions are of real objects in the world, and there is no problem with the accuracy of judgments based on those perceptions. Yet what we sense are individuals, whereas knowledge has as its object universals (*De an.* 419a12–13). It is a shame that this point is insufficiently grasped by modern commentators on the controversy in Islamic philosophy over whether God has knowledge of individuals. This controversy is actually part of a much larger controversy over whether anyone at all can have knowledge of individuals, something which Aristotle denies. Since images are important for our thought, and since they are based on individuals, it might seem that Aristotle would have a problem in explaining the existence of knowledge at all. He does not, because of course we can abstract away from the particularity of images to the generality of the intelligibles which then constitute the framework for knowledge. Ibn Rushd captures this point well when he emphasizes the significance of the eternity and impassibility of both the agent and the material intellects. These ways of operating are eternal and impassible because they are not primarily directed towards individuals in the world of generation

and corruption, they are on the contrary made up of principles which
are abstract and formal. Yet they can be applied to our world, and when
they are, they are temporary and contingent, because they are infused
with temporary and contingent images.

But how can something be both eternal and temporary, unmixed and
in constant contact with material forms? It was this paradox which lead
ibn Rushd to so much shilly-shallying about the real nature of the intellect, sometimes agreeing with ibn Bājja and Alexander, and sometimes
siding with Themistius, but not really being satisfied with any resolution
of the issue. But it is only really a problem if we think of the intellect as
a thing, rather than a way in which a thing (a human being) operates,
and this is not how Aristotle refers to it most of the time. Aristotle's own
language is hesitant and speculative, not at all as demonstrative as ibn
Rushd portrays his style to be. In just the same way that we are com-
posites of form and matter, neither entirely spiritual nor material, so it
might be said our intellect is itself neither entirely spiritual nor material.
It has a part which is spiritual and a part which is material, as Aristotle
sometimes says. But this would be far better formulated as that we think
in different ways, sometimes using abstract ideas and sometimes using
concrete images, and the former links us with formal concepts which are
pure, unmixed and eternal, while the latter connects our thinking with
ideas which are mixed, passible and temporary.

We should not allow ibn Rushd to control our interpretation of his
thought. When he says in the long commentary on the intellect that
he was previously mistaken in his interpretation of the nature of our
thinking, but now has found the answer by turning his back on the
commentators and concentrating on the Aristotelian text itself, he is
setting up an image of himself as a thinker who is cutting through the
superfluities provided by the Greek commentary tradition and also the
more modern Islamic thinkers. He claims that all these philosophers fail
to attend to the text itself, and get caught up in the discussion which takes
place around the text instead. If we examine what Aristotle actually had
to say, he suggests, we can resolve the truth of the matter quite easily,
and we have seen how he thinks this can be done.

But ibn Rushd is being disingenuous here, since the whole discussion
of the intellect as he takes it up is entirely a creature of the commentators
in the first place. As has been frequently pointed out, the reification of the
material and actual intellects has far more to do with the hermeneutic
tradition surrounding Aristotelianism than with Aristotle himself. This
is by no means intended to be a criticism of either that tradition or ibn

Rushd. Philosophy at every stage in history has a curriculum, and only the most dramatically radical and creative thinkers can transform that curriculum and take it on to a different level. Ibn Rushd had to work with the curriculum as it came down to him, and even in rejecting the main answers of the debate on the nature of our thinking which had been provided up to his time he was working within the context of those answers, and merely reformulating them to provide what seemed to him to be a more satisfactory understanding of the concept of human thought.

So we return to the question with which we started, namely, how Aristotelian were ibn Rushd's commentaries? The answer is that if the commentaries on the mind are representative, then they are very Aristotelian. They are part of the tradition of interpretation of Aristotle which took seriously the nature of his arguments and approach to philosophy. When we look at the commentaries on the intellect, we have to acknowledge that there is often a heavier reliance on the preceding commentary tradition than is the case for Aristotle's works on other topics, but this is for the excellent reason that Aristotle's writings on this area are fairly sparse and suggestive, and so left gaps for his successors to fill in. Although it has been argued that the understanding which ibn Rushd has of Aristotle's actual view was only accurate when he follows ibn Bājja's approach, his various ideas on the intellect change because of his general Aristotelian worry about the paradoxical nature of human thought. The latter seems to be both abstract and concrete, formal and contingent, and it is difficult to see how it can be both. Now, although I have argued that ibn Rushd was wrong to think of the different intellects as really different things, he obviously does not think that they are straight forwardly different things, since if they were really different it would be not be difficult to characterize them in a way which settled the issue decisively. That is, if the different intellects (speculative, passive, material, agent) were really different *things* which all work together somehow, then there would be no great difficulty in describing their operation both separately and jointly. Ibn Rushd has the view that all these intellects must really be the same thing, share the same genus, because of his Aristotelian presupposition that the analysis of thinking is really just the description of a natural process.

What makes ibn Rushd perhaps the most Aristotelian of the thinkers in the Islamic world is his thoroughgoing and unique antipathy to mysticism, to the idea that there is a hidden reality behind our world. The principle that the world is basically comprehensible, that there is nothing mysterious about it, comes out clearly in his various accounts of the nature of human thought. In his commentaries on the *De anima* this becomes evident in his continual framing of different answers to the understanding of the intellect, and his constant dissatisfaction with any of the answers. So although like all of us he is condemned to work within the philosophical curriculum of his day, as a thoroughgoing Aristotelian he was never easy with that curriculum and worked with it to try to re-establish the ontological simplicity produced by Aristotle himself.

The theme of this book has been the interest and power of the philosophical arguments which arose in the Islamic world in the Middle Ages. The structure of these arguments and the theoretical framework within which they arose are well worth examining for their philosophical rigour. To concentrate rather upon the supposedly devious intentions of the philosophers themselves is to imply that the arguments are of little value or significance as arguments. Now, there certainly is not just *one* way of reading Islamic philosophy, but there is perhaps just one way in which such texts ought to be approached initially.

The first questions we should ask about a text of Islamic philosophy are philosophical questions, e.g. are the arguments valid? Do they cohere with other arguments produced by the author? Do they increase our understanding of the concepts involved? Are they interesting? If we cannot make any progress with these sorts of questions then it may well be appropriate to ask other kinds of questions about the way in which the text is written, and what the author may have tried to conceal. Throughout this *Introduction* it has been argued that we can make good philosophical sense of Islamic philosophy without asking these autobiographical and historical questions. The philosophical arguments are there to be analyzed, and for that analysis we require nothing more than philosophical tools. If we concentrate upon the philosophical nature of the arguments we shall find many examples of intriguing and subtle reasoning.

Further reading

Since some of the notes are rather technical and refer to works inaccessible to many readers, a brief guide to further reading might be helpful. Translations of some of the passages related to those referred to in the notes will be found in the articles, as will some interesting arguments which extend those found in the book.

PART I AL-GHAZĀLĪ'S ATTACK ON PHILOSOPHY

Fakhry, M., 'The "antinomy" of the eternity of the world in Averroes, Maimonides and Aquinas', *Muséon*, 66 (1953), pp. 139–55.

Goodman, L., 'Ghazali's argument from creation (I)', *International Journal of Middle Eastern Studies*, 2 (1971), pp. 67–85.

'Did al-Ghazali deny causality?', *Studia Islamica*, 47 (1978), pp. 83–120.

Hourani, G., 'The dialogue between al-Ghazālī and the philosophers on the origin of the world', *Muslim World*, 48 (1958), pp. 183–91, 308–14.

Marmura, M., 'Avicenna and the problem of the infinite number of souls', *Medieval Studies*, 22 (1960), pp. 232–9.

'Some aspects of Avicenna's theory of God's knowledge of particulars', *Journal of the American Oriental Society*, 82 (1962), pp. 299–312.

'Ghazali and demonstrative science', *Journal of the History of Philosophy*, 3 (1965), pp. 183–204.

PART II REASON V. REVELATION IN PRACTICAL REASONING

Altmann, A., 'Maimonides' "four perfections"', *Israel Oriental Studies*, 2 (1972), pp. 15–24.

Fakhry, M., 'Al-Fārābī and the reconciliation of Plato and Aristotle', *Journal of the History of Ideas*, 26 (1965), pp. 469–78. Summary of al-Fārābī's *Agreement of the opinions of the philosophers Plato and Aristotle*.

Hourani, G., 'Ghazali on the ethics of action', *Journal of the American Oriental Society*, 96 (1976), pp. 69–88.

'Islamic and non-Islamic origins of Mu'tazilite ethical rationalism', *International Journal of Middle Eastern Studies*, 7 (1976), pp. 56–87.

Leaman, O., 'Does the interpretation of Islamic philosophy rest on a mistake?', *International Journal of Middle Eastern Studies*, 12 (1980), pp. 525–38.

'Ibn Bājja on society and philosophy', *Der Islam*, 57 (1980), pp. 109–19.

'Ibn Rushd on happiness and philosophy', *Studia Islamica*, 52 (1980), pp. 167–81.

Lerner, R., *Averroes on Plato's 'Republic'*, trans. introduction and notes (Ithaca, Cornell University Press, 1974).

Rosenthal, E., *Political thought in medieval Islam* (Cambridge, Cambridge University Press, 1968).

Studia Semitica, vols. I and II (Cambridge, Cambridge University Press, 1971).

Ibn Ṭufayl, *Ḥayy ibn Yaqẓān*, trans. L. Goodman (New York, Twayne, 1972).

INTRODUCTIONS TO ISLAMIC PHILOSOPHY

Two very useful books are

Fakhry, M., *A history of Islamic philosophy* (New York, Columbia University Press, 1983).

Watt, W., *Islamic philosophy and theology* (Edinburgh, Edinburgh University Press, 1962).

AVERROES AND ARISTOTLE

Butterworth, C., 'La valeur philosophique des commentaires d'Averroes sur Aristote' in *Multiple Averroes* (Paris, Les Belles Lettres, 1978), pp. 117–26.

Gätje, H., 'Averroes als Aristoteleskommentator', *Zeitschrift der Deutschen Morgenländischen Gesellschaft*, 114 (1964), pp. 59–65.

Das Kapitel über das Begehren aus dem mittlern Kommentar des Averroes zur Schrift über die Seele (Amsterdam, 1985), see pp. 23–35.

Cruz Hernández, M., 'El sentido de las tres lecturas de Aristóteles por Averroes', *Academia Nazionale dei Lincei, Rendicotti della Classe di Scienze morali, storiche e filològiche*, 28, 3–4, pp. 567–85.

Abu-l-Walid Ibn Rušd (Averroes): Vida, Obra, Pensamiento, Influencia (Cordoba, Cajasur, 1986).

Druart, T.-A., 'Averroes: the commentator and the commentators', in L. Schrenk (ed.), *Aristotle in late antiquity*, Catholic University of American Press, (Washington 1994).

Hanafi, H., 'Ibn Rushd shārihan Aristū', *Dirāsāt Islāmiyya* (1982), pp. 157–202.

Leaman, O., 'Is Averroes an Averroist?', in F. Niewöhner and L. Sturlese (eds.), *Averroismus im Mittelalter und in der Renaissance* (Zurich, Spur, 1994), pp. 9–22.

'Averroes', in F. Niewöhner (ed.), *Klassiker der Religionsphilosophie: von Platon bis Kierkegaard* (Munich, Beck, 1995), pp. 142–62.

Averroes and his philosophy (Richmond, Curzon, 1997).

Martínez Lorca, A. (ed.), *Al encuentro de Averroes* (Madrid: Editorial Trotta, 1993).

Urvoy, D., 'Ibn Rushd', in *History of Islamic philosophy*, ed. S. Nasr and O. Leaman (London, Routledge, 1996), pp. 330–45.

For interesting background information which puts ibn Rushd's Aristotelianism into its historical context see:

Urvoy, D., *Averroes: les ambitions d'un intellectual musulman* (Paris, Flammarion, 1998).

GENERAL INTRODUCTIONS TO ISLAMIC PHILOSOPHY IN THE CLASSICAL PERIOD

Corbin, H., *History of Islamic philosophy*, trans. L. Sherrard (London, Kegan Paul International, 1993).

Fakhry, M., *A history of Islamic philosophy* (New York, Columbia University Press, 1983).

An introduction to Islamic philosophy, theology and mysticism (Oxford, OneWorld, 1997).

Leaman, O., *A companion to the philosophers*, ed. R. Arrington (Oxford, Blackwell, 1999), 'Alfarabi', pp. 675–7, 'Avicenna', pp. 671–4, 'Averroes', pp. 667–70, 'Ghazali', pp. 678–80 and 'Maimonides', pp. 683–5.

Eastern philosophy: key readings (London, Routledge, 2000).

'A guide to bibliographical resources' and 'General introductions to Islamic philosophy', in S. Nasr and O. Leaman (eds.), *History of Islamic philosophy* (London, Routledge, 1996), pp. 1173–76 and 1177–9.

'Islamic philosophy', in E. Craig (ed.), *Encyclopedia of philosophy* (London, Routledge, 1998).

Key concepts in Eastern philosophy (London, Routledge, 1999).

Leaman, O. (ed.), *Encyclopedia of Asian philosophy* (London, Routledge, 2001).

USEFUL ARTICLES AND TRANSLATIONS

Lerner, R. and Mahdi, M. (eds.), *Medieval political philosophy: a sourcebook* (Ithaca, NY, Cornell University Press, 1972).

Morewedge, P. (ed.), *Islamic philosophical theology* (Albany, State University of New York Press, 1979).

(ed.), *Islamic philosophy and mysticism* (New York, Caravan Books, 1981).

CRITICAL SURVEYS

Butterworth, C., 'The study of Arabic philosophy today', *Middle East Studies Association Bulletin*, 17 (1983), pp. 8–24; 161–77.

REFERENCES

HIP History of Islamic Philosophy, ed. S. Nasr and O. Leaman (London, Routledge, 1996).

Abrahamov, B., *Islamic theology: traditionalism and rationalism* (Edinburgh, Edinburgh University Press, 1998).

Abed, S., *Aristotelian logic and the Arabic language in Alfarabi* (Albany, State University of New York Press, 1991).

Abdel Haleem, M., *HIP*: 'Early kalām', pp. 71–88.

Abu-Rabi', I., *HIP*: 'The Arab world', pp. 1082–114.

Ahmed, A., *Discovering Islam: making sense of Muslim history and society* (London, Routledge, 1989).

Akhtar, S., *HIP*: 'The possibility of a philosophy of Islam', pp. 1162–9.

Al-Ash'ari, *The theology of al-Ash'arī: the Arabic texts of al-Ash'arī's Kitāb al-Luma'*, ed. R. McCarthy (Beirut, Imprimerie Catholique, 1953).

Al-Fārābī, *Al-Fārābī's commentary and short treatise on Aristotle's De Interpretatione*, trans. and intro. F. Zimmermann (London, British Academy, 1981).

Al-Fārābī on the perfect state, trans. R. Walzer (Oxford, Clarendon Press, 1985).

Al-Ghazālī, *The faith and practice of al-Ghazālī*, trans. W. Watt (London, Allen and Unwin, 1953).

    Freedom and fulfillment: an annotated translation of al-Munqidh min al-Dalāl and other relevant works of al-Ghazālī, trans. R. McCarthy (Boston, Twayne, 1980).

    Ghazali on prayer, trans. and intro. K. Nakamura (Tokyo, Institute of Oriental Culture, University of Tokyo, 1973).

    The incoherence of the philosophers, trans. and intro. M. Marmura (Provo, UT, Brigham Young University Press, 1997).

    The ninety-nine beautiful names of God, trans. D. Burrell and N. Daher (Cambridge, Islamic Texts Society, 1992).

    The remembrance of death and the afterlife, trans. and intro. T. Winter (Cambridge, Islamic Texts Society, 1989).

Al-Kindi, *Al-Kindī's metaphysics: a translation of the Treatise on First Philosophy*, trans. A. Ivry (Albany, State University of New York Press, 1974).

Al-Tusi, *Contemplation and action: the spiritual autobiography of a Muslim scholar*, ed. and trans. S. Badakhchani (London, I. B. Tauris, 1998).

Alon, I., 'Fārābī's funny flora; al-nawābit a "opposition"', *Arabica*, 37 (1990), pp. 56–90.

Aminrazavi, M., *HIP*: 'Persia', pp. 1037–50.

    Suhrawardī and the school of illumination (Richmond, Curzon, 1997).

Arberry, A., *The Koran interpreted* (Oxford and London, Oxford University Press, 1964).

Aslan, A., *Religious pluralism in Christian and Islamic philosophy: the thought of John Hick and Seyyed Hossein Nasr* (Richmond, Curzon, 1998).

Bakar, O., *HIP*: 'Science', pp. 926–46.

Bello, I., *The medieval Islamic controversy between philosophy and orthodoxy: Ijmā' and Ta'wīl in the conflict between al-Ghazālī and ibn Rushd* (Leiden, Brill, 1989).

Benmakhlouf, A., *Averroes* (Paris, Les Belles Lettres, 2000).

Black, D. *HIP*: 'Al-Fārābī', pp. 178–97.

    Logic and Aristotle's rhetoric and poetics in medieval Arabic philosophy (Leiden, Brill, 1990).

Campanini, M., *HIP*: 'Al-Ghazzali', pp. 258–76.

Chittick, W., *HIP*: 'Ibn 'Arabī', pp. 497–509; 'The school of ibn 'Arabī', pp. 510–23.

    Imaginal worlds: Ibn al-'Arabi and the problem of religious diversity (Albany, State University of New York Press, 1994).

    The self-disclosure of God: principles of ibn al-'Arabi's Cosmology (Albany, State University of New York Press, 1998).

Corbin, H., *History of Islamic philosophy*, trans. L. Sherrard (London, Kegan Paul International, 1993).

Dabashi, H., *HIP*: 'Khwājah Naṣīr al-Ṭūsī: the philosopher/vizier and the intellectual climate of his times', pp. 527–84; 'Mīr Dāmād and the founding of the "School of Iṣfahān"', pp. 597–634.

Daiber, H., *HIP*: 'Political philosophy', pp. 841–85.

Davidson, H., *Al-Farabi, Avicenna, and Averroes on intellect: their cosmologies, theories of active intellect and theories of the human intellect* (Oxford and New York, Oxford University Press, 1992).

Fakhry, M., *A history of Islamic philosophy* (New York, Columbia University Press, 1983).

    K. al-ḥurūf, ed. M. Mahdi (Beirut, 1971).

    Islamic occasionalism and its critique by Averroes and Aquinas (London, Allen and Unwin, 1958).

Frank, D. and Leaman, O. (eds.), *History of Jewish philosophy* (London, Routledge, 1997).

Frank, R., *Al-Ghazālī and the Ash'arite school* (Durham, Duke University Press, 1994).

Goodman, L., *Avicenna* (London, Routledge, 1993).

    HIP: 'Ibn Masarrah', pp. 277–93; 'Ibn Bājjah', pp. 294–312; 'Ibn Ṭufayl', pp. 313–29.

    HIP: 'Muhammad ibn Zakariyyā' al-Rāzī', pp. 198–215.

Gutas, D., *Avicenna and the Aristotelian tradition: introduction to reading Avicenna's philosophical works* (Leiden, Brill, 1988).

Hallaq, W., *Ibn Taymiyya against the Greek Logicians* (Oxford, Clarendon Press, 1993).

Hayoun, M.-R. and de Libera, A., *Averroès et l'averroïsme* (Paris, PUF, 1991).

Ibn Bājja, *Rasā'il ibn Bājja al-ilāhiyya* [Ibn Bājja's metaphysical essays], ed. M. Fakhry (Beirut, Dar al-Jil, 1992).

Ibn Rushd, *Averroes' commentary on Plato's 'Republic'*, ed., intro. and trans. E. Rosenthal (Cambridge, Cambridge University Press, 1969).

    Averroes on the harmony of religion and philosophy [Faṣl al-maqāl], trans. G. Hourani (London, Luzac, 1976).

    Averroes' Tahāfut al-Tahāfut [The incoherence of the incoherence], (London, Luzac, 1978).

    Le livre du discours décisif, trans. M. Geoffroy, intro. A. de Libera (Paris, Flammarion, 1996).

    L'Incoerenza dell'Incoerenza dei Filosofi, trans. M. Campanini (Turin, Unione Tipografico-Editrice, 1997).

Ibn Sīnā, *The life of ibn Sina: a critical edition and annotated translation*, ed. and trans. W. Gohlman (Albany, State University of New York Press, 1974).

Ibn Ṭufayl, *Ḥayy ibn Yaqẓān, a philosophical tale*, trans. L. Goodman (Los Angeles, Gee Tee Bee, 1996).

Inati, S., *HIP*: 'Ibn Sīnā', pp. 231–46; 'Logic', pp. 802–23.

Jayyusi, S. (ed.), *The legacy of Muslim Spain* (Leiden, Brill, 1992).

Kemal, R. and Kemal, S., *HIP*: 'Shah Walīullāh', pp. 663–70.

Kılıç, M., *HIP*: 'Mysticism', pp. 947–58.

Klein-Franke, F., *HIP*: 'Al-Kindi', pp. 165–77.

Lameer, J., *Al-Fārābī and Aristotelian syllogistics: Greek theory and Islamic practice* (Leiden, Brill, 1994).

Leaman, O., 'Averroes', in *Klassiker der Religionsphilosophile: von Platon bis Kierkegaard*, ed. F. Niewohner (Munich, C. H. Beck, 1995), pp. 142–62.

'Averroes and the West', in *Averroes and the Enlightenment*, ed. M. Wahba and M. Abousenna (Amherst, Prometheus, 1996), pp. 53–68.

'Averroes' Commentary on Plato's Republic and the missing Politics', in D. Agius and I. Netton (eds.), *Across the Mediterranean frontiers: trade, politics and religion*, 650–1450 (Turnhout, Brepols, 1997), pp. 195–204.

'Averroes, le Kitāb al-nafs et la révolution de la philosophie occidentale', in *Le choc Averroès* (Paris, Maison des Cultures du Monde, 1991), pp. 58–65.

Companion encyclopedia of Asian philosophy, ed. B. Carr and I. Mahalingam (London, Routledge, 1997), 'Logic and language in Islamic philosophy', pp. 950–64 and 'Islamic philosophy since Avicenna', pp. 901–17.

'Continuity in Islamic political philosophy: the role of myth', *British Society for Middle Eastern Studies* 14.2 (1988), pp. 147–55.

The future of philosophy: towards the 21st century, ed. O. Leaman (London, Routledge, 1998), 'The future of philosophy', pp. 1–13, 'Philosophy of religion', pp. 120–33.

'Ghazali and Averroes on meaning', *Al-Masaq*, 9 (1997), pp. 179–89.

HIP: 'Introduction', pp. 1–10; 'Islamic humanism in the fourth/tenth century', pp. 155–61; 'Introduction to the Jewish philosophical tradition in the Islamic cultural world', pp. 673–6; 'Jewish Averroism', pp. 769–82; 'Orientalism and Islamic philosophy', pp. 1143–8.

'Is Averroes an Averroist?', in *Averroismus im Mittelalter und in der Renaissance*, ed. F. Niewöhner and L. Sturlese (Zurich, Spur Verlag, 1994), pp. 9–22.

'Islam', in *Philosophy of education: an encyclopedia*, ed. J. Chambliss (New York, Garland, 1996), pp. 311–16.

Moses Maimonides, 2nd edn (Richmond, Curzon, 1997; 1st edn London, Routledge, 1990).

'The philosophical tradition', in *The Cambridge Encyclopedia of the Middle East and North Africa*, ed. T. Mostyn (Cambridge, Cambridge University Press, 1958), pp. 264–6.

'Philosophy vs. mysticism: an Islamic controversy', in *Philosophy, religion and the spiritual life*, ed. M. McGhee (Cambridge, Cambridge University Press, 1992), pp. 177–88.

Lewis, B., *Cultures in conflict: Christians, Muslims and Jews in the Age of Discovery* (Oxford and New York, Oxford University Press, 1995).

Lory, P., *HIP*: 'Henry Corbin: his work and influence', pp. 1149–55.

Marenbon, J., *HIP*: 'Medieval Christian and Jewish Europe', pp. 1001–12.

Morewedge, P., *Essays in Islamic philosophy, theology and mysticism* (Oneonta, NY, Philosophy Department, State University of New York, 1995).

    Neoplatonism and Islamic thought (Albany, State University of New York Press, 1992).

Muhajirani, A., *HIP*: 'Twelve-Imam Shi'ite theological and philosophical thought', pp. 119–43.

Nanji, A., *HIP*: 'Ismā'īlī philosophy', pp. 144–54.

Naṣīr Khusraw, *Knowledge and liberation: a treatise on philosophical theology*, ed. and trans. F. Hunzai (London, I. B. Tauris, 1998).

Nasr, S., *HIP*: 'Introduction', pp. 11–20; 'The meaning and concept of philosophy in Islam', pp. 21–6; 'The Qur'ān and Hadith as source and inspiration of Islamic philosophy', pp. 27–39; 'Ibn Sīnā's "Oriental philosophy"', pp. 247–51; 'Introduction to the mystical tradition', pp. 367–73; 'Mullā Ṣadrā: his teachings', pp. 643–62.

    The Islamic intellectual tradition in Persia, ed. M. Amin Razavi (Richmond, Curzon, 1996).

    Sufi essays (London, Allen and Unwin, 1972).

Netton, I., *Al-Fārābī and his school* (London, Routledge, 1992).

    Allah transcendent: studies in the structure and semiotics of Islamic philosophy, Theology and Cosmology (London, Routledge, 1989).

    HIP: 'The Brethren of Purity (Ikhwān al-Ṣafā)', pp. 222–30.

    Muslim neoplatonists: an introduction to the thought of the Brethren of Purity (London, Allen and Unwin, 1982).

Nomanul Haq, S., *HIP*: 'The Indian and Persian background', pp. 52–70.

Nursi, S., *The Flashes collection*, trans. S. Vahide (Istanbul, Sozler Nesriyat, 1995).

Nuseibeh, S., *HIP*: 'Epistemology', pp. 824–40.

Pavlin, J., *HIP*: 'Sunnī kalām and theological controversies', pp. 105–18.

Peters, F., *HIP*: 'The Greek and Syriac background', pp. 40–51.

Reinhart, K., *Before revelation: the boundaries of Muslim moral thought* (Albany, State University of New York Press, 1995).

Rowson, E., *HIP*: 'Al-'Āmirī', pp. 216–21.

    A Muslim philosopher on the soul and its fate: al-'Āmirī's Kitāb al-Amad 'alā L-Abad (Chicago, Kazi, 1996).

Shayegan, Y., *HIP*: 'The transmission of Greek philosophy to the Islamic world', pp. 89–104.

Taftazani and Leaman, O., *HIP*: 'Ibn Sab'īn', pp. 346–9.

    HIP: 'Ibn Rushd', pp. 330–45.

Wolfson, H., *The philosophy of the Kalam* (Cambridge, MA: Harvard University Press, 1976).

Ziai, H., *HIP*: 'Shihāb al-Dīn Suhrawardī: founder of the Illuminationist School', pp. 434–64; 'The illuminationist tradition', pp. 465–96; 'Mullā Ṣadrā: his life and works', pp. 635–42.

These books and articles were very useful for both the first and second editions of this book:

Berman, L., 'Maimonides, the disciple of Alfarabi', *Israel Oriental Studies*, 4(1974), pp. 154–78.
    'The political interpretation of the maxim: the purpose of philosophy is the imitation of God', *Studia Islamica*, 15(1961), pp. 53–61.
Hourani, G., 'Ghazali on the ethics of action', *Journal of the American Oriental Society*, 96(1976), pp. 69–88.
Mahdi, M., *The attainment of happiness* (New York, Free Press, 1962).
Marmura, M., 'Al-Ghazali's attitude to the sciences and logic', in G. Hourani (ed.), *Essays in Islamic Philosophy and Science* (Albany, State University of New York Press, 1975), pp. 100–20.
    'Al-Ghazali on ethical premisses', *Philosophical Forum*, n.s. 1(1969), pp. 393–403.
    'Ghazali and demonstrative science', *Journal of the History of Philosophy*, 32(1965), pp. 183–204.
    'Leaman's introduction to medieval Islamic philosophy: a review article', *Muslim World*, 76(1986), pp. 43–5.
    'Some aspects of Avicenna's theory of God's knowledge of particulars', *Journal of the American Oriental Society*, 82(1962), pp. 299–312.
Rahman, F., *Prophecy in Islam* (London, George Allen & Unwin, 1958).

Glossary

'*adl*, justice
'*aql*, reason
bāṭin, inner (meaning), esoteric, hidden
failasūf, falāsifa, falsafa, philosopher, philosophers, philosophy
fiqh, jurisprudence
furū', branches (of law)
ḥadīth, Tradition(s)
ḥaj, pilgrimage
ḥakham, wise man
ḥasan, good
ḥasid, righteous
ḥukkim, statues (ritual)
ishraq, illumination
ittiḥād, union
ittiṣāl, contact
jihād, holy war
kalām, theology
khalīfa, deputies
khaliq, creator
mawjūdāt, existing beings
mishpatim, statutes (with obvious reasons)
miṭālāt, similitudes

mutakallimūn, theologians
mutawaḥḥid, solitary, isolated (philosopher)
nāmūs, law
naql, tradition
qabīḥ, evil
qāḍī, judge
qiyās, analogy
ra'y, opinion
shar', religious law
sharī'a, prophetic law of Islam
sū', evil
takhlīq, producing
taqdīr, determining
taqīya, dissimulation
taṣawwūf, mysticism
ta'wīl, figurative meaning
'*ulamā'*, religious scholars
uṣūl, roots, principles (of law)
waḥy, inspiration, revelation
wājib, obligatory
wujūd, existence
ẓāhir, exoteric, clear (meaning)
ẓulm, harm

Index of passages

General index

Due to their ubiquity in the text, some terms are not indexed and these include *falsafa, falāsifa*, God, Islam, Qur'ān, philosophy.